VILLAINOUS
COMPOUNDS

VILLAINOUS COMPOUNDS

CHEMICAL WEAPONS & THE AMERICAN CIVIL WAR

GUY R. HASEGAWA
Foreword by Bill J. Gurley

Southern Illinois University Press | Carbondale

18 17 16 15   4 3 2 1

Jacket illustration: artillery shell, delivered by the Union's "Swamp Angel," bursting in Charleston, 1863. *Harper's Weekly*, January 9, 1864.

Library of Congress Cataloging-in-Publication Data
Hasegawa, Guy R.
Villainous compounds : chemical weapons and the American Civil War
/ Guy R. Hasegawa ; foreword by Bill J. Gurley.
   pages cm
Summary: "This book is a study of the diverse array of chemical weap-
ons that were deployed, prepared for use, or proposed during the Civil
War"—Provided by publisher.
Includes bibliographical references and index.
ISBN 978-0-8093-3430-8 (cloth : alkaline paper)
ISBN 0-8093-3430-5 (cloth : alkaline paper)
ISBN 978-0-8093-3431-5 (ebook)
ISBN 0-8093-3431-3 (ebook)
1. Chemical weapons—United States—History—19th century. 2. Chem-
ical weapons—United States—History—19th century—Sources.
3. Inventions—United States—History—19th century. 4. Technological
innovations—United States—History—19th century. 5. United States—
Armed Forces—Weapons systems—History—19th century. 6. United
States—Armed Forces—Ordnance and ordnance stores—History—19th
century. 7. United States—History—Civil War, 1861–1865—Equipment
and supplies. I. Title.
UG447.H368 2015
973.7'3—dc23   2015001827

To Betsy, David, and Stephen

CONTENTS

Gallery beginning on page 65

FOREWORD

GIVEN THE NUMEROUS ADVANCES IN weapons technology over the last 150 years, people today, particularly Southerners, often daydream about what-ifs when it comes to battlefield tactics and potential outcomes of the American Civil War. For example, if Stonewall Jackson had not been mortally wounded at Chancellorsville, would the Battle of Gettysburg then have had a different outcome? This is a fairly plausible what-if. A more fantastic scenario would be imagining what Joe Johnston might have accomplished with a detachment of King Tiger tanks during the Atlanta Campaign. Atlanta certainly would not have burned, and the March to the Sea would not have occurred, but the likelihood of mechanized armor being available in 1864, even if powered by steam instead of gasoline, is simply too far-fetched. Yet what if Robert E. Lee had had flamethrowers to defend the Mule Shoe salient at Spotsylvania? The Overland Campaign might have ended there. Or what if E. Porter Alexander had had chlorine gas shells in his limber chests during the Confederate artillery barrage of Cemetery Ridge just prior to Pickett's Charge? Would those numerous shots that landed behind Meade's center still have been for naught? What if John B. Gordon's storming parties had had pepper spray in their knapsacks for overpowering sentinels during their surreptitious attack on Fort Stedman in the waning days of the war? The Federal counterattack might not have materialized, and perhaps President Lincoln, who was nearby observing a review, might have been captured. These last three what-ifs, as fanciful as they might seem, were closer to reality than most would believe.

The Civil War was not only a turning point in our nation's history but also a pivotal period in the evolution of military science. Today, when Civil War scholars use the term *military science*, improvements in the design of ammunition, rifles, cannons, or naval vessels immediately come to mind. Metallic cartridges, repeating rifles, long-range cannons, ironclad warships, and functional submarines are just a few of the more recognized innovations of military science developed and used during the conflict. Emphasis, however, has often been placed more on the military results of such inventions and less on the science behind them.

One of the sciences that played a key role in Civil War weapons development was chemistry. Few Civil War enthusiasts are cognizant of the role chemistry played in the American arms race of the mid-nineteenth century. In the 1860s, the science of chemistry was still in its nascency, and among its principal practitioners were pharmacists and physicians. Knowledge of chemistry was crucial to both the practice and production of Civil War medicine. As such, doctors and druggists were very familiar with the toxic nature of various organic and inorganic chemical compounds. When the war erupted, a few of these forward-thinking chemists quickly recognized that the noxious, and sometimes deadly, aspects of certain chemical concoctions could be weaponized. Throughout the course of the war, a host of exotic chemical weapons were proposed and, in some instances, actually employed. Bureaucrats in the War Departments of both armies, however, often viewed such unusual weapons as being too villainous, expensive, or unreliable for battlefield use and either delayed or outright rejected their adoption. Nevertheless, many of the proposed armaments presaged the widespread use of chemical weapons on many battlefields in the twentieth and twenty-first centuries.

Guy Hasegawa, a pharmacist and one of the nation's leading experts on Civil War medicine, has uncovered details of a forgotten chapter in the history of American weapons development. His discoveries open our eyes to an array of possible what-ifs. As readers will learn in the chapters to follow, pepper spray, flamethrowers, and chlorine gas shells were just a few of the exotic chemical weapons proposed by patriotic inventors, both blue and gray. Indeed, what if several of these weapons had been developed further or seen wider usage in the Civil War? Perhaps its outcome might have been different.

Villainous Compounds is a significant and fresh contribution to the historiography both of the Civil War and of science and technology. Hasegawa's clear prose and engaging style will appeal to Civil War aficionados with little grounding in chemistry as well as chemists with scant knowledge of the war. Battlefield trampers and armchair historians alike will gain new insights into the scientific and moral underpinnings of America's earliest attempts at developing weapons of mass destruction.

Bill J. Gurley, PhD
Professor of Pharmaceutical Sciences
University of Arkansas for Medical Sciences, College of Pharmacy
Little Rock

PREFACE

RESEARCH PROJECTS CAN BEGIN IN odd ways. My investigation into the Civil War's chemical weapons started several years ago, after I examined the compiled service record of Confederate surgeon Joseph Jones for anything he might have written about remedies for malaria. His record revealed nothing on that subject but did yield a letter that astonished me. In it, Jones outlined schemes for using phosphorus and hydrogen cyanide as chemical weapons. I knew from other reading that red pepper, chloroform, and chlorine had been proposed during the war as weapons, but Jones's plans were new to me and suggested the possibility that other undiscovered information about proposed chemical weapons might survive in the historical record.

Articles describing Civil War proposals for chemical weapons started appearing in periodicals in the 1920s, probably because the recent use of poisonous gases in World War I had spurred interest. Those early works, whose major point seemed to be that chemical weapons were not so new after all, were maddeningly inadequate in documenting their sources, and later articles generally repeated what earlier ones had said. The most valuable published resource by far was Robert V. Bruce's *Lincoln and the Tools of War* (first published in 1956), because Bruce was unusually thorough in recording his sources, which included those for his few mentions of chemical agents. A useful but short general reference was Jeffery K. Smart's 2004 work, "Chemical & Biological Warfare Research & Development during the Civil War."

The documentation in Bruce's book guided me to army and navy ordnance files at the National Archives in Washington, DC, that contain descriptions of "inventions" submitted by civilians to US civic and military officials. Those letters dealing specifically with chemical weapons provided much of the information for *Villainous Compounds*. If an analogous compilation resides among Confederate records, it has not been located, but a number of Southern ideas for chemical weapons can be found scattered here and there among official Confederate records and in periodicals. Undiscovered proposals probably exist among the letters received by the Confederate secretary of war and in other files, but that correspondence is indexed by name and not by subject. Without a lead linked to a specific name, finding relevant letters would require incredible luck or examination of each letter on file, which would be a needle-in-a-haystack endeavor. Thus if weapons proposals from Confederate civilians seem underrepresented here, it is because they are much harder to find and not necessarily because Southerners were less active in putting forth their ideas. Looking for proposals by military personnel in Union and Confederate Ordnance Department correspondence presents the same problem of letters not being easily searched, but given the general aversion among ordnance officials, especially on the Union side, to new classes of weapons, there may not have been many such suggestions. I consulted standard references such as the army *Official Records* and its navy counterpart, and Internet searches proved useful, especially in providing newspaper accounts of citizens suggesting chemical weapons.

Biographical information about weapons proponents was gleaned from various sources, including city directories and the 1860 census. In a surprising number of instances, the proponents were prominent enough to be mentioned in detailed obituaries or local histories. In a few cases, I confirmed the identities by comparing the handwriting in proposals with samples on patent applications, on documents contained in manuscript collections, or in published histories. For some weapons proponents, no additional information could be found. Excerpts from historical sources reproduce their spelling exactly; this preserves their particular flavor and spares readers from distracting *sics*, of which there would be many. Original punctuation and capitalization are also retained to the extent that it was possible to discern writers' intent from their handwriting. Modern American spellings—*sulfur*, for example, rather than *sulphur*—are used outside of quotations. A simple glossary is included to assist readers with selected terms, especially those whose meaning, although provided once in the text, may be forgotten when they subsequently appear.

Many of the ideas described in *Villainous Compounds* were presented for the first time several years ago in an article I wrote for *Military Medicine* titled "Proposals for Chemical Weapons during the American Civil War." That article, because of length limitations, necessarily omitted biographical facts about the weapons proponents and had limited discussion of the historical context for the proposals. The continued concern about chemical weapons in today's unsettled world led me to believe that a book-length description of the Civil War weapons and proposals would broaden readers' view of such agents and how they fit in the historical timeline. The only other scholarly book touching on the topic is the aforementioned *Lincoln and the Tools of War*, which emphasizes President Lincoln's relationship with weapon inventors and ordnance officials and devotes relatively little attention to chemical weapons specifically. In contrast, *Villainous Compounds* describes the background of chemical weapons advocates, suggests possible sources and motives for their ideas, evaluates the feasibility of the weapons, and explores whether and how they evolved into more modern counterparts, such as the poison gases of World War I or the crowd control agents used in law enforcement today.

Villainous Compounds also contains proposals found since publication of the *Military Medicine* article and identifies the original sources for nearly all the suggestions previously described in the secondary literature. This and other documentation in the notes and bibliography should assist future scholars to a greater extent than earlier works on the topic. Additionally, the book describes the incendiary compounds collectively called "Greek fire," which the article did not.

This work is limited to agents to be used with official sanction against military targets and intended to disable, even temporarily, or kill by virtue of their chemical properties. Artillery projectiles containing molten iron or heated until red hot are not considered chemical weapons here because their effects were primarily thermal; their extreme heat set objects on fire. On the other hand, formulations of Greek fire are included because a large part of their actual or intended usefulness was the production of noxious fumes from ignition of their chemicals, rather than from the burning of objects set afire. Although incendiary compounds like napalm are often not considered chemical weapons today, there is ample historical precedent for grouping such incendiary agents among chemical weapons. Biological weapons, such as contaminated clothing meant to spread disease—as in the so-called Yellow Fever Plot—are not included, nor are instances of water sources being intentionally fouled with animal carcasses. Also excluded are instances of citizens setting out poison, on their own accord, for ingestion by enemy troops.

Many people had a hand in the publication of this book. Special thanks are due to James M. Schmidt, who shared my excitement when I first started delving into the topic and helped convince me that my findings could be turned into a book. F. Terry Hambrecht freely shared his knowledge, reference collection, and advice. Bill J. Gurley graciously accepted my invitation to contribute the book's foreword. Jim, Terry, and Bill are authors and Civil War experts in their own areas, and I am proud to count them among my longtime friends; all sacrificed their precious time to provide thoughtful and encouraging comments about the manuscript. Sylvia Frank Rodrigue, executive editor for Southern Illinois University Press, guided me through the book proposal process and contributed insightful recommendations for improving the manuscript. Finally, I could not have written this book without the patience and encouragement of my wife, Betsy, and our sons, David and Stephen. Their support of my historical endeavors has been unwavering and invaluable.

VILLAINOUS
COMPOUNDS

1

IMPROVEMENTS IN WARLIKE INSTRUMENTALITIES

The Government will of course have a number of new devices submitted to it, and among them it must be expected there will be a great deal of trash. Nevertheless, there may be some wheat in the chaff, and the grain may be worth the labor of sifting.
—*Philadelphia Inquirer*, July 17, 1861

HOW THE ORDNANCE DEPARTMENT WORKER reacted to the latest piece of incoming mail can only be guessed, but he likely shook his head and muttered something like "Crank" under his breath. The six-page missive, received in Washington, DC, in August 1861 and signed only "Live Yankee," offered numerous unusual ideas for weapons, including noxious smoke, to use against Confederate troops. The employee scrawled on the letter's reverse an apt analysis—"Gives his peculiar view in relation to depriving enemies of life"—and decided that the communication warranted no further attention beyond being categorized and filed. Many letters of the same ilk, whether sent to military men or government officials, Union or Confederate, met the same fate of being diverted away from busy decision-makers and consigned to the oblivion of a storage box or filing cabinet.[1]

In large part, communications suggesting chemical weapons form the basis for this book. The ideas put forth seem odd today because they clash with our picture of how the Civil War was fought. Chemical weapons were used in ancient times and are a major concern today, but because Civil War combatants did not employ them to a great extent, it is easy to assume that interest in chemical warfare was quiescent during the period. That was not the case, as is shown in the following pages, although proposals for chemical weapons were usually dismissed out of hand.

Indeed, it was well known that suggestions for new weapons of any kind, especially in the North, were likely to fall on deaf ears. A few months into the war, a Philadelphia columnist urged his countrymen "to direct their attention forthwith to the improvement of all sorts of warlike instrumentalities" but noted "indications of impatience on the part of authorities at being pestered" with citizens' ideas for new weapons. *Scientific American,* a periodical particularly friendly to inventors, was incensed with the US Army's Ordnance Department and its chief, General James W. Ripley, because of his intolerance of what he termed "new and untried arms." Ripley had a large and growing army to equip, and he preferred to concentrate on procuring weapons of proven value quickly and in large numbers. Valuable time and resources were nevertheless spent on those new and untried arms—against Ripley's wishes and often when a person of influence intervened. Late in the war, Union ordnance officer Thomas J. Rodman testified that most of the attention spent by the department on improving weapons had been "in testing and considering the plans proposed by inexperienced persons." When ordnance decision-makers were free from outside interference, it is unlikely that wartime innovations by military men would have fared any better than those of civilians—or would even have been broached—unless they fit within the narrow limits of what was deemed practicable.[2]

Ripley's counterparts in the Confederate Ordnance Department also had their hands full, but the available records are inadequate to indicate whether they were equally unreceptive to unsolicited weapons ideas. One proposal evidently not forwarded to them was from S. M. Brian of Jackson, Louisiana, who suggested to General John C. Pemberton that balls made of cotton be wrapped with iron wire, soaked with turpentine, attached to spears, and set on fire before being hurled at the enemy.[3]

Rufus R. Rhodes, commissioner of patents for the Confederate States of America, was impressed that a large proportion of Confederate patents granted in 1861 were for "improvements in fire arms, or other destructive implements of war, a fact which strikingly illustrates the disposition of inventors . . . to contribute each his offering in furtherance and support of the great cause of civil liberty." The improvements described in those patent applications—none of which have been determined to be chemical weapons—differed somewhat from the weapons suggestions sent by citizens to government officials or to newspapers. The latter usually lacked detail and were offered up freely, often without serious consideration of practicality.

Yet Rhodes's statement does say something about the inventive spirit in the South. Rhodes added that the rejected patent applications displayed "the strongest evidence of the stimulating effect which the combined influence of the revolution . . . and the yearning behests of patriotism . . . has produced upon the Southern mind." If this was Rhodes's tactful way of saying that some ideas were imaginative to the point of being outlandish, that observation fit many of the ideas for weapons that officials in both North and South received from citizens. Rhodes did report that certain concepts described in granted patents had been adopted by the government, but Confederate ordnance officials, receptive or not, appear not to have tested or deployed any chemical weapons proposed by civilians. As described in later chapters, the chemical weapons tested or readied for use by the Confederacy are likely to have arisen in the minds of men serving in or employed by the military.[4]

It was not unusual for citizens, North and South, to air their proposals through periodicals. This may have been an attempt to garner popular support that they hoped would compel skeptical government bureaucrats to pay attention, but it also made the ideas available to the opponents, since newspapers found their way across enemy lines quite frequently. Some Northerners took their ideas directly to President Lincoln, an inventor himself, who was deemed more sympathetic than Ripley and his staff. Others name-dropped or enlisted the assistance of persons thought to have influence with decision-makers in the War Department.

Among the proponents of new weapons were individuals who were clearly unbalanced. Canadian Samuel Small, for example, offered President Lincoln the following:

> What for twelve years kept a secret from the World To Wit an Invention by which I can take one thousand cavalry and reduce the Whole South Territory to complete Submission in three months The nature of the Discovery is to shock by the power of mercury any Army or Fleet that may be brought together Into a State of stupefaction so that They can easily be made Prisoners Bound and Secured without doing them any material Injury You need not doubt it in the least as I have tried it on Animals such as Bears Deer &c With full effect.

"As a Field General or Officer you Will not find my Superior in the World," Small informed Lincoln, and followed his signature with the notation "Alias A Napoleon." Even apparently rational correspondents were largely uninformed about the complexities of weapons production. Thus there was ample justification for viewing weapons proposals warily. One must wonder, though, whether some of them should have attracted more attention and what the attendant consequences might have been.[5]

Not all Civil War proposals for chemical weapons were filed and forgotten. In fact, fume-producing incendiary devices, which were being developed by American inventors as early as the War of 1812, were planned or deployed by both the Union and Confederate military. Other chemical weapons were readied for use or tested for feasibility. Among the remaining ideas were some that seemed workable and even ahead of their time. The proposals, even those that never progressed beyond the idea stage, deserve attention. As Michael Musick, former Civil War archivist at the National Archives and Records Administration, observed, studying the might-have-beens "increases our awareness that the familiar course of events need not have taken place." It is impossible to say with certainty how events would have changed if some of the proposed chemical weapons had been deployed, but pondering the what-ifs can be a valuable and challenging exercise. Did any of the weapons have a reasonable chance of working? How might certain battles have developed had the agents been effectively deployed? What would have been the internal and worldwide political reaction to the use of chemical weapons?[6]

Investigating the proposals and the individuals who offered them provides insight into the knowledge and mores of the time. Upon what learning or notions were the ideas based, we may ask, and did their originators or others express ethical qualms about implementing them? Studying the proposals also helps place chemical weapons into their proper place on the historical timeline and adds another consideration for those eager to characterize the American Civil War as a transitional conflict—as, for example, the first modern war, the last ancient war, or the last Napoleonic war. Many of the substances proposed as weapons were used in antiquity and were familiar to the public, whereas others were of more recent discovery or development and foreshadowed agents used in future conflicts. Robert V. Bruce bluntly described most weapons inventors as "pitifully deluded," yet he acknowledged that among the proposals, one can discern "in silhouette almost all the feral implements of modern war." Indeed, some Civil War ideas were limited only because the technology that would have made them possible had not yet been developed. Some of these proposed weapons have obvious military and civilian counterparts, but whether the later devices evolved directly from the Civil War concepts is less clear.[7]

Finally, the Civil War's proposals for chemical weapons—and their originators—are fascinating in their own right. It is hard to read about the ideas or their authors without being terrified, enlightened, impressed, or even amused. Chemical weapons were certainly of interest during the war, and not only to their proponents. News items, commentaries, political cartoons, and even poems about chemical agents appeared in Civil War periodicals, demonstrating that the topic had not merely entered the public consciousness but progressed into the realm of popular culture. The suggested chemicals covered here range from bothersome to deadly poisonous and are frightening even today: incendiaries, hydrogen cyanide, arsenic compounds, chlorine, plant-based irritants, chloroform, acids, sulfur, and others. Some proposed modes of delivery were ingenious; others that appear absurd at first glance seem less so when their historical precedents are considered. Some of the weapons proponents were prominent citizens or renowned scientists, but most were "ordinary" enough to remain unnoticed by modern historians if not for their role in this story. One particular pursuit—the study or practice of medicine—was surprisingly common among these individuals yet seemingly at odds with the advocacy of chemical weapons.

All of the ideas were offered with apparent earnestness. For the moment, then, let these remarkable proposals be rescued from obscurity and given the attention most were denied a century and a half ago.

2

GREEK FIRE, AMERICAN STYLE

> We do not know of any substance bearing a resemblance to the
> renowned Greek fire of old: nevertheless there have not been
> wanting inventors who, dazzled by the visionary character of
> this exaggerated and mysterious substance, have labored to
> re-discover it.   —Edward C. Boynton, 1864

URIAH BROWN WAS A PERSISTENT man. During the War of 1812, he offered
the US government his weapon system consisting of an ironclad steamship
that could spray "liquid fire"—his version of the ancient Greek fire—onto
opposing vessels while remaining impervious to enemy cannon fire. Brown
conducted experiments "upon an extensive scale, in the presence of thousands of the citizens of Baltimore," who witnessed "the astonishing effects
of this terrible agent of destruction." The end of the war was in sight, however, and the government chose not to pursue Brown's system. In 1828, he
sought the government's patronage again, for what he said was the last
time, in hopes that he would "not be *forced* . . . to seek in a foreign land
that consideration and requital for his sacrifices and patriotic zeal which
have so long been witheld from him in his own." That appeal failed, as did
another in 1836.[1]

Finally, in 1847, during the Mexican War, Congress granted Brown $10,000
to conduct a public demonstration, which he held in Washington at the
western end of the city canal "in full view of the President's house." Brown,
aboard a scow containing the liquid fire and equipped with a pump to propel
the fluid sixty to seventy-five feet toward his target—he claimed a maximum
range of two hundred feet—failed at first to get the substance to ignite. With

his second attempt, he managed to set fire to the target, a tall mast to which empty tar barrels had been nailed. "A dense smoke and prodigious heat," reported official navy observers, "accompanied the jet of the liquid." Despite "the grand and interesting spectacle," the naval observers concluded that certain "practical difficulties" of Brown's system were "conclusive against its practical utility."[2]

Brown, still unwilling to give up, applied for further testing in a petition introduced to the House of Representatives in January 1848 by a congressman from Illinois named Abraham Lincoln. The House Committee on Naval Affairs concluded that Brown had gotten ample attention and saw "nothing in the results of experiments already made by the memorialist justifying any further action on the part of the government." Brown died without seeing his dream realized, but his idea arose again in 1863, when Mrs. John B. Hodges appealed to now President Lincoln. Mrs. Hodges asked that Brown's weapon system be reconsidered and referred the president to Brown's widow, among others. Lincoln evidently did not act on the request.[3]

At least three contemporaries of Brown's in the decades before the Civil War claimed to have their own versions of Greek fire. The first, Philip Rupel, asked for a congressional appropriation in 1835 to allow him to prove "his recently rediscovered submarine or Greek fire," but the request seems to have gone nowhere. The second, Homer Anderson from New York State, demonstrated his incendiary shell around 1855, while the Crimean War (1853–56) was under way, and was said to be in communication with European governments about his invention. Anderson, too, asked the US government to consider his shell but was turned down. The third, Levi Short, demonstrated his Greek fire to the government in 1848 only to have the War Department declare, according to Short, that it was "to[o] crewell a mode of warfare for any Christian nation to adopt." Short reappeared during the Civil War, as we shall see.[4]

Greek fire was a term used loosely to describe a fluid or solid substance that would ignite spontaneously (or upon being lit), burn on or under water, engulf objects in flame, and resist being extinguished by conventional means. Historical accounts available before and during the Civil War generally credited the composition's invention to Callinicus of Heliopolis, Syria. Greek fire was said to have been used as early as the seventh century AD, although incendiary compounds were employed well before then by various civilizations. The histories described Greek fire being projected by pumps or hurled in jars or other containers and terrorizing the forces against whom it was used. It became obsolete when weapons using gunpowder were developed to the point that they could prevent troops armed with the incendiary from getting near enough to use it. The formula for ancient Greek fire was unknown, but possible constituents were thought to include naphtha (a gasolinelike substance collected from petroleum wells in parts of the Middle East), sulfur, bitumen, and pitch.[5]

Incendiary materials other than so-called Greek fire were well known to artillery and ordnance officers of the Civil War. Projectiles, for example, could be heated until red hot or filled with molten iron, and then fired at enemy positions in hopes of igniting combustible materials. Portfire was a substance made of niter (potassium nitrate, or saltpeter), sulfur, and mealed powder (a form of gunpowder), sometimes containing antimony or steel filings. The composition was packed into small paper cases, pieces of which could be placed into incendiary shells called carcasses. Portfire was highly flammable but slow-burning and produced an intense, penetrating flame that could not be extinguished with water. Similar to portfire was Valenciennes compound, which, when ignited by the powder in artillery shells, "melts lava-like, and flows about, setting fire to combustibles it meets with, and evolving noxious fumes." Despite the long availability of these incendiary materials, some Civil War inventors—perhaps captivated by historical accounts of the destruction and consternation caused by ancient Greek fire—seemed intent on rediscovering the old formula and offering it to their government as a way to help vanquish the foe. Americans wishing to reproduce the substance had more than ancient history to inspire them, for the Crimean War had prompted individuals in the combatant nations to try their own hand at devising incendiary weapons.[6]

In 1853, British chemistry student Wentworth Scott developed a spontaneously igniting fluid, said to be phosphorus dissolved in bisulphide of carbon (carbon disulfide), and a concept for delivering it in artillery projectiles. Chemists of the time were well aware that the phosphorus in such mixtures would burst into flame spontaneously as the solvent, carbon disulfide, evaporated. Persons struck by the flaming substance could suffer serious burns, and the smoke, known today to contain various oxides of phosphorus, was capable of inducing coughing and other forms of respiratory irritation, yet the fluid was considered nonexplosive and safe to transport if protected from air. English chemist Lyon Playfair independently promoted essentially the same concept at about the same time. After the British Board of Ordnance failed to pursue either man's idea, their countryman Captain Henry Disney advocated a like, if not identical, substance and was met with a similar reception. Disney's compound was, according to his 1855 patent application, "composed of various combustible materials unnecessary to detail or expose" and could be modified "to cause blindness for several hours to all troops coming within a quarter of a mile of its operation." When demonstrated for a group of distinguished observers, a mild form of the blinding formula caused them "some irritation in the nostrils" and had a "remarkable resemblance to Lundy Foot snuff." Disney's patent application was refused—in fact, it was reported to have been "suppressed for the benefit of the government"—but another British military man, Captain John Norton, employed the phosphorus–carbon disulfide solution in rifle projectiles that could ignite objects at long distances.[7]

Also in 1855, John Macintosh received a British patent for combustible compounds composed of coal-tar naphtha and other substances, such as India rubber, gunpowder, phosphorus, carbon disulfide, and potassium. These mixtures, meant for charging incendiary shells and rockets, were also claimed to produce "dense suffocating vapours."[8]

The unwillingness of British military officials to pursue Scott's and Disney's proposals prompted concerns that Russia, Great Britain's foe in the Crimean War, would be more receptive to similar ideas and gain an advantage in armaments. One British scientist, Benjamin W. Richardson, MD, thought that newspaper descriptions of Scott's fluid and its intended use had essentially let the cat out of the bag. "The elements of the chymical problem are so simple and limited to such narrow bounds," observed Richardson, "that every chymist in Europe will see at once its full meaning and importance." Indeed, rumors had already arisen that Russia possessed a liquid fire that was capable of "burning under water, and destroying life by suffocation, in all who happen to be within a certain distance of its explosion." The weapon was thought identical to one invented by French chemist M. Fortier and called *boulet asphyxiant*. (France was a British ally in the Crimean War.) It had been offered twice to French military authorities, first by Fortier and then by M. Champion, a Frenchman scornfully considered to be "one of those who deem all means of gain lawful." The idea, rejected by the French authorities because its use would be "contrary to the laws of humanity and honourable warfare," had evidently found its way into enemy hands just as Champion "repaired his broken fortunes in Russia." Americans wishing to inform themselves of such developments could do so by perusing European publications or American periodicals like *Scientific American*.[9]

As might be expected, American proposals for versions of Greek fire became commonplace once the Civil War began. Among Northern inventors, one of the first to put forward his idea was G. Huff, MD, from Philadelphia, in late October 1861. Huff informed the War Department that he had developed a mortar shell that released "liquid streams of fire" that would "spread most fearfully in all directions." Huff's proposal was referred to General George B. McClellan, commander of the Army of the Potomac, who declared that "such means of destruction" were "hardly within the category of those recognized in civilized warfare." McClellan, who had served as an observer during the Crimean War, knew that "kindred inventions" had been employed in Europe but thought that they should not be used in the American conflict until other means of warfare had been exhausted. Dr. Huff's proposal was evidently shelved.[10]

The correspondent who signed his letter only as "Live Yankee" (see chapter 1) offered an idea for the defense of forts that had moats. "If the water . . . were covered with oil and some varnish of combustible sugar and camphene mixed with it on the approach of an enemy and set fire to on thier trying to cross they would be likely to back out." Camphene, also called turpentine, was a flammable liquid, and combustible sugar was an extremely flammable, explosive, and almost inextinguishable material made by mixing sugar with sulfuric and nitric acids. Camphene-spraying fire engines were proposed by A. Spear of West Randolph, Vermont, and combustible artillery shells containing a turpentine and alcohol mixture were suggested by physician Edwin E. Glezen of Ireland, Indiana.[11]

P. P. McIntyre of Rahway, New Jersey, suggested that night attacks on enemy fortifications might be undertaken by vessels firing large shells containing "tar balls," which would be as destructive as conventional shells and "fill the works with smoke, and suffocation, and at the same time afford light by which the rest of the fleet might see to direct their fire." "I hope," said McIntyre, "you will not think I have got tar on the brains but will give the tar ball a fair consideration." Uriah Brown's idea seemed resurrected when physician, dentist, inventor, and prominent conchologist James Lewis of Mohawk, New York, suggested fitting an ironclad vessel with a steam-powered device to project ignited crude petroleum or unrectified coal oil onto enemy vessels. F. G. Crary, former co-owner of a blast furnace in Kittanning, Pennsylvania, proposed using petroleum, "1000 barrels of which thrown by means of an engine upon or into Fort Wagner would make the rebels skedaddle out of it quicker than 10,000 bombs." Crary was referring to Battery Wagner, a Confederate stronghold on Morris Island, South Carolina, and the substance would presumably be set ablaze. "The means of throwing it upon or in the forts," added Crary, "will suggest themselves to you." The Ordnance Department appears to have quietly filed these suggestions. Various other inventors of incendiary substances during the war years appear not to have sought or gotten the notice of government officials.[12]

Probably the first inventor after Uriah Brown to earn significant attention for his version of Greek fire was Benjamin Franklin Greenough. In the late 1830s, Greenough began demonstrating his "chemical oil," a mixture of alcohol, spirits of turpentine, and other constituents intended to replace sperm oil in lamps. He also patented a lamp and lighting system to be used in conjunction with his formula, as well as "an electrical conductor for submarine telegraphs." According to *Scientific American*, Greenough, although nearly blind for many years, "had pursued his chemical investigations with unabated zeal" before producing a liquid fire for military use. On December 14, 1861, he demonstrated the fluid at the Washington Navy Yard before an audience that included Assistant Secretary of the Navy Gustavus V. Fox; Commander John A. Dahlgren, commandant of the navy yard; and navy lieutenants O. C. Badger and Henry Augustus Wise. Greenough employed an apparatus that included a pipe three-sixteenths of an inch in diameter to project the fluid thirty to fifty feet toward his target, a solid three-foot-thick oak timber set on a platform. The liquid ignited several feet from the nozzle, "expanding to a diameter of two feet, with an intense combustion, which covered the target and the platform with liquid fire." The fire appeared inextinguishable, burned on water, and "emitted dense fumes and smoke which darkened the atmosphere and would have suffocated any human being who had come within its influence." Shells containing the fluid were also successfully demonstrated.[13]

Lieutenant Badger was particularly impressed, saying, "If this fluid was thrown from a powerful force pump on the deck of a vessel, nothing could stand before it, and the deck would have to be abandoned." Badger may actually have used Greenough's formula when he commanded the USS *Anacostia*, which shelled a Confederate position at Cockpit Point, Virginia, about the first of January 1862. According to newspaper reports, the shells, "charged with a peculiar combustible material," failed to explode. Regardless, Badger thought in April 1862 that Greenough's sprayable formula might be just the thing to defend the ironclad USS *Monitor* against a boarding party: "The pipe of a hose thrown out of the small holes in the 'dome,' or out of the pilot house, would, I think, clear the decks sooner than the heaviest discharge of musketry that could possibly be brought to bear." Lieutenant Wise agreed that "with respect to that 'liquid fire' stuff, which is petroleum, naphtha, and benzine, it might do well on an emergency, in all save the risk of the fire running down the gratings of the *Monitor* or the crevices about the turret and setting her going below." Wise's comments notwithstanding, the composition of Greenough's liquid fire remained a secret. *Scientific American* thought it was phosphorus mixed with either naphtha or carbon disulfide.[14]

It is unclear whether Greenough's formula was ever used in combat. One 1909 obituary for Greenough's widow stated that it was used in the bombardment of Charleston, South Carolina, while another obituary indicated that the government had broken a promise to use it to defend Washington only. Both obituaries agreed that no more of the fluid was supplied to the US government after the uses mentioned and that the Russian government had unsuccessfully attempted to buy the formula—for a "big price" or $1 million, depending on the account.[15]

Meanwhile, Levi Short, disappointed by the government in 1848, showed that he, too, could be persistent. In 1860, when the census identified him as a machinist residing in Buffalo, he patented an "apparatus for manufacture of illuminating-gas." His primary efforts, though, had been devoted to perfecting his formula for Greek fire. Rockets and shells containing the material had been demonstrated on Lake Erie and the Canada shore, "to the entire satisfaction of all that saw them from the American side." Encouraged by prominent New York politicians, Short ventured once again to the nation's capital, where he met with President Lincoln and conducted two demonstrations in January 1862. The first was unsatisfactory because the proper materials were not on hand, but the second, held on January 22 just south of the White House, was highly successful. Two eight-inch shells containing Short's composition were exploded, "throwing a shower of fire in every direction to a height of from forty to fifty feet, and covering a space of earth one hundred feet in diameter where it burned with intense heat and brilliancy over ten minutes."[16]

Then, as Short described it, "I was sent from one department to another untill I imagined myself the veritable Wandering Jew." He did manage to meet General Benjamin F. Butler, who wanted Short to prepare some shells for the upcoming New Orleans expedition. On March 2, 1862, Short was about to prepare additional shells for the Sawyer guns on the Rip Raps, an artificial island at Hampton Roads, Virginia, and site of the Union's Fort Calhoun (soon to be renamed Fort Wool). This was the last time, he said to Secretary of War Edwin M. Stanton, that he would assist the government at his own expense.[17] He continued:

If my government wants my services it must be signified through you within seven days for like our young and gallient commander on the Potomac I have also drempt a dream I drempt that Washington stood before me with eyes downcast and weeping but said not a word pointed to my bleeding country and Napoleon Bonapart came pointed towards France and said Son of America haste thee to Paris and the Royal Ear of my Nephew will listen to your story and will send the orriflammy of France to acompany your Greek fire until England's Navey is swept from the seas, and on finding that money to bear my expenses is waiting in New York I am half persuaded to go and eagerly wait your answer.[18]

Stanton was apparently unmoved by Short's demand.

Short's Greek fire came in more than one form. One, a liquid, could be projected "from a huge syringe, or other appropriate engine, to a great distance." His 1863 patent for an incendiary composition called for the mixing of charcoal, asphaltum, antimony, sulfur, and naphtha. The liquid rising to the top of the mixture—possibly the substance to be projected as described above—could be combined with a "vegetable fibrous substance" and packed into artillery shells. The wet fibrous substance, when scattered by the explosion of the shell, would adhere to and help ignite objects that it struck. The sediment, Short's so-called "solidified Greek fire," was pressed while still malleable into small metallic cylinders—tin was typically used—that were sealed at one end. The cylinders, which measured about three inches long and five-eighths inch wide, were then packed into artillery shells and surrounded by the bursting charge of gunpowder. The explosion of projectiles on reaching their target would ignite the incendiary substance and turn the cylinders into so many rockets, which would "dart out in every direction with ten thousand tongues hissing and burning wherever they go." According to one account, the burning cylinders emitted "a heavy sulphurous smoke in large quantities." It was reported that a French agent who had witnessed Short's demonstrations offered him $25,000 for the formula but was turned down.[19]

In the weeks after his March 1862 letter to Stanton, Short had reason to be optimistic about his prospects. During that month, some of the shells he had supplied to Butler were fired from the general's gunboat *Saxon* at the enemy shore at the mouth of the Mississippi River. The projectiles, hurled some three miles, set fire to a canebrake, which was still burning five days later. Union artillerists at Rip Raps fired on a Confederate position at Sewell's

Point on March 23, and one of the shells "filled with a new liquid fire exploded in the midst of the rebel parade ground" and did, it was thought, considerable damage. In April, a Confederate officer at Fort Jackson, downriver from New Orleans, reported that some of the shells used to bombard his position were "filled with liquid fire, and besides being very destructive, emit[ted] an unpleasant and almost stifling odor."[20] Short also took steps to garner public attention by having his Greek fire appear at Nixon's Cremorne Gardens, "a most beautiful and interesting place of amusement" in New York City. An August 1862 advertisement proclaimed:

> A gorgeous fountain of pure fire throws up its brilliant jets in a thousand graceful forms, actually scattering around streams of living fire mingled with water. It is a singularly grand and beautiful effect, and is alone worthy of the price of admission. This new and unquenchable fire is the discovery of Mr. Levi Short, and by it he asserts that he can destroy the fleets of every nation of the earth. It certainly seems very formidable, and suggests to all to keep at a respectable distance.[21]

An April 1863 news article reported that Short's solidified Greek fire had been used at the Battle of Malvern Hill (July 1, 1862), was believed responsible for the destruction of the Confederate privateer *Rattlesnake* (formerly CSS *Nashville*) by the ironclad USS *Montauk* (February 28, 1863), and had been supplied to "nearly all our [the Union's] blockading squadrons and fleets." Shells with Short's composition were reportedly carried by at least one ironclad bound for Virginia, but whether the rest was true is questionable. In May 1863, Short did manage to supply solidified Greek fire to Admiral David D. Porter, who used a small quantity to shell Vicksburg, Mississippi, in July. Porter seemed pleased with the incendiary, and his positive report set the stage for its most well-known performance: the bombardment of Charleston.[22]

Early on the morning of August 22, 1863, Union artillerists under the command of General Quincy A. Gillmore opened fire on Charleston with a single gun from a distance of about four and a half miles. The gunners manning the two-hundred-pounder (eight-inch) Parrott rifle, dubbed the "Swamp Angel," had at their disposal four types of shells. Some contained an explosive charge of powder only, while the others had the explosive charge supplemented by one of three incendiary materials: portfire, Short's solidified Greek fire, or an incendiary mixture devised by Alfred Berney, a rival of Short's. Sixteen projectiles were fired that night, with twelve reportedly landing in town. On the night of August 23, the Swamp Angel fired another twenty rounds, with the last causing the gun to burst; Charleston newspapers reported that thirteen or fourteen of these projectiles, "mostly incendiary shells," landed in town.[23]

Exactly how many shells of each type reached town and exploded is difficult to determine. Gillmore's aide-de-camp reported that twenty-four Short and twelve Berney shells were fired during the two nights. Gillmore stated that twelve of twenty-two Short shells fired from eight-inch Parrott rifles—not necessarily just the Swamp Angel on those two occasions—burst prematurely. Gillmore's chief of artillery said that the Short shells "worked very poorly, nearly every one prematurely exploding; and it is not determined whether any shells containing Greek fire ever reached Charleston." The crew manning the Swamp Angel reported premature explosions of several Short shells, "scattering the tubes containing the much-vaunted composition of Greek fire into the marsh grass, but no trace of the terrible effects promised could be seen." The numbers in the various reports cannot be satisfactorily reconciled, but the consensus was that shells containing solidified Greek fire performed badly. Nevertheless, newspapers gave Short much of the credit (or blame) for devising the incendiary used against the town. A few structures were damaged by exploding shells, but only one fire resulted, and it was extinguished easily. Gillmore said that Short's solidified Greek fire had no advantages over and burned less intensely than ordinary portfire.[24]

Gillmore attributed the premature explosions to the heat generated by friction between the tin cylinders containing Short's formula and the interior surface of the shell, which was suddenly put into a spiral motion when the rifled Parrott gun was fired. Short attempted to remedy the fault by filling the shells with powder in a different manner and altering the wrapping of the cylinders, but of forty-one Parrott or mortar rounds that contained solidified Greek fire and were used to bombard Charleston or nearby targets during the prolonged siege, twenty-nine did not explode or exploded prematurely.[25]

Short tried vainly to salvage his reputation by offering to tailor his formula for use against enemy fortifications. He suggested adding "nausiating properties whitch will soon cause them to oncover by filling their casemate with a steanch that cannot be endured." He further proposed to introduce the same offensive substance into tin hand grenades for use in an attack on Confederate-held Fort Sumter. Short died on November 26, 1863, and although his compounds evidently did little damage during the war, some Southerners did not rue his passing.[26] One sentiment was expressed by an unnamed Confederate in a poem, this excerpt from which began with a statement from the devil:

"Greek fire suits me well;
      Its author—I'll promote him—
His proper sphere is Hell."
      This said, the Devil smote him.

Down to the shades below
      Where Yankee fiends must wallow,
The soul of Short did go—
      Soon may his master follow!

Fill now the caldron up,
      Pile vandal souls still higher;
Henceforth Old Nick shall sup
      By Levi Short's Greek fire![27]

Short's biggest rival was Alfred Berney of Jersey City. Shortly after the duel between the USS *Monitor* and CSS *Virginia* on March 9, 1862, Berney approached Assistant Secretary of the Navy Fox with a bold proposal: allow him to equip the *Monitor*, at his own expense, with his incendiary material in shells and in fluid form for projection from a pump, and he would go personally to Norfolk and direct that vessel in the destruction of the *Virginia* and the burning or taking of the city. Berney, according to his proponent, the political and social gadfly Oliver S. Halsted Jr., "was virtually laughed at, & denied every opportunity." The navy, however, agreed to test his composition—which included benzole, crude petroleum, coal tar, coal oil, and turpentine—and did so at the Washington Navy Yard on March 19, 1862. The results were encouraging enough to warrant supplying shells charged with Berney's fluid to the navy squadron at Hampton Roads.[28]

Lieutenant Wise, who had witnessed the demonstration of Greenough's liquid fire, thought that the Berney shells would "puzzle the devil himself even in his own dominions, to put out, should one crack over into hell." On April 30, the same day that Wise expressed his enthusiasm, seven Berney shells were fired at a Confederate position in Yorktown, Virginia, from the USS *Marblehead*. The vessel's commander initially reported that five of the projectiles exploded on land and appeared to start a fire. He later experimented with the fluid, which caused so little damage when burning that he became doubtful that the shells fired from the *Marblehead* had ignited anything. Also on April 30, Union artillerists lobbed four one-hundred-pounder shells filled with Greek fire (probably Berney's composition) at the

Yorktown wharf without producing an observable effect. Berney charged the navy $13,000 for 111 barrels of his fluid but accepted $1,100 after he was unable to produce receipts for the $8,000 he claimed to have spent on materials; the navy noted that even the $1,100 was 20 percent higher than the market price of petroleum and coal tar.[29]

Further tests were conducted on April 4, 1863, this time by army personnel at West Point, New York. According to Captain Stephen Vincent Benét, an ordnance officer, shells charged with Berney's fluid performed well when the projectiles exploded, as did the fluid alone when projected by a rotary pump and ignited by a torch near the pump's nozzle. The fires caused by the shells were extinguished by water, whereas the ignited fluid burned easily upon water and produced an intense flame and large volumes of thick smoke.[30] When the government did nothing immediately to follow up, Halsted wrote President Lincoln on April 25 to express Berney's frustration:

> [Mr. Berney] has struggled & tried . . . for over two years to induce your subordinate officials, who control in such matters, to employ, or allow him to employ, what we believe to be the only underline certain weapon, & sure means of bringing this parricidal contest to a speedy termination—He was studiously misused, abused & subjected to such wrong treatment, in every way, that he retired in disgust, determined to secure his secret by Patent, & seek that Justice & fair play at the hand of Foreign Nations which was insultingly denied him, in his native land.[31]

The upshot was that a number of shells filled with Berney's fluid were ordered, and some ended up with General Gillmore, who used them to bombard Charleston.

Like the shells containing Short's solidified Greek fire, the projectiles filled with Berney's liquid fire and used by the Swamp Angel did not live up to expectations. In particular, they often failed to explode. The first explanation offered was that the shells were fitted with percussion fuses rather than the time fuses that Berney had specified. Because the Swamp Angel's barrel was elevated to a high angle, the elongated missiles were thought to have maintained that angle throughout their downward flight and struck with their fuse, on the shell's nose, pointing upward. The problem would supposedly be remedied when the steamer *Arago* arrived with a supply of Berney shells with time fuses, but the opportunity to test the theory never arose. Berney, in the patent specifications for his liquid-fire shell, attributed the previous failures of his projectiles to weakness in the section that held the explosive charge of powder. Halsted maintained that three Berney shells fired by the Swamp Angel worked properly and were "confounded with a worthless shell known as the Short shell, which I predicted a failure in advance." Berney shells, he said, would function properly seven out of ten times if properly prepared and fitted with the right fuses. Captain Benét, in his report of the April tests, described the percussion fuses on Berney shells as performing badly, but he recommended against time fuses because they were likely to detonate the shells before or after the instant of impact. "Unless the explosion takes place in contact with the object," he said, "the fluid would fail in its effects, as the flame is not scattered to a very great distance."[32]

Berney evidently kept his hopes alive, for he advertised in May 1864 for large amounts of "pitch pine stumps or fat pine wood." Such materials were the source of pine tar and pitch. In addition, turpentine, which before the war had come primarily from live pines growing in North Carolina, could be extracted with newly developed techniques from pine stumps and wood. Turpentine was a component of Berney's liquid fire, and because the war had curtailed shipments of North Carolina turpentine, he seemed intent on producing his own. He also found an officer willing to try his incendiary compound, as Levi Short had, in the person of General Butler.[33]

On November 24, 1864, Butler and a group of other officers, including Generals Ulysses S. Grant and George G. Meade, gathered to witness a demonstration of Berney's liquid fire. A few days before, Berney had arrived at Fort Brady, on the James River, Virginia, "preparatory to the grand test in presence of the great men." A few trial shells containing the incendiary fluid and fitted with the Tice concussion fuse worked beautifully, delighted Berney, and convinced the battery commander that Berney's invention was "no humbug." During the actual demonstration, forty-two Berney shells were fired into enemy territory at a group of frame houses, which all took fire and burned to the ground. Grant remarked that the fuse problem appeared to have been resolved. Someone then "spirted the stuff through a little hose and set the stream on fire," producing an unquenchable fire and columns of black smoke. When poured on the ground and ignited, Berney's fluid burned "with a clear flame of low temperature," which led one observer to guess that the substance contained turpentine and petroleum. When Butler opined that five men equipped with a small garden engine and a quantity of liquid fire could hold a redoubt, Meade, perhaps recalling how gunpowder had made Greek fire obsolete centuries before, countered, "Certainly, only your engine fires thirty feet, and a minié rifle 3000 yards, and I am afraid your fire men might be killed, before they have a chance to burn up their adversaries!" If Berney's liquid fire saw action during the rest of the war, its role was negligible.[34]

One last proponent of liquid fire warrants mention. Robert L. Fleming also managed to get some attention from government officials, conducted a demonstration in Washington (an ad touted "Gen. Fleming's wonderfully destructive shell . . . showing its destructive efficiency and fearful power when used in sea or land service"), and had his invention praised by Captain Benét after tests at West Point.[35] Believing himself to have been shamefully neglected, he stated on February 8, 1864:

> There can be no doubt of the failure, of those parties [Short and Berney], to do what they proposed; and, I again present my self, confident that I can accomplish all, and more than I ever promised. I now ask an opportunity, to bring my shells to bear, on Charleston which has so long been an eyesore, a reproach to those men who have stolen part of my thunder, just enough, however, to make a stupendous failure.[36]

A number of thirty-pounder Parrott shells, each containing about a pint of Fleming's mixture—the ingredients of which remained confidential—were sent in November 1864 to Union artillerists in Virginia. There they remained untouched until March 1865, when they were tested before a board of officers convened by General Grant. Fifteen shells fired at wooden targets burst as intended but ignited only some dry leaves and brush. Fleming's liquid, poured on the ground and ignited, produced a flame with very little heat. An observer concluded that "the invention was entirely useless for burning abatis, stockading, or palisading [obstructions or defensive structures made of wood], unless surrounded by dry leaves or other very combustible material." While Fleming's projectiles "would doubtless be better than the common shell for firing houses or shipping . . . it is doubtful whether the 30-pounder shell would contain enough of the liquid to accomplish these ends." It is unclear whether Fleming's formula was ever used in combat. In any event, Fleming, like the men who had stolen part of his thunder, would not see his invention play nearly the role he had imagined.[37]

Despite the lofty claims of their inventors, the various forms of so-called Greek fire used by Union forces caused minimal damage. Federal forces were essentially no better equipped with incendiary weapons than they would have been had Uriah Brown and later proponents of Greek fire never sought government patronage. The attention devoted by the North, however, to various formulations of Greek fire—including demonstrations before high-ranking military and civil officials and even use in combat—showed that there were exceptions to the claims of *Scientific American* and others that inventions were being neglected.

3

THE TORCH FOR THE TORCH

I would not be surprised if their Greek-fire turns out to be a Yankee humbug. I hope soon to be able to return their compliment with a little "southern liquid fire" which will make them open their eyes.

—General P. G. T. Beauregard, November 1863

EVEN IF IT CAUSED LITTLE damage, Gillmore's bombardment of Charleston prompted strong reactions in both North and South and even across the Atlantic. It spurred discussions about the ethics of using Greek fire and helped accelerate the Confederates' development of their own unconventional incendiary weapons. Much of the response, especially in the North, stemmed from a mistaken notion of what a key figure said about the incident.

The shelling was preceded on August 21, 1863, by an ultimatum sent from Gillmore to General Pierre Gustave Toutant Beauregard, the commander of Confederate forces in and around Charleston: evacuate nearby Morris Island and Fort Sumter immediately, or Union artillery would open fire on the town. Gillmore's deadline passed without a response, so early on August 22, the Swamp Angel's crew began hurling the aforementioned projectiles at the "cradle of rebellion." Beauregard wrote back, protesting bitterly that he had not been given sufficient time to respond or order the evacuation of the town's civilians. He called the bombardment "an act of inexcusable barbarity" carried out by use of "the most destructive missiles ever used in war into the midst of a city taken unawares, and filled with sleeping women and children."[1]

Gillmore, in response, noted astutely that Beauregard did not allege the shelling "to be in violation of the usages of civilized warfare, except as regards the length of time allowed as notice of my intention." He also pointed out that Charlestonians had been well aware that an attack on the town was imminent. Indeed, Charleston mayor Charles Macbeth, in consultation with Beauregard, had recommended on July 9 that women, children, and other noncombatants leave the city as soon as possible. William Stuart, a British diplomat who had seen the correspondence between the two generals in newspapers, agreed with Gillmore's interpretation of Beauregard's protest. Stuart thought that Beauregard's phrase "the most destructive missiles ever used in war" likely referred to the size of the shells rather than their contents and that the general's protest was primarily against the bombardment having occurred without time for the removal of noncombatants.[2]

Northern newspapers did not start printing the Gillmore-Beauregard exchange until August 31, but a few days earlier, they published a dispatch from Morris Island written by Charles C. Fulton, editor of Baltimore's *American and Commercial Advertiser* and agent for the Associated Press. Fulton described (but did not quote) Beauregard as "denouncing 'Greek Fire' as a villainous compound, unworthy of civilized nations." Northern readers quickly seized on that phrase, attached it to Beauregard as his actual utterance, and began ridiculing the general as a hypocrite and complainer. Artillerists under his command had, after all, fired red-hot shot at Fort Sumter in April 1861, and what effective difference was there between such projectiles and Greek fire? "It is puerile in Beauregard," said a Unionist newspaper in Nashville, "to characterize a more efficient engine or instrument of war as barbarous, as if the art of war did not consist of the most destructive agencies."[3] A columnist for a New York newspaper thought that the incendiary shells were not effective enough:

> When we get hold of the right kind of incendiary composition, and explode it in the right spot, we may be able to start a conflagration that will leave nothing but a mass of ashes and rubbish to mark the spot on which the proud city of Charleston now stands. There is a good chance now for ingenious chemists to invent the material by which this desirable consummation may be attained. It has not yet been discovered.[4]

Another journalist joked, "We learn that Beauregard's remonstrance against . . . Greek fire . . . was on account of the horrid *smell* emitted by that substance. No doubt he thinks we should charge our bombs with cologne and lavender and ottar of roses."[5] A similar theme appeared in this excerpt by a pro-Union poet:

An hour passed—"Old Beau" awoke,
Half stifled by a "villainous" smoke,
Enough the very devil to choke,
While all around the "stink-pots" broke
And blinded him with sand.
He cursed the "villainous compound,"
Which stunk like pole-cats far around;
Then roared with wild demonic shriek—
"Lord! what a smell! the Greek! the Greek!"[6]

The *New York Daily News*, owned by Copperhead and New York congressman Benjamin Wood, deplored the shelling:

Civilization, until now, by that tacit understanding among Christian nations which rejects the use of unnatural weapons, has refrained from its employment, even in the most bloody and desperate campaigns. It has been left for this Administration, which claims to be waging war in the name of philanthropy, to conjure up this liquid demon as a fit ally to their purpose of extermination. . . . If a fleet of iron-clads should appear in New York harbor, and at the midnight hour should throw their deadly missils, bursting with liquid and unquenchible fire, into the heart of the metropolis; while standing amid the ashes of our homes, and gazing upon the crisped and burning bodies of our wives and children, we could perhaps appreciate the savageism of that style of warfare. . . . Let Greek fire and such monstrous contrivances be things of the barbarous past, unworthy of the valor and warlike skill of an enlightened people.[7]

British newspapers were quick to print excerpts from the *Daily News* column.[8]

The *Charleston Daily Courier* referred to the shelling as "incendiary villainy."[9] By and large, Southern newspapers condemned Gillmore for targeting noncombatants:

Gilmore is throwing shell into the city of Charleston with the full knowledge that they are far more likely to destroy the lives of women and children, or citizens in the pursuit of peaceful avocations than of soldiers in arms. . . . Such an enemy is an outlaw, and we may proceed against him by any mode of punishment and retaliation we choose to adopt. An eye for an eye is still the rule of war.—What, then, if we say *the torch for the torch!*[10]

Readers on both sides of the Atlantic noted a tendency for British commentators to sternly disapprove of Gillmore's actions. "Two-thirds of the British press," observed the *New York Ledger*, "denounce as barbarous the employment of Greek fire in the bombardment of Charleston." One London journalist, who was clearly not part of that majority, was less than perturbed by the shelling. "Many old ladies of both sexes," he wrote, "appear to have been scandalized beyond endurance at reports which have reached the Old World about this last grievous cruelty of the Federals." The ethics of warfare, he reasoned, boiled down to the facts that "you have the clear right to demolish the enemy as best you can" and that "people who cannot look terror in the face should not make war." A British reporter in Richmond guessed, "It is probably known in England long before this time [January 1864] that the Greek fire is not more formidable than a child's Christmas crackers."[11]

What of the Southern armaments' response to the shelling of Charleston? A British commentator ventured that "in pure self-defence the Confederates have been fain to go to their own inventors for the same or a like combustible." In fact, Southern citizens, like their Northern counterparts, had been proposing incendiary weapons for some time. One proposed using shells containing combustible sugar against Union blockading vessels. John Travis, a famous marksman, was said to have been offering the Confederate government a fluid that, when exposed to air, ignited spontaneously and produced an intensely hot flame that could not be extinguished with water. Travis kept the fluid's recipe secret, but the description brings to mind the phosphorus–carbon disulfide mixture investigated by British inventors. One Southerner proposed that the USS *Monitor* be attacked with a stream of turpentine projected from a fire engine and ignited at the nozzle. At least one Northerner offered his version of Greek fire to the South. In late November 1860, shortly after Abraham Lincoln was elected president but before any state had seceded, New York inventor Homer Anderson (see chapter 2) offered his incendiary shell to Governor William Henry Gist of South Carolina. According to Anderson, the shell would be particularly apt for defending Charleston and other Southern ports; whether Anderson received a reply is unclear.[12]

Confederate investigation and production of incendiaries actually predated Gillmore's bombardment of Charleston. Confederate navy lieutenant Beverly Kennon, assigned to the Ordnance Department at New Orleans in late July 1861, reported that he had directed the manufacture of hand grenades containing Greek fire and liquid-fire shells, all of his own invention. Production of the items was stopped because of their expense, yet some grenades and shells were furnished to the Confederate army. In December 1861, Confederate ordnance officer William Richardson Hunt paid the Memphis firm of Quinby & Robinson for work done on apparatus "for experiment with Greek fire." General Beauregard himself directed investigation into liquid incendiaries months before the Swamp Angel opened fire. The general, derided in the Northern press for his alleged condemnation of Greek fire, had actually been in an arms race of sorts with Union weapons developers, a fact consistent with Beauregard not specifically protesting Gillmore's use of incendiary shells. The Union general's "act of inexcusable barbarity," though, helped remove moral obstacles to Beauregard using Greek fire himself, for "the torch for the torch" principle now applied.[13]

Unconventional incendiary weapons were first being considered by Beauregard no later than January or February 1863, for early that March, he asked a trusted consultant, John Richardson Cheves, MD, to conduct experiments with liquid fire. Cheves, a planter from Savannah, came from a distinguished family. His late father, Langdon Cheves, had been a judge and Speaker of the US House of Representatives, and a brother, also named Langdon, was an accomplished engineer who helped create the Confederate observation balloon Gazelle and supervised the construction of Battery Wagner. John briefly attended the US Military Academy in the early 1830s before receiving his medical degree in 1838 from the Medical College of the State of South Carolina. In May 1862, he was put in charge of chain and boom obstructions and underwater mines for the defense of Charleston Harbor against Union vessels. Although his harbor defense efforts were often frustrated, Cheves earned Beauregard's esteem for the "zeal, indomitable energy, and manifold resources" he had used to overcome great difficulties.[14]

In response to Beauregard's request, Cheves first investigated "liquid fires which had been the subject of experiments at Woolwich," a probable reference to British tests of Henry Disney's composition of phosphorus in carbon disulfide. Cheves tested two such fluids and by April 1863 had concluded that "they and, for like reasons, all liquids so combustible were not suitable for shells." A letter received at Beauregard's headquarters on April 1, 1863, may have directed Cheves's further research. The communication was from Joseph Jones, MD, a graduate of Princeton and of the University of Pennsylvania's medical school and a surgeon in the Confederate army. Jones, an avid scientist and researcher, had written to the secretary of war through Vice President Alexander Stephens in early 1862 to describe certain plans for artillery shells. That letter, said Jones, was "returned with a few superficial objections," but the threats that Union forces presented at Charleston, Savannah, Vicksburg, and elsewhere again prompted the physician to encourage experimentation with shells that he believed would "produce most powerful and destructive effects upon the ships of the enemy." Thus Jones appealed to Beauregard.[15]

Jones's first suggestion (his others are described in the next chapter) was for a phosphorous shell. "It is my belief," said Jones, "that no substance, not even liquid iron, is more suitable for the ignition of ships than Phosphorus; and . . . it produces an inaspirable gas which would drive out men from any confined space, and prevent them from working their guns." He went on to describe various ways that solid phosphorus—covered with water to prevent combustion—could be introduced into artillery shells. The detonation of a shell would ignite the phosphorus, which would set fire to any wood that it struck and produce fumes that would obscure vision and "attack most violently the eyes & lungs of the gunners and drive them on deck." Sufficient amounts of phosphorus, said Jones, could be readily obtained from bones by a familiar and simple process. Beauregard immediately referred Jones's letter to Cheves.[16]

Cheves's initial opinion was that phosphorus would not ignite timber as efficiently as molten iron, hot shot, or carcasses, but he proceeded to experiment with it and found that solid "phosphorus in water would on explosion deliver the phosphorus in a state of vivid combustion as a semi-fluid." A demonstration of phosphorous shells was then conducted on August 28, 1863, near Savannah. A twelve-pounder shell exploding in the air released "a burning cloud of phosphorus . . . from which particles of ignited phosphorus descended . . . continuing in a state of ignition." Similar shells set grass and twigs on fire, even though "every tree and blade of grass was thoroughly wet" from a recent rain shower. Lieutenant Colonel Charles C. Jones Jr., an artillery officer, opined that "no troops could withstand the terrible influences of these shells bursting in their midst, and evolving not only this mass of insidious fire, but also clouds of gas of a most deleterious character." The projectiles, he concluded, were superior to so-called liquid fires. Whether the artillerist believed that phosphorus was better than conventional incendiary compounds at igniting combustible material is difficult to determine, but he clearly regarded the fact that burning phosphorus produced noxious vapors as an advantage.[17]

Contrary to what Surgeon Jones contended, though, obtaining a sufficient supply of phosphorus would not be simple. In April 1863, Cheves estimated that the phosphorus needed to fill one eight-inch shell would cost $100. That September, Cheves reported that the market price of imported phosphorus was $20 per pound. Producing one pound of phosphorus from bones would require about five and a half pounds of sulfuric acid, which cost $7.50 a pound. Thus phosphorus would cost about twice as much to manufacture as to import. The Confederacy was manufacturing sulfuric acid at Charlotte and elsewhere, but the substance was needed for batteries to power the telegraph system, for the manufacture of certain medicines, and—perhaps most vital to the war effort—for production of nitric acid, from which fulminate of mercury, the explosive in percussion caps, ultimately resulted. Monthly production of sulfuric acid at Charlotte reached four thousand to five thousand pounds by late 1864, but there may not have been much to spare in 1863 for phosphorus production. In any event, Colonel Josiah Gorgas, chief of ordnance, ordered fifteen hundred pounds of phosphorus for Cheves from Nassau and Bermuda in October 1863. At that time, Beauregard's intention was to use phosphorous shells against enemy encampments, "chiefly in the event an attempt shall be made to bombard this city [Charleston] especially with incendiary shells."[18]

The scarcity and cost of phosphorus prompted Cheves to investigate mixtures that required less of that substance. He hit on a combination of one part phosphorus to five parts pitch and sulfur, which he preferred, he said, "because a larger quantity can be introduced, it will burn more readily & longer, it spreads more effectually & and the effects [of the fumes] are more *stifling*." Cheves reported supplying ninety-three incendiary shells (of unspecified composition) to ordnance officers by February 1864. At that time, Beauregard told Cheves that little had been accomplished militarily with the phosphorous shells "for the want of combustible material within range of our guns." Some of the shells evidently made their way to Savannah, for in January 1864, General Thomas Jordan, Beauregard's chief of staff, asked a general there whether "liquid-fire shells" could be fired at a Union position. While working on the shells, Cheves noted a simple point that was too often ignored by amateur inventors: Regardless of the destructiveness of the payload, it could not be assumed that every aspect of the weapon system would work. The large volume of phosphorus he wanted to put in shells would displace some of their gunpowder, so Cheves recommended that tests be performed to determine the minimum amount of powder needed to burst the shells. Cheves also prepared a number of phosphorus-containing grenades. These devices, intended for the defense of Fort Sumter, were made from twelve-pounder shells with an attached friction primer. Troops would simply hook a long lanyard to the serrated wire loop of the primer—similar to the pin on a modern hand grenade—and throw the shell from a wall or embrasure.

The momentum of the falling shell would pull it free from the serrated wire, which was still held by the lanyard, and cause the primer to ignite.[19]

The extent to which any of Cheves's weapons were used is unclear. More certain was Beauregard's high regard for the planter turned weapons consultant. "It gives me pleasure to say," wrote the general to Cheves, "that I have ever found you earnest in your efforts to give these headquarters the benefit of your chemical knowledge and habits of industrious research." Cheves's dedication to duty was particularly evident as he continued his work through family tragedies. In June 1862, while he was busy with harbor defenses, his son, Edward, was killed in battle while serving as a volunteer aide-de-camp to General Alexander R. Lawton. "The affliction of my poor wife & daughter," Cheves wrote to his brother Langdon, "is very great—how can it be otherwise with us all." On July 3, 1863, in the midst of Cheves's investigation into incendiary materials, William T. Haskell, his sister's son, was killed at Gettysburg, and one week later, Cheves's brother Langdon and nephew Charles T. Haskell Jr. (William's brother) were both killed at Battery Wagner. How these losses affected Cheves's work or colored his views about the urgency or morality of his efforts is hard to say, but his correspondence reveals no particular bitterness toward the enemy.[20]

The North seemed to have a technological edge in incendiaries, so the Confederates gathered what intelligence they could about the armaments. A Charleston newspaper reported that two Union prisoners, who must have been highly imaginative, had described the projectiles fired at the town by General Gillmore as being filled with "a compound of ether and guano, the stench of which is suffocating and insufferable, besides being inextinguishable." The newspaper cautioned, "It may well be doubted how much credence is due to their statements." Beauregard stated that his ordnance officer had experimented with "the celebrated Yankee Greek-fire, taken from some of their unexploded shells, and found it to be a humbug; one pint of water extinguished the quantity held in one shell."[21]

Union military men were also curious about what their adversaries were developing, but descriptions of unconventional Confederate incendiaries were scarce, possibly because such weapons were seldom if ever used. In March 1863, before Cheves produced phosphorus-containing shells, the commander of the USS *Augusta* reported the results of his examination of a "rebel incendiary shell" used near Charleston. On being ignited, the incendiary mixture flashed and then burned in lumps for about two minutes. The only component identified was gunpowder. Another report concerned a so-called Greek fire projectile fired by Confederates during the siege of

Charleston. The description fit that of a conventional fireball (containing niter, sulfur, antimony, and pitch) typically used to illuminate the enemy's works. Northern newspapers published an account of the exploration of the magazines at Battery Wagner after the stronghold was abandoned by its Confederate defenders. Two incendiary devices were found and assumed to have been intended for use against Union forces. One required preparation according to supplied instructions and yielded glass bottles apparently containing sulfuric acid, camphene, gunpowder, and chlorate of potash (potassium chlorate). The filled bottles were probably small bombs or detonators for underwater mines. The other device was a can filled with cotton, turpentine, and an explosive charge. When the device was exploded, the flaming pieces of turpentine-soaked cotton, which served the same purpose as the "vegetable fibrous substance" in Levi Short's liquid-fire shells, were thrown a distance of four or five yards. A reporter for the *New York Daily Tribune* stated that the Confederate government was seizing turpentine for use in a Southern version of Greek fire.[22]

A tantalizing find concerning Confederate incendiaries occurred after the capture of the ironclad CSS *Atlanta* near Savannah in June 1863. Among the ammunition found onboard were projectiles labeled "Robbins fluid shells" for the two sizes of large guns on the vessel. A Washington, DC, newspaper claimed in October of that year that Robbins fluid was identical to the Greek fire used in the bombardment of Charleston and that the *Atlanta*'s mission had been to throw the incendiary into Philadelphia and New York. Although the *Atlanta* was captured too early for the Confederates to have reproduced the material in unexploded Greek fire shells landing in Charleston, the Union's earlier use of projectiles containing Short's liquid or solidified Greek fire may have yielded unexploded shells for study. Also, it was not too early for the Confederates to have examined the patents of Levi Short and Alfred Berney or to have seen incendiary formulas in various periodicals. The composition of Robbins fluid has not been established.[23]

Various ideas for other unconventional incendiary materials were entertained by Confederate military and government officials, but evidence for their actual use is lacking. General Gabriel James Rains, head of the Confederate Torpedo Bureau, designed an ironclad vessel equipped with a steam-powered flamethrower for spraying a flammable substance such as benzene, turpentine, or naphtha. The concept closely resembled the one first suggested by Uriah Brown during the War of 1812 and that of New York scientist James Lewis. Rains also drew up plans for small bombs that could be dropped on enemy positions by paper balloons. Each bomb would contain sulfuric acid in a glass container and potassium chlorate, vinegar, and gunpowder in another section. This was an early example of a binary weapon—a munition in which two relatively safe constituents combine to produce a more harmful or dangerous substance. On striking the target, the glass would shatter, and contact between the released acid and the other ingredients would cause an explosion and scatter flaming turpentine-soaked paper in all directions and set fire to the surroundings. (The same concepts were behind the two devices found in the magazines of Battery Wagner.) A similar idea was for a device that resembled a cartridge for a rifle musket. The bullet was hollowed out to contain sulfuric acid, which was separated from a mixture of sugar and potassium chlorate by a membrane. The chemicals would be inserted into a number of bullets shortly before use, and a quantity of gunpowder wrapped in especially flammable paper would be attached to complete the appearance of normal cartridges. A few of the devices could be placed into artillery shells that contained their normal bursting charge but were fitted with a fake fuse. After being fired into an enemy camp, the unexploded shells would lie undisturbed or be gathered by enemy soldiers and stacked with other apparent duds. After a few hours, the sulfuric acid would eat through the membrane, contact the mixture of sugar and potassium chlorate, and detonate the shell, "to the destruction and dismay of those around." Alternatively, a saboteur could toss a few of the tiny time bombs into combustible material, where they would later ignite spontaneously. Rains called the device "a most infernal contrivance to do evil" and "a thing not to be known among common people, lest incendiarism fill the land with terror and dread." He hoped his ideas would "secure peace by immunity from war, by rendering the latter too horrible to be followed." The plans were evidently not carried out, so their peace-keeping capabilities were never determined.[24]

In early 1863, General Beauregard planned to have boarding parties attack Union ironclad vessels in Charleston Harbor; among their supplies would be "bottles of burning fluid." Secretary of the Navy Stephen R. Mallory suggested that should such vessels be boarded, a portion of the boarding party might be equipped "with turpentine or camphene in glass vessels to smash over the turret and with inextinguishable liquid fire to follow it." These ideas closely resembled the plans that had been devised to capture the USS *Monitor* the previous year (see chapter 7).[25]

On November 2, 1863, druggist Charles P. Sengstack Jr. told Colonel Gorgas that he was "anxious to enter the lines of the Enemy, and destroy Government Property of all kinds." By employing "discretion and caution,"

Sengstack said he could "'with a Greek Fire' burn <u>every Ship Yard</u>, or Rail Road Bridge" within his reach. Sengstack, a former resident of Washington, DC, had served in a Virginia infantry regiment, been detailed to the Medical Department's laboratory in Richmond, and worked for the Ordnance Department as a special agent. Now a civilian residing in Mobile, all he asked was official sanction so that, if arrested, he could claim the protection due to a prisoner of war. Gorgas, after conferring privately with Secretary of War James A. Seddon, recommended that Sengstack receive an appointment as ordnance sergeant, which Seddon approved on November 4. The next day, Sengstack was given $100 in Federal notes, evidently to help finance his mission.[26]

Whether Sengstack carried out any part of his plans is unclear, but he was arrested in Baltimore by Union authorities on the charge of having served in the Confederate army. Sengstack claimed that he had crossed Union lines to verify rumors of his father's death and persuade his purportedly destitute sisters to accompany him back to Mobile. Although he stated that he was "no enemy to the Union," he could not take an oath of fidelity to the United States because doing so would label him as a traitor to the Confederates. That, said Sengstack, would end his engagement to a "Southern Lady of considerable wealth" who, in the words of the Union Provost Marshal's Office, had "Secesh proclivities." Sengstack was sent south on November 21 by way of Harpers Ferry and warned not to return during the war under penalty of being considered a spy. Shortly thereafter, he was again working for the Confederate Ordnance Department, this time as a messenger.[27]

Phosphorus, probably in water or carbon disulfide, was employed by a group of Southern conspirators in November 1864 in an attempt to burn numerous buildings in New York City. Phosphorus in carbon disulfide also appears to have been involved in a Confederate plan to destroy Union property useful for waging war. In January 1865, Secretary of War Seddon authorized Professor Richard Sears McCulloh to engage in this task, and the following month, Confederate legislator Williamson Simpson Oldham informed President Jefferson Davis that several combustible materials (one of which is discussed in the next chapter) were in McCulloh's hands. A secret meeting of a Confederate congressional committee watched as "a chemist," undoubtedly McCulloh, "placed a handkerchief on the mantle, and after a given interval of time it took fire of its own accord." This was the classic demonstration of how phosphorus self-ignited as its solvent evaporated, and McCulloh's background would suggest an easy familiarity with the properties of phosphorus. The demonstration convinced Oldham that carrying out the mission would "devastate the country of the enemy, and fill his people with terror and consternation." McCulloh, who was born in Baltimore, had been a professor of mechanics and physics at Columbia College, New York, but resigned his post in late 1863 "to cast his lot with that of the South," whereupon he worked as an agent and consulting chemist for the Confederate Nitre and Mining Bureau before being appointed as an assistant engineer without a commission. The war ended before the plan could be implemented. McCulloh was captured shortly after the war, imprisoned, and eventually paroled in March 1866.[28]

By and large, the unconventional incendiary weapons used by both North and South were infrequently employed and not particularly effective. They did, however, foreshadow the later use of similar materials and concepts. Inventors before and during the Civil War were taken with the idea of projecting streams of liquid fire toward the enemy, but this application appears not to have been implemented during the War between the States; the various incendiary formulas were evidently used by the armies and navies only in artillery projectiles. The Germans, however, used the streaming-fire idea in World War I in the form of the portable *Flammenwerfer*, or flamethrower, which used pressurized nitrogen or deoxygenated air to project flaming streams of combustible fluid—typically a mixture of petroleum products. The *Flammenwerfer* was said to have arisen after a German military exercise in which water was sprayed through a fire hose to repel assailants. The water, said an officer, could easily have been burning petroleum, and investigation into that claim resulted in the discovery of a fluid that could work in a flamethrower. The fact that soldiers operating flamethrowers were easy targets for enemy marksmen confirmed George Meade's wisdom in unfavorably comparing a hypothetical flamethrower's range with that of a rifle. Portable and tank-mounted flamethrowers were also used in World War II and later. During the Vietnam War, flamethrowers were even mounted on American riverine vessels known as Zippo boats, an application that harked back to the proposals put forward before and during the Civil War. The inventors of that earlier era envisioned their compositions being projected toward enemy vessels, with Uriah Brown claiming a range of two hundred feet with the right equipment. The M10-8 flamethrowers on Zippo boats were used primarily against land targets and had a maximum range of 150 to 175 meters, yet the basic concepts behind the weapons were identical. Napalm, a gelled form of gasoline and a modern Greek fire, was developed during World War II, and various forms of the incendiary were used in flamethrowers and bombs in subsequent conflicts.[29]

Phosphorus in carbon disulfide was used shortly after the American Civil War as an instrument of arson by Irish separatists called Fenians. By World War I, materials more effective than phosphorus for purely incendiary applications had been developed, but phosphorus came to be recognized as a superior agent for producing smoke screens. The Allies also found phosphorus-containing mortar rounds to be particularly useful against German machine gun nests; not only did they interfere with the Germans' ability to see their targets, but their collateral burning effects also forced the enemy soldiers to abandon their positions and surrender. "Any one who has been burned with phosphorus," said a pair of World War I chemical weapons officers, "or has witnessed the ease with which it burns when exposed to air, wet or dry, has a most wholesome fear of it." This assessment was strikingly similar to the views of Joseph Jones, John Cheves, and Confederate officers observing the trials of phosphorous shells.[30]

The primary purpose of the Civil War's Greek fire was to set objects on fire, but the production of noxious fumes was clearly considered a useful collateral effect, not so much for killing or injuring enemy troops as for temporarily hindering their fighting ability or compelling them to abandon their position. The fact that such fumes were probably not immediately lethal may help explain why ethical objections to Greek fire rarely if ever mentioned its fumes. Some citizens who deplored Greek fire may have been unaware that other frightful incendiaries were already being used by both sides, but such ignorance could not be claimed of military men. General McClellan objected to liquid fire early in the war, as did some American and European officers before the Civil War, but their stance is perplexing in light of their willingness to use molten iron, hot shot, and portfire. Most of the ethical objections to the bombardment of Charleston concerned the purported targeting of noncombatants and structures that supposedly had no military value; denouncing Greek fire at the same time seemed to strengthen the argument that the shelling was barbarous. The same moral outrage would certainly have arisen had Gillmore used only conventional explosive projectiles, but the weapons could not then have been singled out as unusually diabolical.

Greek fire in various forms was used centuries before the Civil War, yet it reemerged during the War between the States as a weapon that was, ironically, ahead of its time. Civil War inventors had imagined materials and apparatuses that would be used effectively in later conflicts, but it would take advances in materials and technology—and perhaps a change in ethical views—to make that possible.

4

NO LIVING BEING WILL ESCAPE

[Hydrocyanic acid] has a peculiar penetrating odour, similar to
that of bitter almonds, checks the breathing, and causes a flow
of tears; it possesses a penetrating taste, which is somewhat
burning, and strongly bitter; its vapour, when inhaled, acts
instantly as a most powerful poison.
—John W. Webster, MD, 1839

A PHOSPHOROUS SHELL WAS NOT the only weapon Confederate surgeon Joseph Jones had in mind when he wrote to General Beauregard in late March 1863. As if the "most irritating & even poisonous gas" produced by phosphorus were not enough, Jones went on to propose an even more frightening implement of war:

You are without doubt familiar with the fact that it requires but
a few drops of Prussic (Hydrocyanic) Acid to destroy the largest
animal, & even man; and further that the inhalation of this acid,
or even its simple application to the surface will produce almost
instantaneous loss of strength consciousness & even life itself. It
would be impossible to charge a shell with the acid ready prepared:
it would be the most practicable plan to charge the shell with those
chemical compounds which would when united within the shell
generate the powerful poison. . . . My plan is a simple one. . . .
Into the inner chamber [of a conical artillery shell] introduce two
glass vessels, one containing Cyanide of Potassium and the other
Hydrochloric Acid. These glass vessels to be hermetically sealed.

33

When the shell is fired, the glasses will be broken by the concussion, the substances will be mingled in the inner chamber; the poisonous compound will be generated during the flight of the shell, & at its explosion it will be scattered in every direction. If the shell explodes in the hold or cabin of a ship, gun-boat or iron-clad, no living being will escape. The atmosphere will immediately be rendered incapable of supporting life—it will be worse—deadly poisonous.

In the unlikely event that Confederate troops were able to board a Union ironclad, the artillery shell could be replaced by an iron, brass, or lead bottle fitted with a metal tube and stopcock:

Two glass vessels, one containing Cyanide of Potassium, & the other Hydrochloric acid, should be introduced into the metallic bottle. After boarding, or just before, the ingredients might be mingled, by a sharp blow, or by any mechanical means which would break the glass bottles. In a few moments the Poison would be generated. If now the tube be introduced through the grates or any passage leading to the cabin, & the stop-cock turned, the Prussic acid will be, necessarily from the pressure generated by its liberation, projected with force & will in a few moments destroy all in the confined space. By this method the ship would be uninjured. . . . The only precaution to be observed would be to fumigate the ship with chlorine before allowing any one to descend.[1]

Beauregard's consultant, John Cheves, had two objections to Jones's proposal. The first was on ethical grounds. Poisoning per se, he contended, "was not a safe or desirable resource." Cheves instead advocated "stifling with the materials ordinarily used in war," an aim that was "more consonant with the spirit of the age." He continued, "There is as much difference between poisoning and stifling as there is between throwing dust in a man's eyes & putting his eyes out yet where only momentary blindness is wanted the first will do as well as the last." Cheves's second objection involved the practicality of Jones's plan. Only a small proportion of the chemicals would form prussic acid by the time the shell reached its target, Cheves thought, and the formed gases would diffuse too rapidly to cause harm. "A rotten egg is a shell containing the generating material," Cheves offered as an illustration. "The gas evolved [hydrogen sulfide] is of a most deadly nature. Men have been under fire of these missiles, yet have I never heard that one was slain." Cheves's assessment was evidently enough to shelve Jones's proposal.[2]

At least one other person, also a Southerner, suggested hydrocyanic acid as a weapon. In a letter to a newspaper, the unidentified correspondent proposed that "large shells of extraordinary capacity" be filled with hydrocyanic acid or other poisonous gases and fired into Union-held Fort Pickens, which guarded Pensacola Bay, Florida. If such projectiles were lobbed rapidly into the stronghold, "every living soul would have to leave in double quick time—it would be impossible to breathe there." Various other substances were mentioned in the same letter and are discussed in this and other chapters.[3]

By the time Joseph Jones wrote to General Beauregard, prussic acid—also known then as hydrocyanic acid and usually called hydrogen cyanide today—was well recognized as a deadly poison. Cyanide derivatives had been involved for centuries in deaths both accidental and intentional. Bitter almonds, leaves of the cherry laurel, and peach pits—all of which contain forms of cyanide—had been used as poisons since ancient times. In an 1862 book written for novice Civil War soldiers, military veteran John P. Curry wrote of "asphyxiating shells" that could "paralyze, if not destroy, the life of every one breathing the atmosphere in close proximity." According to Curry, the projectiles' principal poison was potassium cyanide, but period records do not confirm that such shells existed. Jones's idea of using hydrogen cyanide against enemy vessels qualifies as an early, if not the first, proposal for causing mass military fatalities with the substance. According to a biographer, Jones exhibited signs of a "war psychosis" that manifested, in part, as a marked hostility toward Northerners and a take-no-prisoners attitude toward Union combatants. However, his weapons plans, as revealed to Beauregard, were expressed in objective and dispassionate terms and displayed a good deal of imagination, logic, and insight, especially in view of how chemical weapons—and hydrogen cyanide in particular—would be employed in the coming decades.[4]

The toxicity of cyanide compounds was well known, and Jones had supplemented what he had learned in medical school with his own research with the substances. That he correctly stated the ability of hydrogen cyanide vapor to kill large numbers of people was demonstrated during World War II, when inmates of German extermination camps were gassed with hydrogen cyanide released from Zyklon B, a product originally developed as a pesticide. Unlike most period proponents of chemical weapons, Jones understood that ordnance personnel would need to devise a practical means of implementing his ideas. His concerns about filling artillery shells with hydrogen cyanide "ready prepared" surely reflected his knowledge about the substance's physical properties. At room temperature, hydrogen cyanide is an extremely volatile liquid, with a boiling point of about 78 degrees Fahrenheit, so placing large volumes of the fluid into shells might well have put munitions workers at risk from contact with the liquid or inhalation of the vapor. The liquid is also unstable when stored, "ultimately decomposing with explosive violence." Charging shells with a preformed gas, as suggested by the other Confederate proponent of hydrogen cyanide, was simply impractical, as a projectile would have to be enormous to deliver an effective payload. As World War I chemical weapons experts later explained, "The word 'gas' has nothing whatever to do with the condition of the material when in the shell, or the bombs, or the cylinders when released. In every case, the gases are liquids or solids. When the containers are broken open the liquids are volatilized either by the gas pressure or by the force of the explosion of the bomb." Jones evidently understood this, and his solution to delivering hydrogen cyanide was remarkable and forward-looking.[5]

Mixing potassium cyanide and hydrochloric acid, as Jones proposed, is a highly effective method of generating hydrogen cyanide. Starting around 1930, convicts who died in American gas chambers inhaled hydrogen cyanide vapor produced when solid potassium cyanide was dropped into a container of sulfuric or hydrochloric acid. Decades later, terrorist groups such as al-Qaeda and the Japanese cult Aum Shinrikyo contemplated or actually tried using the same method—producing hydrogen cyanide by mixing sodium cyanide or potassium cyanide with sulfuric or hydrochloric acid—for subway attacks. In their plans, separate containers of the two substances were placed next to each other and ruptured by a small explosive charge.[6]

One historian has dated the binary-weapon concept to 1885, when chemists attempted to have nitric acid and glycerin mix in an artillery shell and form nitroglycerin during flight. However, a phosphorus-containing binary shell was proposed some eighty years earlier for use by British troops defending England from a French flotilla, and a similar concept was applied in Confederate designs for incendiary weapons. Jones's suggestion, first made in 1862, was an early but not the first proposal for a binary weapon in which the precursors were meant to produce a poisonous product (see chapter 8 for a plan that predated Jones's). Although the constituents he suggested placing in shells—potassium cyanide and hydrochloric acid—were hardly nontoxic, there were certainly safer to handle than hydrogen cyanide. The binary concept applied well to chemical weapons, since the alternative of loading shells with fully formed poisons would present a constant hazard during production, storage, and handling of the munitions. During World

War I, British chemists endeavored to develop a binary projectile that would form arsine, a toxic arsenic compound, from calcium arsenide and hydrochloric acid, and the United States developed binary weapons during the Cold War to deliver the nerve agents VX (via the Bigeye bomb) and sarin (via the M687 artillery shell).[7]

Jones was careful to restrict his claims about the deadliness of hydrogen cyanide gas to the explosion of a shell within a confined space, such as a vessel's hold or cabin. He may have realized that the gas is lighter than air and dissipates quickly in an open space. Knowledge of these properties during World War I should have disqualified the substance from consideration as a useful chemical weapon, yet the French used it in artillery shells in combination with ingredients intended to increase the gas's density and keep it closer to the ground. Combatants other than the French considered hydrogen cyanide essentially innocuous as a battlefield weapon, because lethal concentrations of the gas could not be produced in the field, and persons exposed to nonlethal concentrations of the "kill or cure" compound recovered quickly; one authority has claimed that no battlefield deaths during World War I were attributed to it. Thus John Cheves's reservations about hydrogen cyanide gas dissipating too quickly to be an effective weapon were justified and prescient. Notwithstanding this concern, various countries incorporated hydrogen cyanide into grenades or bombs during World War II, although the extent to which those munitions were used is unclear. The Japanese, for example, filled frangible glass grenades with liquid hydrogen cyanide under pressure and added copper or arsenic trichloride as a stabilizer.[8]

Jones was ingenious in proposing a binary weapon, but other practical concerns remained. If a shell had to explode within a confined area to be effective, for example, might not the enemy be disabled to an equal or greater extent if the space devoted to the chemicals were used instead to deliver a larger amount of explosive? Was the time the shell was in flight sufficient for the chemicals to mix? Might the chemicals adversely affect the flight of the shell? (When the M687 binary sarin shell was tested in 1971, erratic flight was attributed to the liquid precursors moving within the spinning projectile.) Once delivered, would an adequate amount of the flammable hydrogen cyanide gas survive? (During World War II field tests of bombs containing hydrogen cyanide, the chemical tended to inflame when the munitions exploded.) With regard to the metallic canister to be used by boarders of an ironclad, would the pressure generated by the formation of hydrogen cyanide be sufficient to propel large amounts of the gas into the vessel's cabin, and would the lighter-than-air gas reach the lower levels of the vessel?[9]

Partial answers can be inferred from agricultural practices developed decades after the Civil War. In the 1890s, it became common for farmers to eradicate insect pests on fruit trees by covering the trees with a tent and generating hydrogen cyanide inside it by dropping solid potassium cyanide into a container of sulfuric acid. One drawback to this fumigation method was that the gas formed slowly because the potassium cyanide had to dissolve, and some gas had time to leak out of the tent before an effective concentration was reached. By 1915, portable machines had been developed that made the process faster and safer. In these devices, which were kept outside the tent, portions of potassium cyanide solution (not the solid) and sulfuric acid were mixed in an enclosed drum by the manipulation of valves. Hydrogen cyanide gas formed almost instantaneously and, by its own pressure, forced its way through an attached hose that was directed into the tent, where an insecticidal concentration was quickly produced. This experience implies that if Jones intended for solid potassium cyanide to be used in the shell, hydrogen cyanide may not have had sufficient time to form completely during the short flight of the projectile. Also, the hydrogen cyanide formed in the metallic containers used by a boarding party might well reach a pressure adequate to force the gas through a tube and into the boarded vessel, with the speed of gas formation influenced by whether the potassium cyanide was solid or in solution. With either weapon, maximum efficiency would require an optimal ratio of potassium cyanide to acid, which Jones did not specify. Jones, who died in 1896, did not live to see the agricultural use of cyanide fumigating machines, but he would have recognized them as versions of his portable cyanide generator.[10]

Jones's proposal was also remarkable for providing a means of protecting friendly forces entering the previously lethal space. The idea of fumigation with chlorine gas may have been based on textbook statements that, under certain conditions, hydrogen cyanide is decomposed by chlorine to chlorocyanic acid (cyanogen chloride) and hydrogen. If that was Jones's rationale, he neglected the fact that cyanogen chloride itself is highly poisonous. A small dose of chlorine, usually taken by ingesting chlorine water (water in which chloride gas has been dissolved) or inhaling chlorine water's vapor, was considered an effective antidote for cyanide poisoning if used quickly enough. Jones had studied this remedy during the early 1860s. Since he described chlorine fumigation as a precaution, his purpose was not to revive stricken enemy sailors, but possibly to have the boarding party exposed to some level of antidote in case dangerous levels of hydrogen cyanide persisted.[11]

Another concern would be how to carry out the chlorine fumigation. The standard method of generating chlorine gas for removing offensive odors or for destroying contagious or infectious matter was to mix common salt, oxide of manganese, and sulfuric acid on a flat pan in the area to be fumigated. How chlorine gas so generated could be directed into an enclosed area is unclear. Jones's purpose could also have been met by treating chlorinated lime with hydrochloric acid and introducing the mixture into the space to be fumigated. Chlorine gas is heavier than air and would find its way to the lower levels of the boarded vessel, but Jones did not say how the boarding party could be protected from the poisonous effects of chlorine.[12]

Before closing his proposal to Beauregard, Jones called attention to a class of chemicals that might bear the general's consideration: the cacodyl derivatives. In 1760, the French chemist Louis Claude Cadet de Gassicourt described experiments that produced a heavy reddish-brown arsenic-containing fluid that gave off intensely malodorous and flammable fumes; the substance became known as "Cadet's fuming liquid." During a series of studies in the late 1830s and early 1840s, the great German chemist Robert Bunsen proposed that the main constituent of Cadet's liquid was an arsenical analog of an alcohol. He thus assigned Cadet's liquid the name "alkarsin," a word formed from the initial letters of *alkohol* and *arsenic*. Further investigation revealed that alkarsin was a mixture of a substance that came to be known as cacodyl (or kakodyl, meaning "bad smell" in Greek) and an oxide of it (cacodyl oxide). Cacodyl vapor, when exposed to air, was found to burst into flames and release deadly arsenic fumes. Bunsen went on to study a series of cacodyl derivatives and lost sight in his right eye, and almost his life, when a container of cacodyl cyanide exploded. Most cacodyl derivatives were noted to be extremely toxic, with cacodyl cyanide being so dangerous—because of its release of both arsenic and hydrogen cyanide fumes—that Bunsen warned that its preparation must be performed in the open air, and then only when the operator breathed through a long tube whose other end was far removed from the deadly vapors. Even a minute amount in a room would cause in its occupants "sudden giddiness and insensibility, amounting to unconsciousness."[13]

It did not take long for the cacodyl derivatives to be recognized as potential weapons. In 1844, an unnamed correspondent to a British periodical suggested a seemingly simple implement of war:

> If, therefore, a fragile vessel of this liquid [cacodyl], say a glass globe, be thrown into the port-hole of a ship, the moment it breaks against the deck, or any hard object, the spilled fluid is in a blaze, and capable of

setting on fire anything combustible in contact with it. But this is not all. The result of its combustion is the evolution of clouds of white arsenic, so that the atmosphere around becomes instantly a deadly poison. Thus, if inflamed between decks, the atmosphere would at once be rendered fatal. . . . Further, the substance is insoluble in water, and heavier than it; so that water will not extinguish it when on fire. The oxide produced by its combustion, moreover, is a violent poison. It would be difficult to conceive a collection of more formidable properties in one body, or of any more fitting it for an agent of destruction in warfare.[14]

About ten years later, at the start of the Crimean War, British chemist Lyon Playfair suggested placing cacodyl cyanide in brittle shells for use against the Russians, but ordnance officials rejected the proposal, saying that it was "as bad a mode of warfare as poisoning the wells of the enemy." Playfair thought the objection was senseless:

It is considered a legitimate mode of warfare to fill shells with molten metal which scatters among the enemy, and produces the most frightful modes of death. Why a poisonous vapour which would kill men without suffering is to be considered illegitimate warfare is incomprehensible. War is destruction, and the most destructive it can be made with the least suffering the sooner will be ended that barbarous method of protecting national rights. No doubt in time chemistry will be used to lessen the suffering of combatants, and even of criminals condemned to death. Hanging is a relic of barbarism, because criminals might be put to death without physical torture.[15]

In September 1854, the *London Times* reported that British ordnance officials were considering "a shell charged with a liquid which, when released by the concussion of the ball, becomes a sheet of liquid fire, consuming all within its influence, the smoke emitted also destroying human life." According to a British scientist, this description fit cacodyl, but Playfair and the British Army were said to have kept his cacodyl idea secret, and the weapon described by the *Times* could well have been one of the formulations of phosphorus and carbon disulfide described in chapter 2.[16]

In May 1861, shortly after the onset of the Civil War, a correspondent to a Richmond newspaper suggested putting alkarsin in a thin iron artillery shell. The projectile would "explode only on striking its mark, when the Alkarsin would take fire, burning with a fierce flame and emitting dense volumes of the most deadly poisonous gases." The liquid, added the correspondent, "can be furnished to the State by a competent Chemist." Another correspondent, writing to a Georgia newspaper in 1863, proposed using cacodyl or alkarsin against Union ironclads: "With the proper appliances for projecting this liquid, or in shells in which it may be contained, upon the gratings of the deck, or into the portholes of an iron-clad vessel, there can be no difficulty, I suppose, in causing it to penetrate the interior, where its effects would be overwhelming and decisive." The correspondent acknowledged that the poison would involve "somewhat of danger to the operator who provides it" and "may be found at present, not readily accessible, or too costly." In 1864, Captain Edward C. Boynton, a former artillery officer in the US Army and an instructor at the US Military Academy, stated, much as another author had twenty years earlier, that if cacodyl were "confined in glass globes or bottles, and dropped on the deck of a vessel, or thrust below, all the horrors of combustion and deadly arsenical inhalations would be realized, besides which the terrors of the Greek fire would be contemptible." Boynton was not advocating cacodyl's use but rather pointing it out as a frightening agent whose use might be contemplated. Absent from the proposals for employing cacodyl derivatives was any description of how areas contaminated by the poisons might be made safe for friendly troops.[17]

Joseph Jones, in his communication to Beauregard, recited the well-known properties of cacodyl and described cacodyl cyanide as "the most deadly compound of the whole series . . . so powerful that a single grain diffused through a room is sufficient to produce numbness of the hands & feet, vertigo, and even syncope in those exposed to its effects." Perhaps recalling how cacodyl cyanide had almost killed Robert Bunsen, Jones warned that the cacodyl compounds were "prepared with too much difficulty, and have proved destructive to the lives of the most careful chemists," saying that "it is not probable that they could be turned to any good account." Nevertheless, he added, "they might claim some attention."[18] The writer of an article published in an Irish periodical in 1859 was also skeptical about cacodyl:

> A great deal has been said of late about charging shells with kakodyl, with cyanogen compounds, and other poisons. Very pretty suggestions, gentlemen speculators, but not so easy to put into practice. Supposing kakodyl capable of employment, which we doubt, who would like the task of making kakodyl? For our part, we would rather be bound, for a punishment to work, day by day in a powder factory, with a lighted cigar perpetually between our lips, than apply ourselves to the frightful task of manufacturing that horrible compound.[19]

That the cacodyl substances were too dangerous to handle was proved nearly fifty years later, when Otto Sackur, a German researcher of chemical weapons during World War I, was killed by an explosion while working with cacodyl chloride.[20]

It does not appear that any cacodyl derivatives were used during the Civil War. However, among the substances reportedly demonstrated by chemist Richard Sears McCulloh (see chapter 3) as part of a plot to destroy Union property was a colorless fluid that, "if thrown from the gallery of the House of Representatives, in Washington . . . would kill every member on the floor in five minutes." McCulloh was said to have released the liquid in a closed room containing several cats, and a Confederate congressional committee watched through a window as "the result predicted was accomplished." The description of the fluid matches that of cacodyl cyanide, a colorless liquid that, unlike alkarsin or cacodyl, can be exposed to air without bursting into flame.[21]

At least two other proposals—both from Southerners and neither, apparently, considered seriously—were made for using arsenic. One was from the same correspondent who suggested placing hydrogen cyanide gas into huge artillery shells; he proposed highly poisonous arseniuretted hydrogen (arsine) gas as an alternative—and equally unworkable—payload. Arsine can be immediately fatal at high doses and at lower doses can produce headache, confusion, nausea and vomiting, loss of consciousness, convulsions, and respiratory failure. The other proposal was put forward in January 1861, three months before Confederate artillerymen opened fire on Fort Sumter, in a letter from Mississippian John Condon to South Carolina governor Francis Pickens. Federal troops occupying Fort Sumter, said Condon, could be neutralized if, during a heavy rain, artillery shells containing arsenic or strychnine were fired at the stronghold. Their explosion would scatter the projectiles' contents on the roofs of the fort, and the rain would wash it into cisterns that collected drinking water, "poisoning the whole concern." Condon advised not implementing the plan, which he termed "a horrid remedy," until after Union troops in the fort opened fire, and he asked Pickens to burn his letter after reading it.[22]

Although alkarsin and cacodyl appear not to have been used as chemical weapons during or after the Civil War, arsine was considered for use in World War I. In addition to the aforementioned British attempt to produce a binary weapon that would generate arsine, some thought was given to arsenides, which might react with atmospheric moisture and liberate arsine. However, calculations of the amount of arsenide needed to produce lethal arsine concentrations revealed that the concept was untenable. By World War II, arsine was considered to have little promise as a chemical weapon, not only because it was difficult to deliver in effective concentrations, but also because respirators provided adequate protection against it. Arsine derivatives and arsenious chloride were used during World War I in combination with other toxic substances.[23]

The cyanide- and arsenic-based agents were well recognized for their toxicity, so it is no surprise that they were suggested as components of Civil War weapons. The proposals of Joseph Jones, in particular, displayed clarity of thought, considerable chemical knowledge, and an appreciation for some of the practical considerations involved in producing a weapon. Jones's status as an officer and scientist probably earned his ideas the serious consideration that Beauregard allowed, and the response by John Cheves reflected ethical concerns and—for the hydrogen cyanide shell, at least—some well-founded skepticism about whether the weapon would actually produce the claimed effect. Unfortunately, available records do not indicate the reactions of Confederate officials to the other described proposals. Perhaps they, like Union ordnance chief Ripley, preferred not to be bothered with ideas for strange new weapons when they had more pressing concerns.

5

PORTENDING THE GREEN CLOUD

When a person is obliged to inspire the fumes of chlorine, it produces a most insufferable sensation of suffocation, occasions a violent cough with much expectoration, which continues for some time, and brings on a very great degree of debility.
—Thomas Thomson, MD, 1831

OF THE KNOWN CIVIL WAR proposals for chemical weapons, one stands out as a rival to that of Joseph Jones for its thoroughness, rationality, and foresight. On April 5, 1862, John W. Doughty of New York City wrote to Secretary of War Edwin M. Stanton to recommend that liquid chlorine be placed in artillery shells and used against enemy troops in entrenched positions or for warding off attacks by ironclad vessels or steam rams. Doughty included an illustration showing how such shells might be constructed and filled. He evidently did not receive a response, so Doughty sent a similar letter and drawing to President Lincoln on May 1. His idea, he said, had formed shortly after the war began, but he had assumed "that the government would prefer using such projectiles as had already undergone the test of experiment." However, the recent exploits of the CSS *Virginia* and his belief that chlorine shells would have naval applications had spurred him to follow up on his note to Stanton. As was the case with many other inventors, the appearance of ironclad vessels had raised apprehensions and a belief that extraordinary measures must be adopted to combat them. This time, he was told that Chief of Ordnance Ripley would inform him if his invention should "prove to be of practical utility, and adapted to the public service." When two months passed without further word, Doughty wrote to Ripley for a status report on his proposal and—as other inventors in the same situation had done—mentioned a possibility calculated to elicit a response: "Should the Department believe the improvement unimportant & incapable of producing the results I claim for it, there would, I think, be no impropriety in my offering the shell to the considerations of other governments." Again ignored, Doughty, now writing to Ripley from Newburgh, New York, tried once more in August 1864 to urge consideration of his idea. Four attempts were apparently enough, for there is no evidence that Doughty continued to write or that the Ordnance Department did anything but file his correspondence. There is also no indication that Doughty took his idea elsewhere.[1]

Doughty's detailed proposal outlined properties of chlorine that would render it a useful weapon. First, as a gas, chlorine was "so irritating in its effects upon the respiratory organs, that a small quantity diffused in the atmosphere, produces incessant & uncontrollably violent coughing." In high enough concentration, chlorine gas can be lethal—a fact Doughty did not mention—but even brief exposures can be debilitating. "Their first intimation of its presence," said Doughty, "would be by its inhalation, which would most effectually disqualify every man for service that was within the circle of its influence; rendering the disarming and capturing of them as certain as though both their legs were broken." The prominent Philadelphia physician and professor John Redman Coxe, who had inhaled chlorine gas after a mishap during a chemistry lecture in 1811 or 1812, provided a detailed first-person account of the nonfatal effects of chlorine gas. He experienced immediate difficulty breathing, a choking sensation, coughing, dizziness, and a weak pulse; the symptoms were unrelieved by breathing fresh air. Anticipating that his lungs would fill with fluid if he were left untreated, he summoned a bleeder, who assisted in removing about sixty ounces of blood, a treatment that Coxe credited with saving his life. His cough persisted for about a week.[2]

The second useful characteristic of chlorine gas was its high density, or specific gravity. If released in the air, it would sink to the ground, and persons in the vicinity could not escape it. "On account of the low temperature occasioned by its expansion," stated Doughty, "together with its great specific gravity, the gas would descend "almost as rapidly as rain, covering a space from one to two hundred feet in diameter according to the size of the shell." Third, said Doughty, the gas would not persist for long, because it would soon be dispersed or absorbed by the ground, and friendly troops could occupy the area quickly and safely; meanwhile, enemy combatants debilitated by the chlorine would remain helpless and harmless long after the gas disappeared. Doughty recognized that chlorine, with a boiling point of about −29 degrees Fahrenheit, had to be placed into shells not as a gas but as a liquid. He stated that this could be done "under a pressure which is within practical limits," which he cited as sixty pounds per square inch (psi), about four times normal atmospheric pressure. Hence the liquid chlorine in a large shell would expand forcefully to a volume of gas hundreds of times larger when it was freed by the projectile's explosion. Enemy troops within a large area would be affected because chlorine was disabling even when quite dilute. Chlorine, said Doughty, had a great advantage over "chemical shell & stink-pots," in which the contents were not pressurized, because with those weapons, "it is impossible . . . to liberate the gas with sufficient rapidity & in sufficient quantity: the enemy escapes in perfect fighting trim, with the exception of the disturbance which the gas may have occasioned to his olfactories" (stink shells are discussed in chapter 9). Doughty suggested that the enemy would be defenseless against chlorine. "This shell is designed to dislodge an enemy without battering down his fortifications," he said. "The strength of the fortress—the size of the guns, or the number of men composing the garrison is wholly immaterial. It matters not whether it be a [Fort] Darling on the James or a Gibraltar on the Peninsula."[3]

The scientific knowledge displayed in Doughty's proposal suggests that he was a learned man. Details of his early education are lacking, but as a young man, he worked as a teacher and studied Greek and Latin. In 1848, at about age thirty-one, he became an instructor at the Chelsea Collegiate Institute in New York City, where he remained for fourteen years. For the last six years of that period, he taught geometry and chemistry at "Mr. Leopold De Grand-Val's Boarding School" in Hoboken, New Jersey. He was a member of the 1843–44 class of the Medical Department of the University of the State of New York and reportedly received a diploma in 1852 from the New York State Medical Society, although he never practiced medicine. In 1862, shortly after he wrote the third of his four letters urging the use of chlorine shells, he became an instructor of Greek and Latin at the Newburgh Academy in Newburgh, New York. After the war, he was appointed principal at that institution, a position he held for twenty years, during which he earned "the love of his pupils, and the unqualified esteem of the community for his learning and noble characteristics as a man." The postwar years saw Doughty patent a steam-boiler water feeder with a partner from Newburgh and be elected a member of the American Association for the Advancement of Science, in which he participated in the group on geology and geography.[4]

The reasoning in Doughty's chlorine proposal seems theoretically sound, but he cautioned wisely that experiments would have to prove the actual feasibility of his ideas. The employment of chlorine as the first effective chemical weapon of World War I provides some basis for evaluating Doughty's claims. The Germans introduced chlorine, released from cylinders, as a weapon at Ypres, Belgium, on April 22, 1915. Its effects closely mirrored those that Dr. Coxe had experienced and feared more than a century earlier. "The effect of the gas," said a British correspondent describing its Allied victims, "is to fill the lungs with a watery, frothy matter, which gradually increases and rises up till it fills the whole lungs and comes up to the mouth; then they die; it is suffocation; slow drowning, taking in some cases one or two days." Thus Doughty was correct that chlorine could be debilitating in concentrations achievable on a battlefield, but creating a drifting cloud by releasing chlorine from cylinders, as the Germans (and later the Allies) did, differed profoundly from his proposal of delivering the agent in artillery shells. As Doughty maintained, and as German chemists knew would happen, the release of liquid chlorine and its rapid expansion to gas cooled the surrounding air, and the gas sank to the ground. The gas did not always disperse immediately; German soldiers advancing after its release had to avoid patches of gas persisting in low areas. Chlorine gas dissipates quickly at battlefield temperatures, a property that Doughty appreciated. This could be desirable if friendly forces had to occupy the area immediately or undesirable if the intent was to expose the enemy to the poison for a prolonged period.[5]

Doughty was also correct that chlorine would have to be loaded into artillery shells as a liquid. The Germans intended to do just that in World War I, but because of a shell shortage, they placed liquid chlorine into metal cylinders, hundreds or thousands of which were positioned in their own trenches in preparation for a cloud attack. (The British, French, and Americans also used the same technique for the same reasons.) When the wind was blowing at the desired speed and direction, the cylinder valves were opened in unison, the escaping liquid turned to gas, and the resultant poisonous cloud drifted toward the enemy. By World War I, Germany was producing large amounts of liquid chlorine for various industrial purposes and could deploy enough from cylinders to cover huge swaths of the battlefield with the green gas; Britain, France, and the United States responded by stepping up their own production of chlorine during the war. During the Civil War, gaseous chlorine could be produced fairly easily and cheaply, but the ability to manufacture large amounts of liquid chlorine—with facilities to cool, pressurize, and condense the gas and the ability to produce strong, leak-proof containers in which to store the liquid—did not develop in the United States until after 1880. Moreover, an important point not appreciated by early (pre-1888) chemists working on liquefying chlorine was that the substance had to be free from moisture; moist chlorine is highly corrosive of many materials, including iron, of which Civil War artillery shells were made. World War I munitions experts learned that filling shells with toxic chemicals was a hazardous task, and they took elaborate precautions to protect the filling facilities and their workers. Given the technology of the Civil War era, filling shells with liquid chlorine would have been even more dangerous then, especially since effective protective gear was not commonplace.[6]

World War I artillery shells were inherently inefficient as delivery vehicles for toxic chemicals, because the chemical accounted for only about 7 to 12 percent of the total weight of a shell. At first the only available shells were those designed to carry high explosives, but alterations in design, such as thinning the walls, increased the space for the chemical payload. Nevertheless, shells remained inefficient compared with chlorine cylinders, in which liquid chlorine accounted for half the weight of the filled containers. Filling artillery shells with liquid chlorine carried another liability. The pressure exerted by the vapor above chlorine liquid within a closed container would be seventy to one hundred psi at normal outside temperatures and would increase in warm weather; the preferred maximum pressure for chemical shells was twenty-five to thirty psi. These factors, plus the availability of more effective gases, such as phosgene, are why chlorine was not used in artillery shells during the Great War. The British, however, used chlorine in projectiles fired from a crude mortar known as the Livens projector. Because a less powerful propellant charge was used, these projectiles' walls could be thinner, so up to half the weight of a Livens projectile was occupied by the toxic agent. In one bombardment employing eighty-six Livens projectiles, about 160 gallons of liquid chlorine, weighing approximately a ton, was delivered. It is unclear whether existing Civil War artillery projectiles would have been suitable for Doughty's scheme and how much liquid chlorine they could have carried; Doughty's drawings suggest that new shells would have to have been designed and tested.[7]

Doughty thought that covering a large area with chlorine gas would be a relatively simple affair:

> In opposition to this [my proposal] it may be urged that if the
> shell be exploded at any considerable elevation, there would be no
> difficulty in getting beyond its influence. To this I would answer

that allowing each shell to contain a sufficient quantity of gas
to render the air irrespirable for a space of one hundred feet in
diameter (which would not require a large shell) it will be found
by computation that one hundred shells (discharged within a few
minutes) would render more than twenty acres untenable, or a line
of fortifications two hundred feet wide & one mile & seven eighths
in length.

In his August 1864 letter, he stated that if a hundred chlorine shells rather
than conventional shells had been "simultaneously fired when the mine was
blown-up on the 30th ult. in front of Petersburg" (a reference to the Battle
of the Crater) and directed toward the enemy entrenchments, "there is not
a doubt in my mind but it would have resulted in the capture of the enemy
& all his works."[8]

Other than his claims about battlefield coverage, Doughty's proposal
included no calculations to support his assertions. He offered no figures, for
example, on the actual volume of liquid chlorine that could be delivered by
projectiles usable in standard artillery pieces, the concentration of chlorine
gas that would result from the explosion of a shell, or the dose of chlorine
needed to incapacitate a soldier. Late in World War I, the British estimated
that exposure to a chlorine gas concentration of 240 milligrams per cubic
meter (mg/m^3) for a few seconds would render a soldier unable to fight, yet
no such information was available during the Civil War to guide Doughty
and ordnance officers, and even if it had been, there was no simple way to
determine how many chlorine shells would have to be exploded and in what
proximity to each other per unit area of land. After World War I, it was estimated that for a nonpersistent chemical agent like chlorine, a quarter to a
half of the chemical contents of an artillery shell was driven into the ground
or forced too high into the air and was lost; thus one expert concluded that
"to be effective in war, chemical agents must be used in enormous quantities."
The pattern of firing—for instance, whether shell bursts should overlap or
not—was an issue of contention during World War I and might have been
settled by trial and error with Doughty's shells.[9]

Doughty proposed that chlorine shells be exploded in the air, yet this
technique was not necessarily the most efficient. For certain gases used
during World War I, explosion of the shell just above the ground was ideal,
and gas was wasted if a shell embedded itself into the ground before detonation. One advantage of the Livens projectors during the Great War—in
delivering chlorine, for example—was that their projectiles had a rounded

nose and usually did not sink into the ground before exploding. That possibility could not be entirely avoided with World War I artillery shells because fuses did not always detonate when desired, and this circumstance—along with uncertainty about the ideal firing pattern—led some British artillerymen to suggest that a gas bombardment with fewer than a hundred shells was useless.[10]

Even in the unlikely scenario of Civil War artillery projectiles and fuses matching the efficiency of their World War I counterparts for delivering gas, the World War I experience would be insufficient for estimating how many Civil War shells would have to have been fired to ensure a successful chlorine bombardment. Much would depend on the size and topography of the target area, the strength and direction of the wind, and the ambient temperature. Moreover, chlorine was used during World War I in concentrations that could and did kill, whereas Doughty evidently aimed only to deprive the enemy of the ability to fight, a purpose that could be accomplished with lower gas levels. Data exist on the amounts of chlorine released from cylinders by World War I combatants per kilometer of enemy lines during specific engagements, but because the gas drifted across no man's land to the target, it is difficult to extrapolate from those figures the amount of chlorine needed for an artillery barrage aimed directly at the enemy. It seems reasonable to assume, however, that during the Civil War, a large number of chlorine-containing artillery shells—scores of them, at least, and efficiently spaced—would have been required to neutralize a land position containing a sizable force of entrenched enemy troops. As for naval use, Doughty guessed—again, without calculations to support his case—that a single ten-inch shell containing one or two gallons of liquid chlorine could, "with ordinary accuracy," be exploded near an enemy vessel and "envelop him in an atmosphere that would cause his inmates to be more anxious about their own safety than about the destruction of their enemy."[11]

Implementing new shells to carry chlorine would have been no simple matter. Unless the liquid chlorine was free of water, it would corrode the iron of which shells were usually made, and the shells would also have to withstand an internal pressure that was considered unacceptable even for World War I artillery shells. In the event that existing shell designs could be used, the precise bursting charge for a chlorine shell would still have to be determined by trial, because the charge's purpose would be merely to open the shell so that the chemical could escape. The charge ordinarily used to create deadly shell fragmentation would occupy space that could be devoted to chlorine and might disperse the chemical so widely as to reduce its concentration below an effective level. Chlorine shells would not be the same weight as conventional shells, so tests would be required to determine the elevation, propellant charge, and fuse setting for artillerymen to use for various ranges. Moreover, the World War I experience showed that the flight of liquid-filled shells was generally shorter and more dispersed than that of shells with solid fillings. The coordinated barrages that Doughty envisioned, in which burst patterns quickly covered a section of enemy territory, without overlap or gaps, would likely be difficult to achieve on the battlefield, where communication among artillery batteries was poor and where numerous artillery pieces hitting assigned target within a short time could be hampered by poor visibility (from smoke, for example), inconsistent accuracy, unreliable fuses, variations in judging distance, and human error. In World War I, shells could be fired from a single artillery piece at a rate of four to twenty per minute, whereas Civil War field pieces had an average firing rate of one per minute; thus Doughty's vision of delivering a hundred well-aimed rounds within a few minutes, even from multiple guns, would have been a challenge. With regard to employing chlorine against vessels, if Doughty were correct that the gas from a single ten-inch shell might put an enemy crew out of action, it is still difficult to determine how many rounds, even with ordinary accuracy, would have to have been expended before one exploded on or above the target.[12]

All in all, Doughty displayed an impressive knowledge of chlorine but seemed to underestimate the practical difficulties, including the realities of the battlefield, that stood in the way of putting his plan into action. To his credit, and in keeping with his scientific background, he acknowledged that experimentation was needed to determine whether his proposal would be feasible. If ordnance officials paid attention to his communications at all, they likely thought of the time and effort needed to give the proposal a fair trial and decided that their attention was best focused elsewhere. Whether they also would have considered the ethics of poison gas is unknown, but Doughty raised the point himself. In his first letter, he said that "after watching the progress of events during the last eight months," he had "arrived at the somewhat paradoxical conclusion, that its introduction would very much lessen the sanguinary character of the battlefield, and at the same time render conflicts more decisive in their results." His letters do not reveal whether his ethical views reflected an awareness of chlorine's lethality at high concentrations or the suffering it could cause those who received more than just an irritating dose. Doughty's April 5, 1862, letter ended with this statement: "If I have erred, I have, <u>at least</u>, meant well."[13]

For many reasons, chlorine did not have a decisive role in World War I. Nevertheless, evidence suggests that chlorine was among the chemical agents used by the Japanese during the Second Sino-Japanese War (1937–45), although exactly how the chlorine was deployed (artillery projectiles versus cylinders) is not clear. Chlorine has remained a threat in producing mass casualties, as demonstrated by its use by terrorists in Iraq in 2007, where most incidents involved chlorine tank trucks fitted with explosives. Clearly, the setting and context for this use of chlorine bears no resemblance to the battlefields of Doughty's era, and the amount of chlorine carried by a tank truck (typically sixteen to twenty-two tons in North America) is well beyond anything he could have imagined. There have also been allegations of chlorine being used as a chemical weapon in 2014 in the Syrian civil war.[14]

Another reason for chlorine not being a decisive weapon in warfare, beginning with World War I, has been the relative ease with which military personnel can be protected from it. During World War I, defenses against chlorine became available relatively quickly, with one of the earliest—suggested soon after the first German chlorine attack at Ypres—being a pad of fabric or cotton waste moistened with the chlorine-neutralizing agent sodium thiosulfate (hyposulfite of soda). This substance was recognized by Civil War chemists, physicians, and photographers, and it was used with some regularity in the paper and fabric industries to halt the bleaching actions of chlorine. Thus it is conceivable that if Doughty's proposal had been implemented, chlorine may have been recognized as the toxin, and sodium thiosulfate may have been issued to troops to use as a neutralizer. It was also known by the late 1840s that chlorine was absorbed by charcoal, and well-read Americans of the time may have been aware of a respirator invented by Scottish chemist John Stenhouse in 1854. The primitive gas mask contained a layer of charcoal between two pieces of wire gauze and was shown to protect the wearer from "otherwise irrespirable and poisonous gases or vapours," including chlorine. One of the device's projected uses was the protection of soldiers against chemical weapons. It seems unlikely, however, that the use of chlorine during the Civil War could ever have become common enough to require widespread use of protective gear or that either side could have quickly provided it to a large number of soldiers and sailors.[15]

Although Doughty's proposal was apparently spurned at the time by ordnance officials, the use of chlorine as the first effective chemical weapon of World War I, in cloud attacks, was a vindication of sorts. Moreover, chemical weapons officers during the Great War had studied the matter carefully and initially hoped to deliver the agent in artillery shells, exactly as Doughty had proposed. Thus Doughty was in some ways ahead of his time. Chemical weapons doctrine, as developed during World War I, stated that the ideal gas should be highly toxic, easy and inexpensive to produce, readily compressible into a liquid or solid form, easily volatilized back to gas when released, much heavier than air when in gas form, and nonreactive to moisture and other chemicals so as not to be easily neutralized. Doughty recognized chlorine's toxicity, easy volatilization, and weight (compared with air) as positive points, but he remained silent about its production, which was easy as far as the gas was concerned. He stated that charging shells with liquid chlorine was practicable, but the ability to produce great quantities of the liquid did not develop for more than two decades after the Civil War. Doughty considered chlorine's quick absorption by the ground to be an asset but made no mention that the same property would facilitate the chemical's neutralization by respirators. Targets for chlorine-containing artillery shells would probably have been far enough away that friendly troops would not have been affected by fumes drifting back toward them, but Doughty did not address the potential need for Northern munitions workers or artillerymen to protect themselves from accidental exposure. As was the case with other Civil War proponents of chemical weapons, Doughty seemed oblivious to the practical difficulties involved in creating and implementing a new weapon, while he maintained an unrealistic view of how precise Civil War artillery would be under battlefield conditions.[16]

John Doughty's chlorine proposal can thus be seen as having arisen a few decades before technology—and the will among military decision-makers—could turn it into a reality. There were pragmatic reasons not to pursue the idea, but it is likely that ordnance officials did not bother to contemplate them in detail. Doughty, born in 1817, died in 1905, by which time advances in chemistry had facilitated the production of liquid chlorine but before he could judge whether the chemical's use in World War I really did, as he had predicted, lessen the sanguinary nature of warfare.[17]

6

INSINUATING DUST

These shells can be thrown into different parts of a regiment
and after exploding the pepper will get into the troops nose &
eyes and will make them sneeze so as they can't steady their
musket to get aim and will blind them so as they cannot see to
pick out officers or shoot our men while our men are mowing
them down. —Vincent Fountain Jr., 1861

JOHN B. BRIGHAM HAD A knack for drawing attention to himself, even if he
did not always mean to. After studying law and being admitted to the bar,
he settled in Syracuse, New York, where he spent the rest of his career as a
teacher in the public school system. In 1849 and 1850, he survived protests
against his appointment as a school principal and failed at least twice in
quests to be elected clerk of the Syracuse Board of Education. In 1851, he
was somehow involved in the escape of a fugitive slave called Jerry and was
among four men tried for their role in the episode, which came to be known
as the "Jerry Rescue"; a colleague maintained that Brigham's only crime
had been to holler and to appear pleased that Jerry had escaped. Brigham's
1853 trial for violating the Fugitive Slave Law ended with a hung jury, and
the charge was dropped. When the National Woman's Rights Convention
met in Syracuse in 1852, Brigham stated before the audience that "women
should be keepers at home, and mind domestic matters," and that the convention's real object was "not so much to acquire any real or supposed rights,
as to make the speakers and actors conspicuous." This view, naturally, was
unpopular among the attendees, who included Susan B. Anthony. So with
that type of life experience, when Brigham ventured on March 11, 1862, to

propose a weapon for use against the CSS *Virginia*, he anticipated that the idea's "simplicity may expose it to ridicule."[1]

His suggestion to President Lincoln was that artillery shells be filled with "some subtle disabling or sickening powder, gas or fluid"; it seemed to him that powdered red (cayenne) pepper would fit the bill. He described what would happen once such a shell was exploded on the *Virginia*:

> Instantly this subtle powder would penetrate every minute crevice, intended for the admission of air; the first inhalation would silence every gun on board for the simple reason that while men are coughing, sneezing & rubbing their inflamed eyes, they cannot load, aim nor discharge guns! The attacking vessel will then have nothing to do, but to run leisurely along side, amid the little shower of the enemy's shot & shell from the forts, answering them now and then with red pepper; cast on her grappling irons, and tow the bepeppered prize over to Ft Henry [possibly meaning Fort Monroe] where the prisoners may receive such relieve as the condition of their visual and nasal organs may require. Thus, at the expense of a very few dollars and by the shedding of nothing more serious than a few tears, the Monitor may capture her late formidable adversary, or any Fort or Vessel you may designate.[2]

The proposal amused John Hay, one of Lincoln's secretaries, who took the opportunity to display his wit as he forwarded the communication to Henry Wise, the navy's acting chief of ordnance and the same officer who had seen possibilities in Greek fire:

> Respectfully referred by the President to the earnest consideration of Mr. Wise. This Kind of "Pepper-caster" is a novelty in furniture. How do you think Comr Buchanan [Captain Franklin Buchanan of the *Virginia*] would like this style of condiment of the half-shell? The music of the Muse's shell would be nothing to the strains of this man's "Piper." [*Piper* is the genus of black, not red, pepper.] A classical joke—very chaste. Yours for Abraham. John Hay.

Evidently nobody in authority thought that Brigham's proposal was of sufficient military importance to be concealed from the public—or from the Confederates, who had easy access to Northern newspapers—for within a few days, the idea, and much of its actual wording, was released to the press. There, as Brigham had anticipated, his idea was ridiculed under titles such as "A Well-Seasoned Proposition." The origin of the proposal was revealed as Syracuse, but the withholding of Brigham's name spared him public humiliation.[3]

By early 1862, when Brigham's proposal was received, authorities may have been jaded about red pepper as a possible weapon, because the substance and other plant-based irritants had already been mentioned many times. In May 1861, for example, newspapers began reporting that an Alabama newspaper had received a suggestion that a mixture of red pepper and veratria be placed in artillery shells and fired at Union troops occupying Pensacola's Fort Pickens. (Veratria, used medicinally, was a mixture of alkaloids of plant origin.) "Everybody almost knows," said the proponent, "that burning red pepper, even in small quantity, a tea-spoonful, will clear the largest room of a crowd in a few moments; that the least snuff of veratria will make one cough himself almost to death and run great risk of coughing himself into consumption." The remainder of 1861 alone saw US authorities receive no fewer than six other letters suggesting cayenne pepper (most commonly), snuff, pepper, or mustard—alone or in combination, in addition to the explosive charge—as constituents of artillery projectiles. One inventor, writing to *Scientific American* in 1862, thought that cayenne pepper could be combined with chloroform in an artillery shell.[4]

In most instances, whether in 1861 or later in the war, proponents merely put forward the substances as fillings for shells without providing details on how this might be accomplished. One exception was Vincent Fountain Jr. of Long Island, who enclosed a diagram of a spherical shell with a long protruding fuse. Dentist and physician Nathaniel Harris from Middlebury, Vermont, thought that snuff could be placed in large bladders and fired from cannons. Harris, a step-uncle of Senator Stephen A. Douglas, claimed that a few such projectiles "thrown in among the enemy would so blind them, as to disenable them for some hours."[5]

Another unusual delivery method came from D. A. Pease of Ohio, who suggested that red pepper be mixed with whiskey or water, placed in small portable garden engines, and used in infantry assaults. The engines, "each of a size and power that two men could work them, and two draw them, and one to hold and guide the Hoes attached," would be positioned just behind the attacking column and throw "a stream of pepered whisky over the heads of my men on to the enemy which would blind them and cause them to drop their arms in less than a second." Were this method to be used, "no one within reach could possibly escape, the most powerfull and bravest would be as helpless as an infant." Pease even addressed possible skeptics:

To remove any doubts that might exist in the minds of any at the War Department as to the utility and practicability of my plan you have only to place unloaded guns in the hands of one hundred more or less of Prisners, or Slaves and put them in a position that they can be reached by the fluid thrown from a common garden force pump and if it is wisely managed every man will drop his gun in less than one second, and the scene that will follow will satisfy every beholder of the utility of my plan. It would have given me great pleasure if I could be presant and conduct the experiment. . . . Wisdom would dictate that the experiment should be in private.

Perhaps in consideration of a garden engine's limited range, Pease acknowledged, "If the men who manage the Hoes take their position in the front line of the attacking column it would be far better in most cases than to throw their power over the heads of their comrads." Pease suggested that "about 5 lbs of the best African Bird Pepper well pulverized should be added to each 40 gall cask of spirits or water." In warmer weather, said Pease, cold water or half the whiskey would suffice as a solvent. The available evidence points to Pease having been a physician, which would help explain his familiarity with red pepper, a popular medicinal agent.[6]

One imaginative approach was suggested by farmer and inventor Orman Coe of Port Washington, Wisconsin, who proposed that pulverized red or black pepper be placed in bags or bladders and flown over enemy encampments with kites. The kites would have an extra string with which to open the containers, and the powder would "sift down among their camps—Finding its way into their tents—blankets clothing etc." Alternatively, the pepper could be delivered by balloon (presumably unmanned), "but in either case it should be done in the night so as to keep them ignorant of the performance." Coe did not indicate how the kites or balloons could be guided by their users while remaining invisible to the enemy.[7]

The backgrounds of the proponents of pepper and other plant-derived irritants varied widely, as did the way they described the effects of those substances. British-born C. G. Birbeck from Jonesville, Michigan, who described himself as "a poor Meccanic," said, "Pepper is exercrussiating and painful to the eyes then the effect on the nostrils causes such sneezing that it bothers them to keep an equlebrian." Henry C. Comegys, a medical graduate of the University of Maryland who soon served as a contract surgeon at Hammond General Hospital at Point Lookout, Maryland, was more clinical: "[The pepper shell] will when burst suddenly irritate the mucous membranes

of the eyes, nose, and air passages of all who are in close proximity obstruct-
ing sight, causing violent sneezing and coughing." Jacob T. Vanderhoof of
New York City, who sold bags and sacks, thought his idea of filling shells with
snuff might seem "ridiculous at first . . . but might answer a good purpose."
Vincent Fountain Jr., who became a prolific inventor of items ranging from
toys to a potato masher, listed nine advantages of his pepper shell, including
its effectiveness against masked batteries: "The scent of the pepper will drive
the troops out like the fox out of the ground." Adelia Babcock wrote from
Lagoda, Wisconsin, saying that her husband was blind and could not be a
soldier; she proposed placing cayenne pepper into artillery shells. "There is
some Southern Sympathizers here in Northern Wisconsin what would assist
the South in amount if they could," said Babcock to the secretary of war, so
"it would be a matter of satisfaction to know if you receive this." Only one
correspondent, William Johnson of Milwaukee, mentioned the possibility
of personal gain: "You can allow any fair or reasonable compensation that
in your judgement will be equivalent to the benefit gained."[8]

The fumes of burning pepper had been used in warfare by various cul-
tures, including civilizations in Central America and China. However,
Americans of the Civil War era did not have to be historians to know that
red pepper and other common substances could be extremely irritating.
Newspapers, for example, carried accounts of disturbances in legislative
and court proceedings caused by unknown persons who spread cayenne
pepper or snuff on floors and other surfaces. According to one report, "the
insinuating dust" kicked up by people moving about caused "a general and
prodigious cough, sneeze, hawking, spitting, and blowing of noses." Pick-
pockets at a Washington, DC, theater and concert saloon victimized the
audience by strewing cayenne pepper on the floor. Loud applause raised
the powder, provoking sneezing, and gave the thieves their opportunity
to strike. A trickster at a "musical beer house" placed some red pepper on
a hot stove, and the resultant fumes soon drove the occupants out to the
sidewalk, "coughing in a manner that threatened cervical dislocation to all
hands." C. G. Birbeck thought the effects of ground cayenne were obvious,
but like Pease, he offered an easy test to prove his point: "By taking a shot gun
charging it with powder than add pepper on the top not using the ram rod
but leave it loose fire it in the are to windward of you and stand in the shower
as it decends—it will not kill but speak for itself better than I can for it."[9]

Cayenne pepper was cultivated in many parts of the world, including
North America, and was widely used for culinary and medicinal purposes. It was familiar to the public and widely available from grocers and

druggists. The ability of snuff (powdered tobacco) and preparations of mustard (from the seeds of *Sinapis nigra* and *Sinapis alba*) to cause sneezing was well known. Veratria, a bitter-tasting powder, was derived from the seeds (called sabadilla or cevadilla) of *Veratrum sabadilla* (a species also known as *Schoenocaulon officinale*) and related plants, which grew in parts of Latin America. It was used both externally in an ointment and by mouth primarily for gout, rheumatism, and neuralgia. When "admitted into the nostrils," veratria produced "violent sneezing and coryza," inflammation of the nasal mucosa. Veratria was expensive—a Cincinnati supplier was charging $5 an ounce in 1864. If it was not imported as the finished drug, two pounds of the seeds would have to be processed with three gallons of alcohol and other reagents to produce about four grams of veratria. The correspondent suggesting veratria as a weapon may have had some medical knowledge but perhaps not enough to be aware of its high price.[10]

The effects of red pepper and the other suggested agents were described fairly consistently by their proponents. These included causing temporarily blindness and sneezing, spreading fear, and irritating the mucous membranes. The claimed effects would last for "a while," "some ten, fifteen, or twenty minutes," or "some hours." At least two correspondents pointed out that the pepper would persist where deployed, with the artillery shell doing "execution some length of time after it explodes." If pepper found its way into a camp, every movement would stir it up and cause additional suffering, and "abandonment of the premises would be the only way of relief." If explosion of the shell ignited the pepper in addition to dispersing it, all the better, for that would have "the same effect as if it was burnt on a stove in a room and therefore makes it very offensive." None of the proponents expressed concern about friendly troops being bothered by the irritants when they occupied the bombarded territory.[11]

Unlike Joseph Jones with his hydrogen cyanide shell and John Doughty with his chlorine shell (see chapters 4 and 5), the proponents of pepper and other irritants paid little attention to the technical feasibility of their ideas. To be sure, placing snuff or pulverized pepper into a shell did not present the difficulties that hydrogen cyanide or liquid chlorine did, but the projectiles would still have to be tested. There was the matter, for example, of deciding on the amount of irritant to place in a shell and determining a bursting charge that would distribute the agent sufficiently without dispersing it so much that it was no longer effective. New range tables would have to be developed if the weight of irritant-containing and conventional shells differed. Domestically grown cayenne pepper was plentiful and cheap in the North, costing druggists 22 cents a pound in 1864. Prices for cayenne were higher in the South. In November 1862, the Confederate Medical Department was offering $1 in Confederate notes per pound of pepper pods grown by citizens. In May 1863, cayenne was being sold at auction in Wilmington, North Carolina, for about $4.50 per pound. The ever decreasing buying power of the Confederate dollar meant that putting cayenne pepper into artillery shells was a less viable option in the South than it was in the North.[12]

Nathaniel Harris's suggestion to fire snuff-filled bladders from cannons would seem to have been based on a few supposed benefits. For example, a relatively large amount of snuff could be delivered because the usual iron projectile, with its fairly thick walls, would be absent. The bladder would rupture upon striking a target, and the enclosed powder would fly out and envelop the enemy. With no metal shell and no bursting charge, there would be no shell fragments; this meant a low risk of lethality or of the payload being dispersed too widely to be effective. A bladder, of course, could not have withstood the blast of the cannon, and even if it could, the flight of the nonrigid bladder would probably be less than predictable.

As unworkable as Harris's proposal seems, it has a modern counterpart. Some military and law enforcement agencies have devices resembling paintball guns that can fire projectiles filled with a powdered substance obtained from peppers (or synthesized) called pelargonic acid vanillylamide (PAVA) or capsaicin II. The plastic projectiles are intended to be nonlethal and to break when they strike a person or a hard surface. The release of PAVA incapacitates the suspect by causing severe coughing and a burning sensation in the eyes, nose, and throat and on the skin. This launcher-projectile system is essentially a realization of Harris's idea but on a small scale and meant to be used at relatively close range. The launcher propels with high-pressure air rather than gunpowder, and its projectiles are spherical, hard shells rather than nonrigid bladders, yet the basic principles of Harris's idea are retained.[13]

One important aspect of D. A. Pease's idea of using garden engines to spray the enemy with liquid pepper was that it could be employed only when the opposing forces were quite near. Liquid projected from small garden engines might reach sixty or seventy feet, and because a device small enough to be moved about by two men could not carry much liquid, its "ammunition" would soon be depleted. Even if the spray reached a hundred feet and efficiently blinded opposing troops who were close enough, that distance was much shorter than the range from which enemy soldiers could deliver accurate rifle fire; the engine operators would be easy targets, and the device could be overrun within a few seconds. It might also have been difficult to recruit soldiers willing to operate a nonlethal device when enemy soldiers less than a stone's throw away were firing back with deadly intent. One is reminded of General Meade's skepticism when General Butler imagined using a garden engine and Greek fire to defend a position (see chapter 2).[14]

Pease's proposal, however, has a modern counterpart in pepper spray. The recipes he suggested resembled those then used to produce liquid medicinal formulations of cayenne pepper. Pease demonstrated some pharmaceutical knowledge in recommending that in warmer weather, the pepper could be added to less whiskey or to cold water, because a higher temperature meant quicker release of cayenne's active constituents into the solvent. The release of these constituents into fluid would be more efficient in typical medicinal preparations because they employed boiling water or exposure to alcohol for a week, but Pease nevertheless knew the principles, and his procedures may have produced sufficiently irritating fluid. The constituents in his formulas would have shared properties of oleoresin capsicum, the cayenne-derived active ingredient of pepper spray. Oleoresin capsicum is prepared by adding a solvent, such as alcohol, to ground dried chili peppers to extract the active ingredients, exactly as Pease described. After the solvent is then evaporated off, the oleoresin remains. To make pepper spray, the oleoresin is mixed with an oil- or water-soluble fluid (the latter with an emulsifier) and packaged with a gaseous propellant.[15]

Orman Coe's idea to deliver a payload by way of kites or balloons may seem peculiar today, but it had historical precedent and continued to be considered a viable method for many decades afterward. A manuscript dating from 1327 and presented to Edward III on the eve of his coronation as king of England depicted a bomb-laden kite being flown over a town. A modern investigation revealed that such a device could successfully have been flown some distance and dropped a bomb weighing at least five pounds. During the Napoleonic Wars, British naval captain Thomas Cochrane used small kites released from his vessels to deliver leaflets to French citizens. Bundles of the papers were tied with string to the kites, and a slow-burning match was timed to burn the string after the kite flew over the coast; as the string gave way, the leaflets fluttered to the ground. The method was reportedly successful and annoyed the French government a great deal. At least one account of Cochrane's action was published by 1861, so American inventors may have been aware of it. In 1864, Union general Benjamin Butler had kites flown over enemy lines to drop copies of President Lincoln's Amnesty Proclamation. Each kite had two strings, with the weaker one securing a bundle of leaflets. When the kite was over its target, the stronger line was slackened, immediately putting strain on the weaker line, which broke and released the papers earthward. The proclamations thus released prompted a number of Confederate soldiers to desert. During World War I, kites were advocated for use in taking aerial photographs and as vehicles for holding scientific instruments, radio antennas, or signal lights aloft. They were also considered for offensive purposes. "Teams of kites," said one proponent, "can easily lift one or two hundred pounds, and when the wind is toward the enemy's lines, kites can be raised, supporting bombs, grenades, or aerial torpedoes, and maneuvered until the projectile is over the enemy's position."[16]

Newspaper readers of the mid-1800s may have been aware of hot air balloons as platforms for delivering weapons. In March 1849, American newspapers started publishing reports of Austrian plans to bombard Venice, Italy, with unmanned bomb-carrying hot air balloons. A few months later, the Austrians made an aerial assault with twenty balloons, but none of the bombs hit their mark. Such reports may have captured the imagination of Charles Perley of New York City, who in 1863 patented a device for dropping bombs from unmanned balloons. Although there is no evidence that weapons were deployed via balloon during the American Civil War, the idea reappeared in the 1930s in Japan. In 1944–45, the Japanese launched thousands of unmanned hydrogen balloons for flight across the Pacific Ocean to the United States. A small percentage of the balloons, typically laden with incendiary and high-explosive ordnance, reached North America and did little damage.[17]

Although there is no indication that cayenne pepper and other plant-based irritants were used during the Civil War in the manners suggested, there is an account of a substance used to detect persons trying to leave the South surreptitiously on the blockade runner *Fannie*, departing Wilmington, North Carolina, for Nassau:[18]

> [A boarding party] was provided with a machine in the shape of a large syringe, filled with some chemical mixture known in that locality as the "sneezing compound." This stuff was vigorously pumped into every possible and impossible place where a "Nassau" runner could be concealed. Any man subjected to its influence in close quarters must sneeze out or "bust his biler." It is described as a villainous compound of stink and tickle, which no person can sustain and live. . . . The "sneezing compound" was thrown in [the coal bunks] freely. After a while a slight motion was noticed, then a suppressed sneeze, quickly followed by a vigorous "Cot tam." In a few minutes four anything but jolly Dutchmen, black as negroes, half smothered, and sneezing with a 20 horse power, came forth from their coal-bunk births.[19]

It seems likely that the sneezing compound contained powdered cayenne pepper, because it was relatively easy to obtain and prepare. Fumigating closed spaces to detect stowaways was practiced on at least one other blockade runner.[20]

The belief that irritant powders might be of military usefulness persisted after the Civil War. The US War Department's Board of Ordnance and Fortification, formed in 1888, reported the receipt of a suggestion that sounded much like its Civil War counterparts: "A bomb laden to its full capacity with snuff, which should be so evenly and thoroughly distributed that the enemy would be convulsed with sneezing, and in the period of this paroxysm it would be possible to creep up upon him and capture him in the throes of the convulsion." During World War I, cevadilla, the source of veratria, was reportedly being incorporated into poison gas, and the British used a pepper-derived extract in chemical grenades. In 2013, the Indian Army was reportedly considering using components of the *bhut jolokia*—supposedly the world's hottest chili pepper—in grenades for use against rioters or terrorists.[21]

The use of tear gases and other irritants in World War I artillery shells indicates that such nonlethal substances had a role in attacking the enemy at a distance. In the Great War, nonlethal irritants could immediately incapacitate at relatively low concentrations; disabling the same number of men with lethal agents would require many more shells. Irritant agents were also intended to force enemy soldiers to put on their gas masks, which made them much less efficient fighters, or to abandon their positions. Whether World War I scientists ever gave serious consideration to filling artillery shells with red pepper, snuff, veratria, or mustard (as opposed to mustard gas, which is not related to mustard at all) is unclear, but they did develop other irritants that were quite effective.[22]

The Civil War proponents of cayenne pepper and other irritants, ridiculed at the time, have had their measure of vindication in the modern development of pepper projectiles and pepper spray. The modern irritants are related to the simple pulverized red pepper that was so often suggested during the War between the States, and their delivery vehicles—liquid or frangible sphere—resemble the peppered whiskey of D. A. Pease and the snuff bladders of Nathaniel Harris. The major difference is that the modern counterparts are used at close quarters—for subduing rioters, apprehending suspects, and like purposes—where they can be aimed with reasonable accuracy, whereas the Civil War proponents of irritant substances, with the exception of Pease, imagined them being deployed at longer distances against enemy combatants. The tear gas most commonly used today in law enforcement, CS gas (2-chlorobenzalmalononitrile), does not contain irritants suggested during the Civil War but achieves rapid nonlethal incapacitation, the same goal stated by those Civil War proponents.[23]

In light of how familiar citizens were with red pepper and snuff, it is no surprise that those substances were proposed as weapons. Perhaps that familiarity—and the assumption that something so common could not possibly be useful in warfare—helps explain why the ideas were disregarded and sometimes treated with derision. Modern developments suggest that those Civil War proposals were not as outlandish as they seemed at the time.

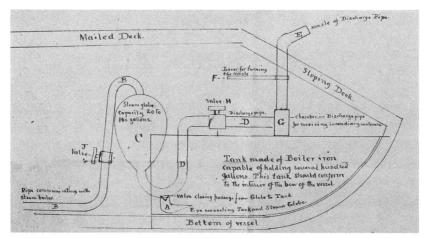

Detail from James Lewis's proposal for an ironclad vessel fitted with a steam-powered apparatus for spraying ignited petroleum or coal oil. *December 18, 1861, class misc., letter 258, entry 994, Records of the Office of the Chief of Ordnance (RG 156), National Archives and Records Administration.*

Flamethrower being test fired from a US Navy patrol boat in 1969. Multiple American inventors imagined Greek fire being used in this manner. *National Archives and Records Administration (identifier 6349329).*

Artillery shell bursting in Charleston during the first bombardment of the city by the Union artillery piece called the "Swamp Angel," August 22, 1863. The projectiles contained explosive charges with or without incendiary materials. Harper's Weekly, *January 9, 1864.*

RETRIBUTION.

HOW ARE YOU MR. BEAUREGARD?

"......A villainous compound!......It's against the cause of Humanity, and the laws of
Civilized Warfare!!"

Cartoon ridiculing General P. G. T. Beauregard for his supposed condemnation
of Greek fire as "a villainous compound, unworthy of civilized nations." Harper's
Weekly, *September 12, 1863.*

Photograph of Dr. Joseph Jones (1833–96). As a Confederate army surgeon, he suggested the use of phosphorus and hydrogen cyanide against Union ironclads. *Joseph Jones Papers, Louisiana Research Collection, Tulane University.*

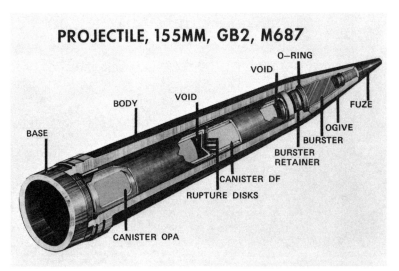

PROJECTILE, 155MM, GB2, M687

M687 binary artillery projectile. Firing of the shell from an artillery piece would rupture thin discs between separate containers of the precursor chemicals OPA (a mixture of isopropyl alcohol and isopropylamine) and methylphosphonyl difluoride (DF), allowing them to mix during flight to form the nerve agent sarin (GB2). The principle was identical to that in Joseph Jones's proposal for weapons that would generate hydrogen cyanide. *National Archives and Records Administration (identifier 6373073).*

German chemist Robert Bunsen (1811–99). Starting in the late 1830s, he studied alkarsin and the cacodyl derivatives, which would later be suggested as chemical weapons. During one experiment, a container of cacodyl cyanide exploded and blinded Bunsen in one eye. *Images from the History of Medicine, National Library of Medicine (image 170877).*

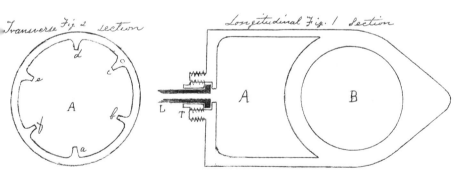

John Doughty's proposed chlorine shell. Liquid chlorine would be placed in section A through lead tube L, whose flange is secured by thimble plug T. Section B holds the explosive powder. *Doughty to Lincoln (with endorsement), May 1, 1862, class 8, letter 191, Correspondence Relating to Inventions, National Archives and Records Administration.*

Confederate fortifications near Petersburg, Virginia. Trenches and bombproof shelters were thought to be particularly apt targets by proponents of certain chemical weapons, such as chlorine gas and chloroform. *Library of Congress (reproduction LC-DIG-cwpb-02631).*

Respirator invented by Scottish chemist John Stenhouse in 1854, with charcoal between two layers of wire gauze. Stenhouse was inconsistent in his claims about the device protecting the wearer from chlorine gas. *Youmans,* Class-Book of Chemistry.

Northern workmen filling and finishing artillery projectiles during the Civil War. Using toxic chemicals in shells would probably have increased the danger to munitions workers. Harper's Weekly, *November 30, 1861.*

Workers at the Rocky Mountain Arsenal (Colorado) wearing protective gear while filling artillery shells with mustard gas in 1954. Respirators and other protective equipment may have been necessary for Civil War workers assembling chemical weapons. *Library of Congress (reproduction HAER COLO, 1-COMCI, 1–207).*

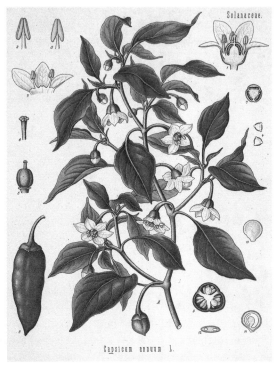

Capsicum annuum, the common red or cayenne pepper. Ground dried red pepper was often suggested during the Civil War for use as a weapon. Chemicals derived from peppers are currently used in personal protection and crowd control devices. *Pabst*, Köhler's Medizinal-Pflanzen, *vol. 2, plate 127 (digital file from Biodiversity Heritage Library and Missouri Botanical Garden, Peter H. Raven Library).*

Capsicum annuum L.

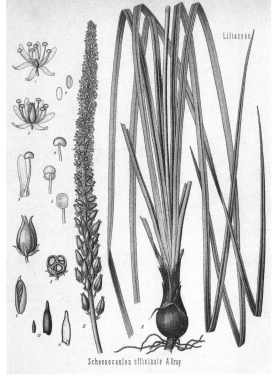

Schoenocaulon officinale, also known as *Veratrum sabadilla*, the source of seeds used to produce veratria, a medicinal powder. Veratria was extremely irritating when inhaled and was thus suggested during the Civil War as a filling for artillery shells. The seeds were reportedly studied for use in World War I chemical weapons. *Pabst*, Köhler's Medizinal-Pflanzen, *vol. 2, plate 111 (digital file from Biodiversity Heritage Library and Missouri Botanical Garden, Peter H. Raven Library).*

Schoenocaulon officinale A.Gray.

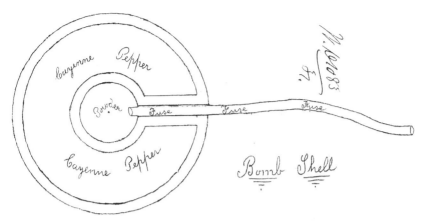

Artillery shell containing ground cayenne pepper and an explosive charge of powder, as proposed by Vincent Fountain Jr. *August 12, 1861, classes 4 & 5, letter 369, Correspondence Relating to Inventions, National Archives and Records Administration.*

Fire engine near Richmond shortly after the Civil War. Many advocates of chemical weapons suggested that fire or garden engines be used to spray the substances on the enemy. *Library of Congress (reproduction LC-DIG-cwpb-02760 DLC).*

Garden engine of a type available during the Civil War. Garden engines included a hand pump for spraying water or other fluids from a reservoir. The typical range was sixty or seventy feet. *Henderson,* Gardening for Pleasure.

Chloroform tin. Suggested by multiple citizens as a chemical weapon, chloroform was widely available in the North, less so in the South. It was a standard military medicine, usually packaged in tin for that purpose and labeled with a Latinized name. Chloroform for civilian use was typically sold in glass bottles. *National Museum of Civil War Medicine (catalog no. 2001.007.001h).*

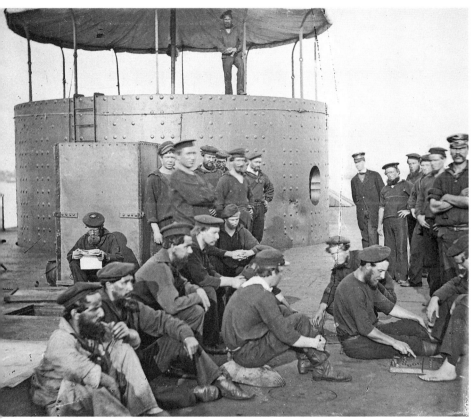

USS *Monitor*, a special target of Confederate proposals to employ chemical weapons, including chloroform and ignited turpentine. *Library of Congress (reproduction LC-DIG-cwpb-01061).*

DRUGS

AND

MEDICINAL PREPARATIONS

Offered to Physicians,

BY BULLOCK & CRENSHAW,

Sixth Street, two doors above Arch St.,

PHILADELPHIA.

ACETONE (pyroxilic spirit) . . .	$1 50 per lb.*	
ACETUM, Opii	1 50	lb.
Scillæ	50	lb.
ACID : Acetic : No. 8	25	lb.
Acet : Glacial (used as a mild cautery) .	18	oz.
Arsenios : (Pure) . . .	06	oz.
Arsenic :	25	oz.
Benzoic :	40	oz.
Citric :	1 50	lb.
Gallic :	75	oz.
Gallic : Pyro	50	dr.
Muriatic : Med : Pure . . .	12	lb.
Nitric : Med : Pure . . .	25	lb.
Nitro-muriat : . . .	25	lb.
Oxalic :	50	lb.
Phosphoric : Glacial . . .	50	oz.
" Dilut : (containing 8.7 per cent.)	1 00	lb.
Prussic : (U. S. P. in oz. Stop. Bot. & Case)	31	oz.
Pyroligneous, Rectif : . . .	25	lb.
Sulphuric : . . .	06	lb.
" Aromatic : . . .	50	lb.
Tannic :	31	oz.
Tartaric :	62	lb.
Valerianic : . . .	2 50	oz.
ACONITINE	15	gr.
ALCOHOL, U. S. P. . . .	62 to 75	gall.
95 per ct. . . .	1 00	gall.

* The pounds and ounces referred to in this Catalogue are all avoirdupois; for convenience we have used the term dr. for the 1-8th of an avoirdupois ounce.

Page from a medical supplier's 1857 price list. Muriatic (hydrochloric), nitric, and sulfuric acids, which were all proposed as chemical weapons during the Civil War, remained inexpensive and plentiful in the North during the war. Prussic acid (hydrogen cyanide), another agent suggested as a chemical weapon, was also offered for sale and had medicinal uses. *Bullock and Crenshaw,* Catalogue of Drugs.

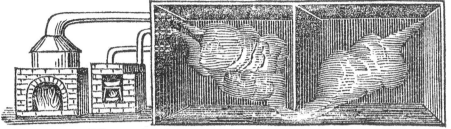

Manufacturing Sulphuric Acid.

Sulfuric acid chambers. The industrial production of sulfuric acid typically involved the introduction of steam, air, and fumes from burning sulfur and potassium nitrate into large chambers lined with lead; the formed sulfuric acid would accumulate on the chamber floors. Sulfuric acid was proposed as a Civil War chemical weapon and was needed to manufacture nitric acid, hydrochloric acid, and phosphorus, which were also proposed as chemical weapons. *Youmans*, Class-Book of Chemistry.

World War I gas cloud attack probably involving chlorine released from cylinders. During the Civil War, chlorine was proposed as a filling for artillery projectiles, but formation of a gas cloud, as shown, was the basis of Forrest Shepherd's proposal to mix sulfuric and hydrochloric acids to form clouds of hydrochloric acid mist. *National Archives and Records Administration (identifier 530722).*

Interior of the Union mine used to detonate powder under the Confederate line outside Petersburg. To prevent future use of such mines, the Confederates dug countermines and equipped troops with fume-producing cartridges to place in detected Union mines. Harper's Weekly, *August 20, 1864.*

US marine with gas mask waiting to descend into a Viet Cong tunnel in 1968. Tear gas was often used to clear tunnels but could persist long enough to hamper later exploration. A device for producing irritating fumes was available to Confederate troops for use against enemy tunnelers. *National Archives and Records Administration (identifier 532460).*

Types of mortars that may have been used to deliver stink balls demonstrated for an audience of Confederate officers and onlookers. *Library of Congress (reproduction LC-DIG-cwpb-00699).*

Portion of Union-held Fort Pickens in Pensacola Bay, Florida, a target of Confederate proposals to use various chemical weapons, including red pepper and an unnamed poison dropped from a balloon. Harper's Weekly, *December 28, 1861.*

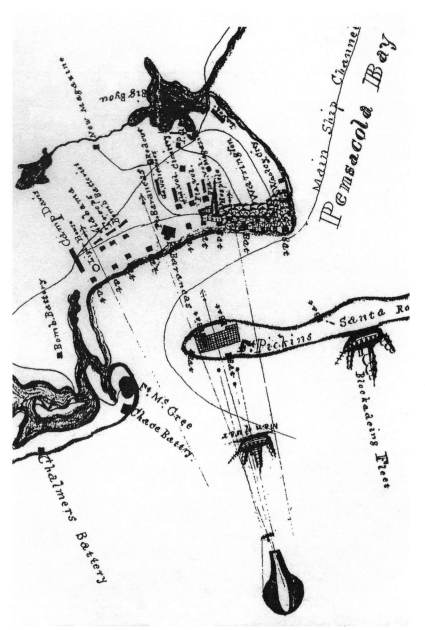

Detail from Isham Walker's proposal to drop poison-containing bombs on Fort Pickens and the Union fleet from a manned balloon. North is at the top of the diagram. *Walker to L. P. Walker, June 4, 1861, Letters Received by the Confederate Secretary of War, microfilm M437, roll 3, letter 1455, War Department Collection of Confederate Records (RG 109), National Archives and Records Administration.*

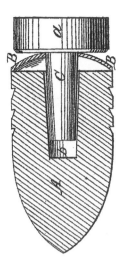

Williams bullet with an expandable zinc disc (part B), originally intended to engage the rifling in a firearm's barrel and later found to remove fouling. There were accusations that the disc's purpose was to poison wounds. *US Patent and Trademark Office (patent 37,145).*

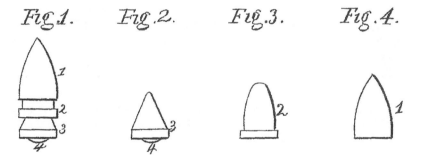

Shaler bullet, consisting of multiple sections that nested together and were intended to separate in flight. The recovery from wounds of section 1 or 2, each of which had a hollowed base, led to claims that the cavity was filled with poison. *US Patent and Trademark Office (patent 36,197).*

World War I poster depicting effects of poison gas on a soldier not wearing a gas mask. Civil War proponents of chemical weapons probably imagined their devices producing a similar effect. Respirators available during the Civil War may have provided some degree of protection. *Library of Congress (reproduction LC-USZC4–11179).*

7

PROSTRATED BY INHALING IT

The chloroform if only spilled on the floor would stupefy or
kill or drive away any thing living, and no gunner could go
or remain where it was as the chloroform is so volatile that
nothing could be thrown on it to destroy its effects.
—Potts & Klett's Chemical Works, 1861

JUST AS THE ACTIONS OF the Confederate ironclad CSS *Virginia* worried
Northerners, the sudden appearance of the USS *Monitor* concerned Southerners, and military officials in particular. After the "duel of the ironclads"
on March 9, 1862, at Hampton Roads ended in a draw, Confederate plans
were hatched to board and capture the *Monitor*. If the Union ironclad
could be enticed to battle again with the *Virginia*, a number of Confederate
gunboats or tugs—the type of vessels and their number vary among the
accounts—would "pounce down on the 'Monitor' at the same time; on a
given signal, and from different directions, all hands were to rush on board,
wedge the turret so as to prevent its revolving, then scale the sides, deluge
the interior with chloroform by breaking the bottles on the upper deck,
and then cover the turret and pilot-house with tarpaulins, and wait for the
crew to surrender."[1]

The assault was planned for April 11, 1862. Boarding parties on the various
Confederate vessels were supplied with scaling ladders, "chopping axes,
to destroy the gutta percha pipe that supplies the Monitor with air; balls
saturated with turpentine and oil, to throw into the turret; bottles with the
same ingredients; chloroform in bottles were placed on board to throw down
the turret of the Monitor." According to one account, the boarding parties

had "wet blankets and boiler iron plate to cover grating supposed to be on the Monitor, in order to prevent the men from firing up at them, and also to smother the men on board the Monitor." Covering the pilot house with blankets, tarpaulins, or a wet sail—again, the description varies with the account—would also make it impossible for the helmsman to see and steer the *Monitor*. The tug *J. B. White* "was furnished with chains to run around the turret of the Monitor, to fasten her to the Merrimac." (Although the *Merrimack* had been rechristened the *Virginia* by the Confederates after they took it over, it was often still referred to by its old name.) On April 11, the *Virginia*, having been repaired and resupplied after her first encounter with the *Monitor*, steamed into Hampton Roads accompanied by her escort vessels with their boarding parties. The intent was to lure the *Monitor* into battle, but the crew did not rise to the bait and kept the vessel where it was, out of reach. Thus, said a crewmember of the *Virginia*, "We saved our chloroform and—our necks." So ended an episode in which a chemical weapon was readied for use but not deployed—only because the opportunity did not arise.[2]

The Confederates apparently were not yet ready to abandon their plan, for on April 28, Flag Officer Louis M. Goldsborough, writing from the USS *Minnesota* at Hampton Roads, informed US assistant secretary of the navy Gustavus Fox that something was afoot. "The present program of the Merrimac," wrote Goldsborough, "is to take the Monitor at all hazards, for which she is provided with numerous grapnels & steel wedges, the latter to choke the tower & prevent its revolving; go to Yorktown; then to Washington City; and finally, to New York. Chloroform is to be used in abundance by the Merrimac to produce insensibility on board the Monitor." (Goldsborough made this report three weeks before newspaper accounts of the Confederates' planned April 11 attack began to appear. He may have learned about the April 11 plans and considered them still active.) Goldsborough, who seemed amused by the plan, remarked, "I was under the impression that chemicals were rather scarce among them!" He was right about the Southern scarcity of chloroform and would shortly have no reason to worry further about the *Virginia*, for she was scuttled on May 11, 1862, to prevent capture by advancing Union troops.[3]

Chloroform was discovered in 1831 and found uses for various medical purposes. A volatile liquid, it was given by mouth as a sedative and analgesic and even to treat malaria. It could be used as a gargle for ulcers of the throat or applied externally for local pain relief. Its usefulness as an anesthetic began to be appreciated in the late 1840s. By the American Civil

War, chloroform's increasing employment as an anesthetic was becoming generally known, and the public could read about its use or even request its administration during tooth extraction. Citizens could also read accounts—evidently apocryphal—of robberies or other crimes committed with the assistance of chloroform. The stories typically described victims becoming insensible immediately after a chloroform-moistened cloth was applied to their face. Chloroform was also becoming a drug of abuse, with one physician stating that "many persons of both sexes, and of all ages, have resorted to it for the purpose of obtaining the pleasure of a temporary delirium." The other well-known anesthetic of the time, ether, was flammable, so chloroform might naturally suggest itself to concerned citizens as a potentially effective and practical chemical weapon that was safer than ether for the user. In fact, among the communications described in this book, those advocating chloroform are outnumbered only by those suggesting cayenne pepper.[4]

As might be expected, proponents of chloroform usually suggested that it be placed in artillery shells. George Bennett, a machinist from Newburgh, New York, wrote to Secretary of War Edwin M. Stanton that chloroform could first be put in glass globes or tubes—presumably to facilitate handling the liquid—and then in shells. He had presented the idea to General Winfield Scott, who recommended sending it to Stanton. The secretary also received a letter from namesake Mrs. F. A. Stanton of Danville, Pennsylvania, who thought that chloroform in shells "might be used to advantage as an instrument of war." She added modestly, "I have taken the liberty to write you thinking that a small mind might possibly think of something that greater ones would not find time to notice. Please give this your attention and oblige a woman who wishes to serve her country." There is no evidence that Mrs. Stanton received a reply.[5]

One correspondent who did receive a reply—a rare occurrence—was carpenter Dickson B. Coulter of Prescott, Wisconsin. Coulter was confident that shells containing both chloroform and a bursting charge would be effective, writing, "I am satisfied that any fort, intrenchments, or rifel pitts, that are not boomproof, can be taken with one battery, and shells so charged, in a very short time after geting the range." For some reason, Assistant Secretary of War Peter H. Watson, forwarded Coulter's letter to Chief of Ordnance Ripley for a report, and two days later, Ripley's terse response—more of an outright refusal than a report—came back: "Respectfully returned. This Department is not willing to introduce into the military service shell containing chloroform in addition to the powder charge." Watson quickly informed Coulter, "Your letter . . . was referred to Chief of Ordnance who reports adversely upon your proposal." When a correspondent known only as C. B. from Connecticut asked *Scientific American* its opinion of a shell filled with chloroform and cayenne, the editors responded that it "would be a very harmless affair." The editors were somewhat more encouraging about a chloroform shell proposed by J. R. A., also from Connecticut.[6]

Perhaps the most credible of citizens' chloroform proposals came from Potts & Klett's Chemical Works in Camden, New Jersey. Potts & Klett's was a well-established firm, best known for manufacturing acids and farm fertilizer. In a curious coincidence, the company made and supervised the production elsewhere of a fertilizer called Rhodes' Super-Phosphate, formulated for the cultivation of cotton. Before the war, the Cotton Planters' Convention of Georgia desired to have an analysis made of the content and suitability of available fertilizers and hired for this task physician Joseph Jones, who reported favorably in 1860 on Rhodes' Super-Phosphate. This was the same Jones who in a few short years suggested using phosphorus and hydrogen cyanide against Union naval vessels (see chapters 3 and 4). The Potts and Klett's factory was also known for having been struck in 1860 by a tornado, which killed three of the firm's workers.[7]

Robert B. Potts was a graduate of the Philadelphia College of Pharmacy and known as "a man of substantial character, public spirit and benevolence, a useful member of society and of high standing in his community." His partner, Frederick Klett Jr., was a graduate of the University of Pennsylvania. Klett's father was a founder of the Philadelphia College of Pharmacy and owned a well-known drugstore in Philadelphia. Thus the chemical expertise of Messrs. Potts and Klett should have lent some authority to their proposal.[8]

Potts and Klett suggested filling artillery shells half with gunpowder and half with chloroform, with the two substances separated by an iron partition; the chloroform end could be sealed with a cork after filling. The liquid was so volatile, they said, that it would have wide-ranging effects and could not be counteracted. "If ten pounds of it," they claimed, "was thrown into the Steamer Wabash [a US vessel being used as an example] every thing living must be stupefied or leave it at once." The difference between the chloroform shell and other projectiles was "simply that if one gunner is killed or driven away from his gun by the fumes of the chloroform, no other can take his place." They were quick to point out, "We do not make chloroform, but as it could be used for this purpose very impure there is no doubt that it could be purchased very cheaply." They guessed no more than 50 cents per pound.[9]

Chloroform did indeed possess properties necessary in a successful chemical agent. Its vapor was heavier than air, so it would sink to the ground, and it was not so volatile—compared with chlorine or hydrogen cyanide gas, for example—that it would dissipate immediately. Moreover, at room temperature, chloroform could be placed in artillery shells without concerns about creating too much pressure. Whether the shells' chloroform chamber should be sealed with a cork was questionable. One possible objection to sealing chloroform bottles with a cork was that "the chloroform penetrates the cork after some time, especially during the agitation incidental to shipment, causing shrinkage and perhaps consequent leakage." Poor-quality chloroform, which Potts and Klett suggested using, could even corrode the cork. There seemed to be no reason to worry that chloroform would be unstable in a cast-iron shell, as long as air was excluded as much as possible, or that it would corrode the shell.[10]

Even in the absence of such technical worries, there was one critical concern, which the *Scientific American* editors voiced clearly when they examined a correspondent's proposal for a chloroform shell: "We fear it is impractical, as it seems to us that the vapor of chloroform would not be sufficiently concentrated. The vapor of chloroform, to produce sleep or stupefaction, must be inhaled without being much diluted with atmospheric air as much as we think it would be when diffused as you propose. If this difficulty could be shown not to exist, we think you could obtain a patent."[11]

Misconceptions about chloroform were common. According to one physician:

> The notions which are current concerning chloroform and its effects are in great degree strange and erroneous. Among the public there is much perplexity, many ideas based upon false reasoning, and much ignorance even with regard to the nature of the agent itself. Many people scarcely know whether it is a solid or liquid: but, I think the most widely spread error is that concerning the instantaneousness of its action. It is supposed to be only necessary to hold the chloroform over the patient's nose and mouth, and insensibility is produced.[12]

Indeed, citizens' suggestion to use chloroform as a weapon seemed to presume that its stupefying effect was immediate. This was certainly the impression readers got from newspaper stories of chloroform-facilitated crimes such as robbery and rape. Regarding the actions of chloroform, an article in the British medical publication *Lancet* complained that the popular press was more inclined to believe disreputable persons than expert medical opinion.

Period experts on chloroform anesthesia pointed out that the agent did not work instantaneously. According to one clinician, "Four minutes are at the least required to produce insensibility; more to make it profound. I have never in any instance seen any helplessness whatever produced in less than two or three minutes, and that with the full consent of the patient. . . . Without the consent of the patient, or without his being held for at least several minutes, insensibility cannot be produced." The odor of chloroform can be detected at concentrations as low as eighty-five parts per million (ppm), which is much lower than levels considered immediately dangerous, so troops detecting the chemical might be able to escape before it had time to do its work.[13]

At the time, the concentration of chloroform vapor needed to produce anesthesia was not known with precision, and even today, the levels said to produce certain effects range widely, from five hundred ppm as a concentration "immediately dangerous to life or health" to twenty thousand ppm to produce anesthesia. The lower figure of five hundred ppm is essentially identical to the concentration of hydrogen cyanide vapor thought necessary during World War I to produce incapacity in a few seconds; in comparison, the analogous concentrations for chlorine and phosgene were only eighty-three and ten ppm, respectively. It was widely accepted during the Great War that five hundred ppm of hydrogen cyanide was too high to be achieved on the battlefield, so it is likely that the same would be true for chloroform. A related concern about chloroform-laden artillery shells would have been that the bursting charge necessary to atomize the liquid chloroform and spread it about could not be so large as to disperse the substance too widely to be effective. As was the case for the proposed chlorine shells, artillerists would have had to determine the optimal number of shells and the pattern of firing for an effective barrage.[14]

If released within an enclosed space—poured into the USS *Monitor* in large amounts, for example—chloroform, like hydrogen cyanide, may have been effective because of a high gas concentration and the occupants' inability to escape. Chloroform proponents, however, gave no apparent consideration to how the space might be decontaminated so that friendly troops could enter safely. And if a shell capable of delivering ten pounds of chloroform penetrated a naval vessel, as in the scenario presented by Potts and Klett, an equivalent volume of high explosive, rather than chloroform, within the projectile might have subdued the stricken vessel's crew to the same or a greater extent.

As might be expected with a liquid agent, the idea of employing fire engines arose for chloroform. Joseph Lott of Hartford, Connecticut, proposed

that such devices be positioned so that Confederate troops defending Yorktown, Virginia, and Corinth, Mississippi, could be anesthetized by a spray
of chloroform. Drawbacks to fire or garden engines are mentioned in other
chapters and would apply in this case as well. Had this proposal received serious consideration, officials would have had to choose the engines carefully.
Some fire engines had parts made of India rubber or gutta-percha, and those
materials were sometimes incorporated into fire hoses. Both substances can
be dissolved by chloroform, which is a powerful solvent.[15]

The estimate provided by Potts and Klett of chloroform's price, 50 cents
per pound, seems on the mark. An 1863 report on the New York drug market indicated that ten specimens of chloroform, half of which were judged
good or nearly good in quality, ranged in price from 90 cents to $1.50 per
pound. If merchants of impure chloroform, which would probably suffice
for weapons use, would agree to that characterization of their offering or
sell chloroform that had not undergone all the purification steps, then it
seems reasonable that they could sell that product for 50 cents per pound.[16]

The price of chloroform was much higher in the South, and Flag Officer
Goldsborough was quite right when he supposed that chemicals were scarce
in the Confederacy. In Charleston, a pound of chloroform sold at auction
for $6.25 around March 1862 and for $17.50 and $9.75 in May and June 1863,
respectively. In May 1863, it sold for $11 to $17 per pound in Wilmington,
North Carolina. In July 1862, a blockade-running company said it could
sell chloroform in Savannah for $20 per pound. The Confederate army's
Medical Department could and did manufacture chloroform, but it was
desperately needed by surgeons as an anesthetic. For Confederate combat
use, chloroform might have done for selected missions, such as boarding
the *Monitor*, but the anesthetic's general scarcity would probably have ruled
out wider employment as a chemical weapon.[17]

As was the case with other suggested chemical weapons, the advocates
of chloroform had a general understanding of the agent's pharmacologic
effects. Although many substances proposed as chemical weapons were also
used medicinally, chloroform was unique in that its suggested use in warfare
mirrored its application in medicine. That is, it was intended to render the
enemy unresponsive just as it did patients. (On the other hand, chlorine's
"dose" as a weapon greatly exceeded its medicinal dose, and cayenne pepper's direct delivery to the face as a weapon differed from its medicinal use
in oral and topical preparations.) Thus physicians who had used chloroform
as an anesthetic should have had special insight as to whether it could be an
effective weapon. Physicians were common among the advocates of other

chemical weapons but absent among the identified proponents of chloroform; the tempting explanation is that physicians would not have considered chloroform to be a viable weapon. Robert Potts and Frederick Klett had a pharmaceutical background and an understanding of chloroform's chemical properties but not necessarily any personal experience using chloroform as an anesthetic. Chloroform advocates mentioned no ethical issues, probably because the agent was unlikely to kill and was generally thought to stupefy or anesthetize without associated unpleasant effects.

As with cayenne pepper, chloroform could probably have been incorporated into artillery shells with little technical problem; doing so would have been more economically feasible in the North than in the South. Chloroform advocates seem to have had little or no appreciation for the many variables that would determine the actual effectiveness of their imagined delivery systems on the battlefield. Unlike chlorine, which was used in later wars, and cayenne pepper, which became a personal defense and law enforcement tool, the value and practicality of chloroform as an incapacitating agent in similar settings have not been elucidated by testing or use after the Civil War.

8

DESTROYING FLUIDS

No person can contemplate coming in contact with such a
destructive agent without a shudder.
                                        —Edward M. Meader, 1862

EDWARD HARWOOD WAS A MAN of conscience. A native of Rhode Island,
he moved to Cincinnati as a young man, where he became a member of the
firm of Marsh & Harwood, chemical manufacturers. A friend described
him as a person "with a countenance full of humor and amiable mischief, a
native of Rhode Island, and a true representative of the old Roger Williams
class of Soul-Liberty Baptists." Unlike cayenne proponent John Brigham,
whose involvement in a fugitive slave's escape evidently was minimal (see
chapter 6), Harwood actively assisted runaway slaves by hiding them. He
was an ardent abolitionist and close associate of Levi Coffin, the so-called
"President of the Underground Railroad." Starting in 1851, Harwood helped
organize an annual antislavery convention in Cincinnati. At least one such
meeting was attended by Frederick Douglass, and Harwood also became
acquainted with another Cincinnati abolitionist, attorney and future secretary of the treasury Salmon P. Chase. In 1863, Harwood was one of a group
of men, including Henry Ward Beecher, who appealed to President Lincoln
to form a Bureau of Emancipation.[1] So it was that in late 1862, Harwood
offered an idea that he probably saw as hastening the end of slavery, suggesting to Edwin Stanton:

> India rubber bags may be put inside of bomb-shells before being
> filled, the neck of the bag being left out so as to fill it with oil vitriol

[sulfuric acid] then tieing the neck it could be placed inside, room of course being left for powder. . . . It may be well to state that Oil Vitriol will not take hold of Rubber. I am of the firm of Marsh & Harwood Oil of Vitriol Manufacturer, but it is the furthest thing from my intention to make this a means of disposing of our acid. If the above looks reasonable, make use of it procuring your acid from any one. I have only my country's good at heart. I refer you to Hon SP Chase who knows me. May God give you wisdom is my sincere desire.[2]

Despite Harwood's connections, there is no evidence that his letter elicited a response.

Others also suggested that acids be used, and like Harwood, they demonstrated an awareness that the liquids required special handling. Edward M. Meader, a printer from Philadelphia, wrote to the Ordnance Department with his suggestion for a new shell:

1. The Shell is to be made of glass, of any desirable form, size and thickness, and to hold one quart or two gallons (more or less). It may be made acorn-shaped, globe form, or of any required pattern.

2. The Contents to be Nitric Acid, so that when the shell strikes an object and breaks, it will scatter the destroying fluid in every direction. The shell may be made with small opening for filling, and the end of the plug coming in contact with the liquid be covered with thin gold, and the plugs be firmly and tightly secured.

Such shells thrown on board of ships, or into forts, or amongst bodies of troops and broken, would send destruction everywhere, which no human being could endure, nor could any material splashed with its content, be handled or become useful again. Nitric Acid thrown on an iron-clad vessel would soon find its way to the gun-decks, and the drippings render it impossible for men to work the guns. No person can contemplate coming in contact with such a destructive agent without a shudder. Such shells would be more destructive of life and material than steam or hot water, and have this advantage—they could be thrown a long distance. Sulphuric Acid and other fluids, and obnoxious dry contents, might be thrown in such shells.

If thought by you advisable to experiment with my proposition, I should like to be one of those appointed to conduct the experiments.

This communication is made confidentially, and its content known only to you, Capt. Dahlgren, and myself.[3]

If Meader believed that the shells could be hurled long distance, he evidently envisioned them not as grenades but as artillery projectiles. He did not mention what Dahlgren, commandant of the Navy Yard, thought of the idea, and it is curious that Meader chose not to follow up with the navy but rather to send his letter to the army's Ordnance Department. Some of Meader's knowledge of acids may have come from his son Samuel, a druggist who had attended the Philadelphia College of Pharmacy.[4]

Samuel Fahnestock, a physician from Indianapolis, may have been the first to suggest a binary weapon for delivering a nonincendiary chemical weapon. He proposed in August 1861 that an artillery shell be filled with gunpowder, salt, and a hermetically sealed vial of sulfuric acid. "When the shell should burst," he explained, "the vial containing the oil of vitriol will be broken, and mingle with the salt & generate Hydro Chloric acid gas which no mortal can breathe, by which means any Fort or camp could be dislodged & taken." The method he described was the standard one for producing hydrogen chloride and should have been well known to most physicians. Hydrogen chloride is a gas at room temperature; when it is dissolved in water, it is called hydrochloric acid. For those who might doubt the chemical reaction described, Fahnestock said that it could be easily tested "by simply putting a small quantity of salt in a vial & pouring a few drops of oil of vitriol into it; the experiment should be performed in the open air on account of its offensiveness." He acknowledged that the result of mixing salt and sulfuric acid was no secret: "I do not offer the above as a new invention by any means; but the application for the purposes set forth; and if of any practicle importance I should be pleased to hear from you. The idea above advanced should be kept by all means a secret, so that they not . . . get into secession hands and prove to our own disadvantage."[5]

It is regrettable that one particular proposal did not include a drawing or detailed description, for it came from a man who, by all accounts, had a sharp mind and versatile talents. David Beecher Marks was born in Connecticut and moved to Hallsport, Allegany County, New York, in 1819, where he practiced medicine, dentistry, and pharmacy. A natural inventor and mechanic, he designed an artificial leg, patented it in 1854, and persuaded his younger brother, Amasa, to join in efforts to market the device. When the business failed at first to do as well as the brothers had hoped, David withdrew and returned to being a health practitioner. The limb business, under the name of A. A. Marks, went on to become a resounding success. David Marks's activities in Hallsport included operating a "botanic distillery" and practicing phrenology. At some point, for reasons that have not been determined, he began to call himself Job Smythe or Quincy Job Smythe. It was as Job Smythe that he wrote on August 20, 1861, to President Lincoln: "I have invented a Bomb Shell for throwing <u>Acids</u> wish will operate upon iron defenses . . . I am satisfied that it is worthy of your attention at this time. Thinking it policy that the Rebels should not know anything of this, therefore I trust it only with you. If you wish to know more about it, I am at your service." The letter was filed by the Ordnance Department, and although it was apparently never answered, Smythe was not discouraged in his inventive activities, for in the coming years, he patented an improved stovepipe shelf and a household vinegar maker.[6]

John Dobyns, a farmer from Bracken County, Kentucky, provided the seemingly requisite proposal to use fire engines, in this instance to spray sulfuric acid. In a letter to Secretary of War Cameron, he suggested that "the engine hoes can be lined with something that will contain the oil [of vitriol] without eating the hoes." The spray could "be made to bear upon the enemy in making a charge or in resisting an attack by the enemy especially on ship board," and "the engine can be protected by a screene thrown out before from small armes." Dobyns hoped his suggestion would prove useful, saying, "If we can sucseed in getting this article on the enemy it will be sure to eat them up, even Jeff Davis or Beauregard."[7]

Perhaps the most unusual of the acid proposals came from Forrest Shepherd of New Haven, Connecticut. Born in 1800, Shepherd received bachelor's degrees from both Yale University and Dartmouth College, attended Yale Divinity School, and spent most of his adult life teaching and in the study of natural sciences, which took him on travels to various parts of the United States, Canada, Latin America, and Great Britain. From 1847 to 1856, he was a professor of economic geology and chemistry at Western Reserve College in Hudson, Ohio. Well known in scientific circles, he was also an inventor, with patents for white paint and a "tree protector." It is perhaps not surprising, then, that he should have had an idea for a chemical weapon.[8] In a June 22, 1864, letter to President Lincoln, Shepherd wrote:

> I find that by mingling strong sulphuric acid with strong hydrochloric or Muriatic acid [an alternative name for hydrochloric acid] on a broad surface like a shovel or shallow pan, a dense white cloud is at once formed, and being slightly heavier than the atmosphere rests upon the ground and is high enough to conceal the operator behind it. This may easily be continued by additional sprinklings of the two acids and a light breeze will waft it onward.

When the cloud strikes a man it sets him to coughing, sneezing &c. but does not kill him, while it would effectually prevent him from fireing a gun, or if he should fire to aim at his object. It has occurred to me that Gen. Burnside with his colored troops might on a dark night, with a gentle breeze favorable, surprise and capture the strong holds of Petersburg, or Fort Darling perhaps, without loss or shedding of blood.

Shepherd closed by referring the president to Secretary Chase, the eminent chemist Benjamin Silliman, and Governor William A. Buckingham of Connecticut.[9]

Shepherd's idea had some similarity to that of Samuel Fahnestock. In both cases, the mixing of two chemicals would result in the generation of hydrogen chloride. The white cloud that Shepherd described was the gas condensing with atmospheric moisture to form hydrochloric acid mist. His method of allowing the wind to carry the mist toward the enemy exactly paralleled the chlorine cloud attacks of World War I.[10]

By the Civil War, sulfuric, nitric, and hydrochloric acids had been known for centuries and had multiple uses. John Cheves, who assisted General Beauregard with liquid fire, declared that "the three leading mineral acids [sulfuric, nitric, and hydrochloric] are absolutely required before any progress can be made, in the laboratory of the chemist, the artisan, or the manufacturer. . . . Of all the chemical substances above referred to, there is none so generally important as sulphuric acid; it is necessary to the existence of chemistry and of the arts depending on it." Indeed, the mineral acids were needed for processes such as electrotyping and silver and gold refining and in the production of a wide variety of items, including friction matches, pigments, candles, glass, fertilizer, and photographic chemicals. Sulfuric and nitric acids had vital military applications; the former was needed to synthesize the latter, which was needed to make fulminate of mercury for percussion caps. The corrosive properties of the acids were well known, but if acids had been employed by themselves as chemical weapons before the Civil War, accounts of such use are obscure or nonexistent.[11]

Many newspaper articles before and during the war, however, reported acids being used in attacks on individuals; these usually involved acid being thrown on the victim's face by a romantic rival or a jilted spouse or lover.[12] According to a British physician describing acid attacks:

The skin touched by a concentrated acid is destroyed and sloughs away. . . . Although a person may not die from the direct effects of acid, yet in certain irritable constitutions the inflammation which follows in deep-seated parts may prove fatal. . . . Sulphuric acid is most commonly used: but in a case which occurred at Guy's Hospital, nitric acid had been thrown at the individual, and had led to the destruction of the sight of one eye.[13]

Another physician commented on chemical injuries to the eye:

There is no class of injuries to which the eye is exposed, more formidable than those caused by the caustic alkalies or the strong acids. Intensely painful at the time, they leave behind, effects that not only destroy sight but mar the aspect of the face; the brilliancy of the eye is superseded by white opacities, and the lids are either glued to the ball by adhesions, or everted, showing their crimson and raw-looking conjunctival surfaces. It is these well-known properties which cause the mineral acids, as vitriol, to be used from motives of malice or revenge as a means of disfigurement.[14]

It is tempting to suppose that some citizens—perhaps those with a pronounced hatred of the enemy—concluded that the intense suffering caused by acids would make them particularly apt for attacking the enemy.

Most Civil War letters advocating acids were silent about how the chemicals would affect their victims. Job Smythe merely referred to acids as "well calculated to work in Offensive Warfare," and Edward Harwood went no further than calling an acid shell "a powerful means of destruction." John Dobyns said only that he hoped sulfuric acid would "eat up" the enemy. Edward Meader described nitric acid as destructive and frightening. Perhaps the properties of acids were so familiar that no more needed to be said. No acid advocate expressed any ethical qualms about the effects of the chemicals.[15]

Meader's glass shells and Dobyns's fire engines were intended to deliver liquid acid, which would do its work through direct contact with the skin or eyes. Smythe did not describe his acid-containing shell, yet his claim that it would work on iron defenses suggests that he intended the chemical to be delivered as a liquid so that it could drip though the openings of an ironclad vessel. Harwood's exploding shell might have dispersed its sulfuric acid as droplets or as an aerosol, and it is unclear whether he saw its damage being done by direct contact or through inhalation.

Hydrogen chloride gas was also known to be toxic. "The vapor," said one physician, "is very irritating, producing coughing, a difficulty of breathing, and inflammation of the air-passages when inhaled too deeply." The same would apply to hydrochloric acid mist, which formed when the gas combined with atmospheric moisture. Thus the disabling effects of the airborne chemical and its being heavier than air made it a reasonable candidate for an inhalable chemical agent. At a high enough concentration, the acid gas or mist would indeed be something that, as Samuel Fahnestock said, "no mortal can breathe." Forrest Shepherd considered the airborne acid nonlethal, which was usually the case.[16]

The actual weapons ideas were generally not practical. Glass containers might work if thrown by hand but would not survive being fired from a cannon. One author suggested that "a properly constructed engine" for hurling chemical-filled glass or earthenware containers might consist of a steam-powered catapult. Fire engines, as previously mentioned, had serious drawbacks. If scattering the acid—rather than concentrating it in one place—was the aim for the proposed artillery shells, then something more than a minimal bursting charge was needed. Because all the proposed chemicals were liquids at room temperature, they would not be placed in a shell under pressure and thus would not spray out with great force on their own accord from a ruptured shell. Too much dispersion would lessen the amount of acid that would contact any individual soldier, and too small an amount might not be disabling. None of the acid proponents suggested an amount of acid that would be needed to cover a particular area. Once again, the payload and range of special artillery shells would have had to be determined, as would the optimal firing pattern.[17]

Samuel Fahnestock's binary shell was intended to allow sulfuric acid and salt to mix after bursting of the projectile, but the scattering of the components by the blast might not have allowed them to mingle and react to a large extent. If the vial of acid ruptured instead with the blast of the artillery piece, some hydrogen chloride might have formed during the projectile's flight, but it is unclear whether the reaction would have proceeded quickly enough to produce large amounts of gas before the components were dispersed by the blast.[18]

Forrest Shepherd's idea of mixing hydrochloric and sulfuric acids would have raised many of the concerns that were associated with the chlorine cloud attacks of World War I. Wind and weather conditions needed to be favorable and sustained, and a large (but undetermined) number of reaction vessels would have had to be positioned and activated simultaneously to produce a large enough cloud. The Germans and Allies used chlorine cloud attacks with some success during the Great War, so Shepherd's concept of allowing the wind to propel the hydrochloric acid cloud, at least, could have worked. Transporting large amounts of concentrated acids to the front lines without breaking the containers would have been a challenge and would probably have alerted the enemy that something was afoot. Moreover, soldiers pouring the chemicals into pans located on high ground would have been exposed to spills and enemy fire, and the operation would have produced the highest concentration of noxious fumes in front of friendly troops.[19]

Common to all the acid proposals was the necessity of handling dangerous chemicals and the substantial risk that the users' own munitions workers, artillery crews, and infantrymen would be injured by mishaps. One factor in favor of using acids was their low cost. In 1857, for example, a major Philadelphia pharmaceutical retailer was offering sulfuric, nitric, and hydrochloric acids for 6, 25, and 12 cents a pound, respectively, and lower-quality acids would undoubtedly have cost less, especially if purchased in large amounts. During the same year, the Philadelphia area alone had at least nine companies manufacturing the acids, and their estimated combined daily output was forty-five thousand pounds of sulfuric acid, eight thousand pounds of nitric acid, and fifteen thousand pounds of hydrochloric acid. Although none of the described proposals for acid weapons came from the Confederate states, the same acids were much more expensive in the South during the war. The Confederate army's medical purveyor in Savannah, for example, paid $2 to $2.40 per pound of sulfuric acid, $1.60 to $6 per pound of nitric acid, and $8 to $18 per pound of hydrochloric acid.[20]

Sulfuric acid was present in some Civil War weapons—in detonators for mines, for example—but there is no indication that it or nitric or hydrochloric acid was used during the war as a weapon intended to affect the skin, eyes, or respiratory tract. Even if ordnance officials had been more willing to consider unconventional weapons, the problems posed by the acids would probably have disqualified them. They were dangerous to handle and could not be placed directly into artillery shells because of their corrosive properties. If they were to be used as liquids, relatively large amounts (compared with liquids that turned into gases) would have to have been deployed for effective coverage of the target.

Perhaps these limitations—and the availability of more effective agents—account for why the acids have not been used as chemical weapons by the major combatants in subsequent wars. There were reports in 1991 that Iraqi military aircraft dropped sulfuric acid on civilians. Nitric acid found in that country in 2007 may have been intended as a chemical weapon—an American chemist commented at the time that the acid would cause serious burns if sprayed on people—but it is more likely that the chemical was to be used in producing explosives. In 2013, a Tanzanian police official linked Islamic extremist groups with acid attacks on individuals, but the claim has not been substantiated. Acid-manufacturing facilities and trains or vehicles used to transport acids can be targets of attack, so the acids remain a public threat in war zones or where terrorists are active.[21]

Despite their drawbacks as military weapons, the chemicals continue to be used in civilian acid attacks. Such assaults occur frequently in parts of Asia and Africa and are a particular problem in Bangladesh, India, and Cambodia. Another current phenomenon is the use of acids in homemade chemical bombs. These devices typically consist of a soft drink bottle in which various ingredients, one of which is often an acid, are mixed. The container is sealed and shaken, and the gas generated by the chemical reaction causes the bottle to explode. The bombs, typically made for excitement or as pranks rather than to produce mass casualties, can cause serious injury from bottle fragments, chemical burns, and chemical inhalation.[22]

The individual acid attacks may characterize the chemicals' most effective use as weapons—with amounts that are easily transported and delivered at close range, and with relatively large amounts of liquid aimed at fairly small targets. The Civil War advocates of acid knew well the agents' destructive effects, but they seemed not to appreciate the difficulties of deploying them on a scale useful in military operations.

9

FIRE AND BRIMSTONE

> All fortifications, especially marine fortifications, can under
> cover of dense smoke be irresistibly subdued by fumes of sul-
> phur kindled in masses to windward of their ramparts.
> —Thomas Cochrane, Tenth Earl of Dundonald, 1846

IT WAS JANUARY 1861, AND Charlestonians were reluctant or unable to di-
vulge details about the giant raft being constructed in the harbor. Earlier in
the month, the *Star of the West*, a vessel bearing supplies and troops for the
relief of the Federal garrison at Fort Sumter, had been fired on and withdrew.
The issue now was whether the garrison would surrender the stronghold or
compel Southern troops to take it by force. One early rumor was that the
raft would carry six hundred men, that "a tower is erecting upon it which
overtops Fort Sumter, and that the machine is to be used for a night attack."
A Baltimore reporter commented that the raft was "a portion of the secret
work of the campaign that cannot be too closely inquired into."[1] A correspondent for the *New York Times* described one of the opinions he had heard:

> A chemical gentleman, who owns a plantation in this State, confiden-
> tially informed me the other night—while slightly under the influence
> of some of his chemical compounds—that he had frequently smoked
> out negroes who had run into the woods, by igniting a preparation of
> cotton, sulphur and resin. He says the fumes are perfectly suffocating,
> and he thinks that if the raft was armed in this way, and moored in the
> river, that the tide would carry it against Sumter, the garrison would
> cry out for quarter, and speedily capitulate.[2]

Before long, it became apparent that the raft was intended to carry an armored floating battery. Originally intended to augment harbor defenses, the battery participated in the April 1861 bombardment of Fort Sumter.[3]

Although the ideas of the "chemical gentleman" were not carried out, they demonstrated the common knowledge that burning sulfur produced toxic fumes. Sulfur had, in fact, been used since ancient times in warfare. During the Peloponnesian War (431–404 BC), for example, the Spartans added sulfur to a fire at the walls of a besieged city; the result was a more intense blaze and, intended or not, the generation of poisonous sulfur dioxide gas. Archaeologists have concluded that Sasanian Persian troops employed burning bitumen and sulfur to eliminate Roman soldiers in siege mines at Dura-Europos, Syria, around AD 256.[4]

In 1811, Thomas Cochrane, the British naval officer who had used kites to drop leaflets (see chapter 6), noticed during a stop in Sicily that the processing of crude sulfur in kilns produced large amounts of fumes that fell to the ground, moved with the wind, and destroyed vegetation. The fumes were so toxic and persistent that local inhabitants were prohibited from living within three miles of the sulfur facility during processing season. Quick to see the military applications of his observations, Cochrane suggested in 1812 that expendable ships filled with sulfur and charcoal could be placed to the windward of enemy (French) fortifications and the cargo ignited. The wind would carry the fumes to the target fortifications and incapacitate the troops there or force them to leave. The plan was not adopted, but Cochrane persisted. In 1846, he renewed his proposal, this time with the addition of a smoke screen to conceal the approach of the sulfur-laden vessels; again, the proposal was declined. Cochrane tried once more during the Crimean War. Although the plan was deemed to present a "reasonable prospect of success," it was again turned down, and the proposal was kept under wraps. The essence of Cochrane's plan remained a secret until it was published in 1908.[5]

Sulfur had nonmilitary uses in destroying life. It was being burned in the mid-1800s to rid trees of bark lice and caterpillars. The sulfur could simply be placed on hot embers or mixed with tar or old scraps of leather before being placed under trees and ignited. It was also employed to exterminate vermin in henhouses. An agricultural magazine said that gophers could be eliminated by lighting wooden sticks coated with rosin and sulfur, placing one in each gopher hole found, and covering the hole with a clod of dirt. This, said the periodical, would "speedily generate sulphuric acid gas, which is and must be certain death to all that breathes below the surface, within the reach of its power, and it will perforate every nook and corner of earth where there is a pore, working downward as well as upward; thus, at once relieving our industrious farmers of one of the severest trials they have had to encounter."[6]

Thus, although Thomas Cochrane is credited with being a pioneer in chemical warfare, it is not surprising that, besides the "chemical gentleman," at least one American devised a plan similar to Cochrane's during the American Civil War. Henry Riell, a New Yorker and veteran of the War of 1812, claimed in an 1862 letter to Secretary of War Stanton that he had been acquainted with Henry Clay, Andrew Jackson, Martin Van Buren, and former New York governor Daniel Tomkins. Riell had been a prominent tobacconist and rival to the Lorillard Tobacco Company. "What a curious old man is Henry Reill!" exclaimed a New York historian in 1865.[7] Riell seemed to verify that impression in his note to Stanton:

> I have plans—for impregnating the air! I can save thousands
> of lives in takeing "Forts" & Iron "Steamers" by placing in the
> "Bow" of a "Ship" a Box of "Iron." The contents in the said Box
> is comprised of the following articles—1st one Bbl [barrel] Spts
> Turpentine—"Pine Wood" & Staves of Barrels with several "Bbl"
> Tar then put in a little "Charcoal" "Liverpool" Coal which makes
> a dead heavy smoke 5 Bbls Tar 5 Bbls sulphur then take "Cotton"
> mixed with "Cayenne Pepper" when the air is heavy and wind
> blows I can take a Fort & Steamer by placing the above articles
> on the Bow of a "Steamer." I have also a Glass Bomb Shell which
> has been tried on the Mountains of the Highlands, Hudson River
> State of New York it will throw 80 yards and it Scatters the leaves
> it touches in all directions. I consider it a good invention & worthy
> of the notice of Government. I have several letters in my possession
> from the Patent Office in 1846 Stateing my plan was a good one but
> at that time the Government was at peace therefore they did not
> think it worth while to take any notice of it but as we are at War
> at the present time I consider it my duty as an American citizen to
> forward my plans to Government.[8]

Riell's proposal lacked the necessary detail but implied that his air-impregnating concoction was to be ignited such that suffocating fumes would drift with the wind and overtake enemy troops on vessels or in fortifications. He did not say whether the smoke-releasing vessel was to be sacrificed to the fire, as was the case in Cochrane's scheme; how it would escape enemy gunfire; or how its crew, if one remained onboard, would avoid the fumes in case of a change in wind direction. Although Cochrane's plan was judged to have a reasonable chance of working, it was laid out in great detail and evaluated by accomplished scientists. Neither Riell's plans nor those of Charleston's "chemical gentleman" contained enough detail for anyone to form a judgment about their feasibility.

Samuel Fahnestock, who had suggested the binary hydrogen chloride shell (see chapter 8), also proposed a shell containing spirits of turpentine and flowers of sulfur (sublimed sulfur). "On explosion of the shell," said Fahnestock, "the Turpentine would be fired & sulphur become ignited and generate an offensive gas well known to all, which cannot be breathed." The correspondent known only as "Live Yankee" (see chapters 1 and 2) suggested that shells with a bursting charge plus "varnish of Combustible sugar with Flour of Sulphur stirred into it till stiff would smoke the rebels out of their dens if enough were thrown in." Levi Read, a farmer from Jewel City, New London County, Connecticut, proposed a conical shell filled with sulfur "and other suffocating matter." If such a projectile entered a building, he asked, "would it not drive the inmates out, and if some fell within an army of men would it not make them nearly powerless?" The proposals of Riell, Fahnestock, "Live Yankee," and Read seem to have been filed and ignored, and schemes calling for igniting sulfur in the open air appear not to have been carried out during the Civil War. Numerous twentieth-century articles stated that Union troops besieging Charleston burned sulfur-saturated wood to drive out the town's defenders, but they cite no supporting documentation.[9]

Another use of noxious fumes was to repel enemy soldiers trying to infiltrate or place explosives under friendly lines by means of a tunnel. This was a concern among Confederate forces manning the lines at Petersburg. Union troops had dug a mine ending under a portion of the Confederate lines and placed there a large amount of gunpowder. The detonation on July 30, 1864, created a huge crater and initiated the so-called Battle of the Crater. One subsequent Confederate measure was to dig countermines and have guards patrol them so that they might hear and stop any other Union tunneling attempts. The main course of the countermine ran parallel to and in front of the trench parapet above. From that course, four-inch auger holes, about fifteen feet long, were bored toward the front. Sentinels were equipped with "cartridges of combustibles the smoke from which would suffocate a man." If an enemy mine was found to have struck an auger hole, the guard was to place a cartridge into the hole, light its fuse, seal his end of the hole tightly, and summon his comrades, who would "dig into and take possession of the opposing mine as rapidly as possible, giving another dose of suffocating smoke from time to time to keep the enemy out of his workings until they could dig into them." There is no indication that such cartridges were ever deployed.[10]

Using noxious fumes to repel soldiers within mines had a long history. Not only did the Persians use sulfur against Roman soldiers in siege mines, but also the Chinese pumped fumes of burning artemisia, mustard, and other plants into enemy mines. The practice was still being used well after the Civil War. American troops and their allies, for example, used tear gas to clear enemy tunnels during the Vietnam War. An eighteenth-century textbook stated that miners encountering an enemy tunnel should "throw in quantities of fetid combustibles; close the hole hermetically, to prevent the stench from passing into the countermines; and block up at the same time all access to the besieger."[11] Although the account of the Petersburg smoke cartridges provided no details about them, period textbooks described a device for the exact purpose—the *lance à feu puant*, or stink-fire lance:

> When a miner or sapper has so far penetrated towards the enemy, as to hear the voices of persons in any place contiguous to his own excavation, he first of all bores a hole with his probe, then fires off several pistols through the aperture, and lastly forces in a *lance à feu puant*. He takes care to close up the hole on his side, to prevent the smoke from returning towards himself. The explosion and fetid gas and vapour, which issue from the lance, and remain on the side of the enemy, infect the air so much, that it is impossible to approach the quarter for three or four days. Sometimes, indeed, they have had such instantaneous effect, that, in order to save their lives, miners, who would persevere, have been dragged out in an apparent state of suffocation.[12]

A pyrotechnic lance resembled a long, slender firecracker with a paper wrapper that burned along with its contents. A stink-fire lance contained the ingredients of a stink pot, which was typically an earthenware or wooden container meant to be dropped or thrown and filled with material that when lit would release offensive fumes. Stink pots were often associated with China, and various recipes—many of which included sulfur—were available. One, recorded by Casimir Simienowicz, a seventeenth-century artillerist, contained pitch, tar, saltpeter, sulfur, rosin, coal, raspings or parings of horse or mule hoof, and malodorous plant products (asafetida, sagapenum, and stinking gladwyn). Cadets at the US Military Academy in the 1830s were provided with a similar recipe for a suffocating ball to be used in countermining. Another concoction—considered ancient and out of date by 1830—contained saltpeter, sulfur, quicklime, mercury, pitch, rosin, oak sawdust, and pigeon dung. The simplest recipe called for six parts sulfur and five parts saltpeter, which one textbook referred to as "the most effectual and annoying of all these contrivances . . . used to throw into port-holes, on boarding, where it effectually clears the decks." The striking similarity in how the Petersburg and textbook countermining devices were to be employed suggests that the Confederates knew about stink-fire lances and used the simple recipe, which required ingredients that were already being used in the manufacture of gunpowder. As described above, sulfur was also a component of the antigopher sticks, which were used in much the same way to eliminate nonhuman tunnelers.[13]

Employing fumes of burning substances did not necessarily imply a lethal intent. Simienowicz described the use of so-called "stink-balls" as "much more lawful, and much less pernicious; for these only molest the Enemy by their Faetid Vapours, wrap them up in artificial Mist; offend both the Nose and Head, by their extraordinary Nauseousness; and pain the Eyes by the Sharpness of their Smoke, without any immediate infection." According to agricultural chemist James Johnston, "in the compounds of sulphur alone the chemist has at his command a very large number of exceedingly foul smells."[14]

So it was that in April 1864, a number of Confederate officers and civilian observers were invited to witness the testing of a stink ball invented by one Captain Holden of the army. A Baltimore newspaper correspondent at the scene reported:

> The ball is an iron shell containing combustible and destructive mate-
> rial, as well as odiferous matter, and in appearance is similar to the stink
> ball in use many years ago. It is designed to be thrown by mortars, but in
> the tests on the occasion referred to, the fuse was lighted and the shells
> allowed to fulminate where they were placed. The stench which followed
> the explosion was the most fetid and villainous that ever outraged the
> olfactories of man. . . . The concentrated stink of all the skunks, pole-
> cats . . . pitch, sulphur, rasped horses and horses' hoofs, burnt in fire,
> assafoetida, ferula, and bug-weed in the world could not equal the smell
> emitted by these balls. But not only is the smell itself intolerable, but
> it provokes sneezing and coughing, and produces nausea, rendering it

impossible for men to do duty within reach of it. A single ball will impregnate the atmosphere for fifty yards round, and the fetid compound entering everything it touches, emits the stench for a long time. The opinion of all who witnessed the experiments was that these balls were a fair offset to Greek fire, and General Winder, and several other officers of rank who were present, expressed the belief that it would prove more effective for driving off besiegers than anything ever invented. Be this as it may, if Richmond is ever threatened by a siege, the "sneezers," as the inventor facetiously calls his balls, will form a prominent feature in the defensive operations.[15]

Neither Captain Holden nor the content of the shells was identified in more detail, but the story was repeated in newspapers. One reader who saw the story was General William N. Pendleton, General Robert E. Lee's chief of artillery. Pendleton asked Lieutenant Colonel Briscoe G. Baldwin, the Army of Northern Virginia's chief of ordnance, whether some stink shells could be obtained, since it seemed worthwhile to try them. Baldwin referred the inquiry to Colonel Josiah Gorgas, chief of ordnance. Gorgas sent the request on to Lieutenant Colonel William LeRoy Broun, commandant of the Richmond Arsenal, who supplied a terse answer: "Stink-balls, none on hand; don't keep them; will make if ordered." Broun, a graduate of the University of Virginia and a former professor of mathematics at the University of Georgia, was clearly unfazed by the prospect of producing stink balls. Although not a career military man and perhaps not immediately familiar with the content of such projectiles, that knowledge could have been obtained from Captain Holden (for his particular formula), textbooks, or ordnance colleagues, and it is likely that Broun would have used the simple formula of sulfur and saltpeter.[16]

Other foul-smelling substances might also be placed in artillery shells. According to chemist James Johnston, sulfur-containing chemicals called mercaptans were "all possessed of very offensive smells, but each distinguished by a shade of offensiveness peculiar to itself." Man-made malodorous chemicals, said Johnston, might have uses as weapons:

> Imitating the natural habit of the skunk in this respect, we might far surpass it in the intensity and offensiveness of artificial stinks. Squirted from the walls of a besieged city, projected into the interior of a fortified building, or diffused through the hold of a ship of war, the Greek fire would be nothing to them; and as of the stink-pots of the Chinese, they must be mere bagatelles to the stenches we can prepare.

A Southern citizen familiar with Johnston's words repeated them in an open letter to Lieutenant Colonel George W. Rains of the Confederate Ordnance Department and urged consideration of nonlethal malodorous chemicals if the deadly but harder-to-produce cacodyl or alkarsin (see chapter 4) proved impractical. "I can add nothing," said the anonymous correspondent, "to the pungent eloquence" of Johnston's passage. It is unclear whether any particularly foul-smelling substances could be produced in large quantities in a form suitable for use as a weapon. Levi Short proposed adding ingredients to his Greek fire shells that would produce a nauseating stench (see chapter 2).[17]

Nonlethal stench weapons evidently saw little or no use in World War I, although chemicals with strong odors were developed to mask the smell of poisonous gas or to force enemy soldiers to don their gas masks. In more recent years, military officials have expressed renewed interest in malodorants for their possible use in dispersing hostile crowds and keeping people away from prohibited areas. The United States reportedly has a munition, the XM1063 projectile, capable of delivering a malodorant payload, and Israeli forces have used water cannons to project a liquid called Skunk, described as "the worst, most foul thing you have ever smelled." The supposedly nontoxic substance blends odors of rotting meat, unwashed socks, and open sewers and persists for at least three days despite attempts to wash it off.[18]

Accounts from ancient history indicated that burning sulfur produced noxious fumes useful in warfare, but Civil War advocates of sulfur fumes need not have been historians. The fumes were well recognized for their ability to kill insects and other pests, so extending that knowledge to exterminating or disabling men was not a huge leap. The Civil War schemes for sulfur, however, were so vague that their practicality cannot be judged. When sulfur was burned to kill pests on trees, it was done directly under the trees, so its application was local and under some control. Similarly, stink pots were historically effective when used in relatively close quarters, as when a vessel was being boarded. Sulfur fumes employed to eliminate or repel human or nonhuman miners were confined to the closed space of the tunnel and thus would persist in relatively high concentrations; the historical accounts of this use suggest that the smoke cartridges prepared for use at Petersburg may have been effective if deployed, although their content remains unknown. As for the proposed artillery projectiles, their effectiveness would have depended on factors common to many proposals described in other chapters, particularly the ability to deliver large enough concentrations of the chemical to produce the desired effect and the know-how to release the fumes such that friendly troops would not be affected. The simplified formula for stink shells and stink-fire lances required sulfur and saltpeter, the latter of which was in short supply in the South and was needed to make gunpowder. It seems likely, however, that some saltpeter could have been spared for fume-producing weapons if they had been given high priority. Access to either chemical would not have been a problem in the North.

As was the case with cayenne pepper, sulfur fumes may have been most practical when used at close quarters rather than delivered at a distance by artillery projectiles. The Confederate preparation of countermining smoke cartridges and their testing of stink balls were unusual instances of chemical weapons progressing beyond the idea stage. The stink ball was the project of an army officer, and the smoke cartridges had a strong historical precedent and were likely suggested by a military man. Thus the attention given these devices did not necessarily indicate government willingness to seriously consider suggestions arising from outside the military community.

10

SHARP HORRORS OF SUNDRY WEAPONS

If science were to be allowed her full swing, if society would *really* allow that "all is fair in war," war might be banished at once from the earth as a game that neither subject nor king dare play at.

—B. W. Richardson, 1864

THE VARIETY OF AGENTS PROPOSED as chemical weapons during the Civil War was considerable, with some not being easily categorized with the more commonly advocated substances. Gustavus A. Burbank, cashier of the Bank of Caledonia in Danville, Vermont, and described as a lawyer, banker, Democrat, and Presbyterian, had an idea similar to that of the unidentified Southerner who suggested that large volumes of gaseous hydrogen cyanide be placed in artillery shells (see chapter 4).[1] Burbank proposed the following to Secretary of War Simon Cameron:

I beg to suggest a method of filling explosive Shells, by which I believe they can be made more destructive than any instrument known in modern warfare. Charge the shells with explosive carbureted hydrogen—or some other poison of similar nature and like effect. The explosion of this shell, in the rank of the enemy, will create a smoke, similar in appearance, to that produced by powder—and like that, will spread over an area, in the vicinity of its explosion, of, say, the space occupied by a Regiment, more or less. But unlike the smoke of Powder, this smoke will be a deadly poison to every one who inhales it—and like the fire-damp, will settle near the earth so that none who come within its compass can avoid inhaling it. Hundreds inhale, perhaps a whole Regiment— and are instantly prostrated in a state of helpless asphyxia—a condition I am longing to see Jeff. Davis, Beauregard, and all their hosts in.[2]

Carburetted hydrogen was a somewhat generic and imprecise term for gases often found in coal mines and marshes. It was sometimes called coal gas, oil gas, or firedamp, and some forms, such as illuminating gas, were used in gas lighting. Firedamp referred to the flammable and potentially explosive mixture of air and methane found in mines. It is lighter, not heavier, than air and can cause asphyxiation by displacing oxygen but is not particularly toxic. Accidental asphyxiation from illuminating gas, typically associated with gas leaks, was not uncommon. Blackdamp described carbon dioxide, which is also found in mines and is an incombustible asphyxiant (but is nontoxic itself) and is heavier than air. Burbank may have been referring to water gas or hydrocarbonate. These terms were sometimes equated with carburetted hydrogen but more accurately described a mixture of carbon monoxide and hydrogen. The renowned British chemist Humphry Davy intentionally inhaled hydrocarbonate to study its effects and immediately developed giddiness, headache, and weakness. On taking three breaths of a more concentrated form, Davy experienced numbness and an oppressive feeling in the chest, an inability to sense external objects, and a "sinking into oblivion." Various symptoms persisted for hours, and Davy concluded, "Had I taken four or five inspirations, instead of three, they would have destroyed life immediately, without producing any painful sensation." The effects that Burbank described were consistent with carbon monoxide poisoning, but he did not suggest a method for placing a large amount of gas, whatever its composition, into an artillery shell. Carbon monoxide has, in fact, been considered for use in warfare, but it has serious drawbacks. The pressure associated with the liquid form would be too great for a projectile, the gas would dissipate quickly because of it low density, and it has relatively low toxicity value compared with other agents.[3]

The only known chemical weapons proposal from Europe came from Donald B. McGillivray of Culduthel, Inverness, Scotland, who wrote to President Lincoln:

> I beg to inform you that I have recently invented an ingredient, which when fired along with shell explodes and causes insensibility in those who inhale its fumes, tho not a total extinction of life.

It paralizes all the physical functions and would do good service among a body of men in close file, or within a fort in course of seige, and it does not in the least affect the destructive powers of the shell with which it fired. It is easily made up, and quite harmless except when in a state of ignition. I have deplored the loss of valuable life which the struggle in which your nation is at present engaged, as well as modern warfare in general has entaled on mankind, and I believe, you, Sir are to some extent of the same disposition. This has led me to 2 series of chemical investigations to discover some method by which human life could be saved and yet the enemy enfeebled. In this I have been successful and my sympathy with your cause in you endeavours (which I pray God may be successful) for the liberty of the slave and the unity of your great nation induces me to give your Government the first offer my invention. I shall thank you to let me know if you accept the offer, and if so on what terms.[4]

There is no indication that Lincoln or the Ordnance Department was enticed by the offer, much less willing to pay to learn its particulars.

Another suggestion for an artillery shell came from an Illinois citizen somewhat less interested in compensation. This one was sent to Secretary of War Stanton by George W. Hamilton, who was writing for an acquaintance:

One William B Stutts of this county (Macoupin) claims to have invented an infernal composition when exploded the smell will instantly destroy life of both man and beast for 40 yards in every direction from the place of explosion he says he has experimented with his infernal composition using a small gourd as a bomb filling it with powder and his composition and with a fuse attached that he has fired the fuse and thrown the gourd within 10 feet of six cats confined and that every cat from the smell died in three minutes He claims that if one hundred shells was thrown inside of the enemies works with one pound of his composition in each shell that all life of both men and beast would be instantly destroyed for 40 yards in every direction from the explosion of each shell I know nothing of what his composition is composed he is a poor man he says that if the Government will compensate him if his infernal composition will destroy life is all that he asks should it prove a failure he asks nothing but the use of a cannon and a few shells to demonstrate the utter destructiveness of his composition.[5]

Stutts may have been William B. Stultz, a wagon maker or cooper in his mid-fifties from Barrs Store, Macoupin County. His "infernal composition" is reminiscent of that attributed to Richard Sears McCulloh, possibly cacodyl cyanide, which killed cats confined in a room (see chapter 4), but production of cacodyl required a skillful and very careful chemist.[6]

Another unidentified poison was the centerpiece of a scheme by Private Isham Walker of the Ninth Mississippi Infantry Regiment. Walker, a native of Tennessee, was a millwright who called himself a "practical balloonist" and claimed a friendship with the French balloonist Eugene Goddard. In 1855, a group of Tennessee citizens presented a petition to the US House of Representatives "recommending Isham Walker's plan of carrying the mails through the air at a speed of three hundred miles an hour." The petition was referred to the Committee on the Post Office and Post Roads and presumably filed and forgotten. In 1858, newspapers reported that Walker was giving lectures in which he proposed "building a vessel in the shape of a mountain trout, 365 feet in length, to be impelled through the air by means of screw propellers, driven by a caloric engine, at the somewhat exciting speed of 300 miles per hour, and at the giddy height of two miles from mother earth." He had reportedly "deposited in the patent office a draft of his boat and entire machinery," but no patent was granted. In 1862, Walker appealed to the Confederate Congress, "asking the adoption of a plan for an aerial caloric ship, etc." The proposal was referred to the Committee on Patents, but no patent was granted. A more detailed description appeared in 1873 and indicates why people may have been skeptical about the vessel. It was to be shaped like "three mountain fish," with all three fish made of sheet copper. Two of the fish would contain about three million cubic feet of gas, and the third would contain six hundred thousand more cubic feet of gas and a cabin for passengers. The craft would be steered by the fish tails, and the engines "would attain a very high speed in the air, driving the fish at a tremendous rate through."[7]

In mid-1861, Walker wrote to Confederate president Jefferson Davis to propose a method of delivering a chemical weapon and was advised to write separately to Secretary of War Leroy P. Walker. Private Walker not only offered his services as an aeronaut to photograph Union positions but also proposed using a manned balloon to bomb Union-held Fort Pickens at Pensacola, along with the Union fleet anchored there. The balloon would be controlled by four copper wires and positioned two miles above the target, where the operator could "drop those deadly Bombs, with more unerring aims than can be had from any morter, they decending with accillerated motion for two miles would pass cleare through any covering on any fortress and when they exploded death would be the cirtin doom of every liveing creature near." The bombs would be filled with not only gunpowder but also "a powerfull Subtile Poison perfectly inocent untill Ignited but deadly and awfully distructive when fired, Poisoneing the atmosphere for Several rods in every direction produceing the Same effect upon the Surounding air as the Bohon Upas Tree of Africa." The balloon could be prepared in six weeks and cost only $1,200. Moreover, the plan was "Practicle, safe and sure, endangering no lives in Confederate army."[8]

Private Walker may have been inspired by balloonist John Wise, who in 1846, during the Mexican War, published in newspapers his proposal to bomb the Castle of San Juan de Ulloa at Vera Cruz from a manned hot air balloon measuring a hundred feet in diameter. Tethered by a cable at least five miles long, the balloon would be capable of lifting twenty thousand pounds besides its own weight and would hover a mile above the castle while its crew rained bombs on the stronghold below; the plan was not adopted. During the Civil War, the Union army employed observation balloons filled from portable hydrogen generators, but the Confederacy's capabilities in ballooning were quite limited. The South could not, for example, produce hydrogen in large amounts. In the spring of 1862, the Confederates used an observation balloon near Yorktown, Virginia, that was filled with hot air produced by burning pine knots and turpentine. Another Confederate balloon could be used only at points accessible from the Richmond Gas Works, where it was filled with illuminating gas. The balloons' typical altitude was a thousand feet or less, so Walker's plan to hover two miles over Fort Pickens seems far-fetched, especially since the bombs he planned to carry would add considerable weight. There was also the matter of hitting his targets from that altitude, where he would have been chilled and possibly slightly hypoxic. Even as late as 1899, delegates to the peace conferences at The Hague concluded that dropping explosives from balloons was so inaccurate that the resultant "injury or destruction would be of no practical advantage to the party making use of the machines."[9]

The tree Walker referred to when describing his poison was the upas (*Antiaris toxicaria*), also called bohun upas or bohon upas, then known to grow in Java, not Africa. This type of tree was reported in the late 1700s by a surgeon with the Dutch East India Company to produce an atmosphere so poisonous that no humans or animals could live within miles of one. That description had been discredited well before the Civil War, so Walker's citing of the upas to illustrate his point was unfortunate. One aspect of the account, however, was corroborated by later authors: the upas tree produced an exudate that was used to poison the tips of arrows.[10]

Coincidentally, poisoning edged projectiles was exactly what another weapons proponent had in mind. William Beals of Boston had two claims to fame. First, he was a celebrated decorator, known for having done the decorative work for William Henry Harrison during the "Tippecanoe and Tyler Too" campaign and for decorating the public buildings in Washington, DC, for the inaugurations of Presidents Cleveland and Harrison. Such projects gave him "fame and business all over the country." He was also a practitioner and merchant of pyrotechnics. He billed his 1853 Fourth of July display for Springfield, Massachusetts, for example, as "the most extensive piece of Fire Works ever produced in this country, called THE BOMBARD-MENT OF THE CITY OF VERA CRUZ AND THE CASTLE OF SAN JUAN DE ULLOA, by the American Army and Navy under Gen. Scott."[11]

Beals's creativity with fireworks and explosives led to a number of inventions. At the 1841 Exhibition of the Massachusetts Charitable Mechanic Association, Beals was awarded a prize for his models of a rocket-powered railroad car and "fire ship." The latter was a rocket-propelled vessel that sped on the water's surface in a straight line until it collided with its target and exploded. According to a newspaper, "One advantage of the ship is that it can be used to destroy an enemy's vessel, without endangering the lives of the assailants." The weapon, also called a rocket boat, was demonstrated in 1842 in Washington for an audience that included the president and secretary of the navy; it traveled three hundred yards in less than half a minute and struck within six inches of its target. The demonstration was repeated the next month at the Charleston Navy Yard, where the hundred-pound model, powered by only a pound of gunpowder, traveled the same distance and exploded on impact. Despite the apparent success of the device, there is no evidence of the government pursuing its adoption. Beals also invented an artillery projectile that, on leaving the cannon's muzzle, expanded to three to four feet and was "capable of destroying the whole main rigging of a ship, and would cut down four men standing abreast in the field." A newspaper called the cannonball "a terrific engine of destruction, which will prove of immense national importance," but when Beals presented it at the 1847 Exhibition of the Massachusetts Charitable Mechanic Association, the judges deemed it "of ingenious construction, but having no practical value."[12]

Thus it may not be surprising that Beals proposed to the Union army a weapon that involved pyrotechnics: the "Poison Rocket Battery or Cavalry

Anniahlator." This device consisted of rockets, fifty to a hundred of which could be fired at one time:

> They are to be Charged With the Most Powerful Composition—
> Each Rocket is to have A 10 inch Steel (Sword or Lancet) firmley
> Attached to it—the Swards or Lancets are to be Coated With A
> Deadley Poison—So Fearfull are these Wepons that A Single
> Scratch from one Drawing Blood Will Caus instant Death. The
> Head of these Rockets are to be Heavley Loaded with incendiary
> Fire Balls and Firery Serpants. . . . Large Numbers of these Fired in
> Rapid Sucsesson they Cannot Fail Making Sad Havoc Among its
> Enemy Setting Fire Thoughing Terror Every Where Around.[13]

Beals went on to describe how a preloaded box of rockets could be placed on an artillery carriage, and after the rockets were fired simultaneously, the box could be removed and exchanged for a full one. A rocket battery would consist of two carriages for launching and a magazine carriage for "Convaying from eight to ten thousand of these Distructive Rockets on the Battle Field with Perfect Safty." He finished his proposal as follows:

> The inventor feels confident of the Sucsess of his invention he
> haveing had over 20 years Experence in Pyrotechnists. Hopeing to be
> of Sirvice to the Government of the United States he offers them his
> invention and prays that he May have an opportunity to Experment
> it Before the Proper officers of the US Government—the inventor is
> fully Convinced that from A Simple Flesh Wound from one of these
> Rockets Would Prove Fatal from its Effect of Deadly Poison. In Most
> Cases Whare these Terrable Weapons are Brought into use the Dread
> and Terror they Carry with them would Make them of Great value
> to the Federal Government at A time when our Rebellios Enemy
> are Resorting to Every Dishonorable Means to Distroy our Brave
> and Gallant Army and our Glorious "Union." The inventer Would
> Humbly pray that he May have an Appropriation from government
> to Experiment with he beaing in Limited Circumstances and unable
> to Leave Home Without Means to take Care of his family.[14]

In light of Beals's practical experience as a pyrotechnist, he may have been correct about the feasibility of launching rockets en masse, but the inherently unpredictable flight of such missiles likely would have limited this tactic to use against large groups of soldiers. Also, the expense of fitting each rocket with a ten-inch steel lancet would probably have been excessive, especially since the likelihood of any one of them striking an enemy solider would have been quite low. Unfortunately, Beals did not name the poison to be used. He may have been inspired by mythological tales of poisoned arrows—for example, Hercules using arrows dipped in the poisonous blood of the Hydra—but there were plenty of contemporary accounts of poison arrows or darts being used by various civilizations. Native Americans in California, for instance, were said to coat their arrowheads with rattlesnake venom, and South American tribes were reported to use arrows or blow darts treated with fluids obtained from certain plants or frogs. Two vegetable poisons said to have been used in antiquity—hellebore and aconite—were used medicinally during the Civil War and could have been applied to Beals's missiles.[15]

Poisons could theoretically be applied to other projectiles, such as cannonballs and bullets. There was, in fact, at least one report—evidently unconfirmed—of poisoned cannonballs being used by Union forces at Corinth, Mississippi. Reports of poisoned bullets were much more common and in some instances could be fairly easily discounted. One suspected projectile was a minié ball of three parts, one of which was a zinc washer. A surgeon probing a wound produced by this projectile, it was asserted, would likely find and remove two of the parts, but "the zinc washer would still remain, causing inflammation and death." Such a bullet, patented by Elijah Williams, was actually used by Union soldiers, but the zinc washer was meant to expand in the firearm's barrel and engage its rifling. Because the washer tended to remove some of the barrel's fouling, arsenals started bundling one "Williams cleaner bullet" per ten cartridges issued to troops. Some zinc discs probably ended up in wounds and may have been injurious, but that was not their intent.[16]

Another suspected projectile, said to be used by both Confederate and Union troops, was a "ball of the Minie pattern with an attachment which comes off readily provided the bullet should pass out of the body. The attachment is of a cup shape, on one side in which arsenic or some other poison might be inserted, and this remaining in the wound would tend to poison the general system through absorption." This description fit a three-part rifle bullet patented by Reuben and Ira Shaler and issued in relatively small numbers to Union soldiers. The parts nested one behind the other, with the rear of the front two parts being hollowed to receive the tip of the part behind it. The parts, none of which carried poison, were intended to separate in flight to produce three projectiles. During the war, a Union officer explained that the projectile in question was issued to Federal troops—captured rounds may have been used by Confederate soldiers—and had "nothing to do with poison in any way, but the attachment is intended to separate from the ball, and both to form what may be called a bullet and grape shot." The misconception that the Williams and Shaler projectiles carried poison and the claim that they were issued to Confederate troops were strongly and convincingly countered after the war.[17]

Another claim was that minié balls made by Federal arsenals were "made fatally poisonous by the washing of the indental portion with a solution of copper." An Ohio newspaper reported that a bullet removed from a Confederate prisoner's cartridge box was coated with pulverized blue vitriol (copper sulfate) and arsenic. The copper salts were known to be poisonous and were sometimes used orally in murder or suicide attempts, in which the chemical quickly caused violent vomiting. Large enough doses could cause convulsions, but death from copper sulfate or copper subacetate (verdigris) was relatively uncommon. During the First Boer War (1880–81), some bullets were thought to have been dipped in verdigris to make them poisonous, but this suspicion was disproved by analysis of the projectiles. There may have been confusion between copper and the similar-sounding copperas (ferrous sulfate). In 1658, the death of a soldier was blamed on a bullet that had been boiled in copperas. In any event, the salts of copper or iron would have been odd choices for poisoning bullets, since much more toxic substances were available.[18]

Arsenic was said to have been found as a coating on minié balls in possession of a captured Confederate soldier. On questioning, the prisoner reportedly acknowledged that the substance was poison. He said that the projectiles had come from the North and that although not many were currently in possession of Southern troops, a larger supply had been promised. A battle in New Mexico led to suspicions that Colorado Union infantrymen had used poisoned bullets. The bullets had been made in Colorado from lead ore mined in that territory, and lead ore can contain arsenic, but an analysis by A. A. Hayes, MD, state assayer of Massachusetts, of a lead sample produced by the Colorado smelting works revealed the metal to be as free from arsenic as the best leads from other locations. The Civil War's minié balls were made from pure lead, and although an arsenic-containing lead alloy was used for producing lead shot for small game, the assayer reported that "unless the proportion of arsenic should be very large, no injury would arise from the use of such an alloy, were it required; as *metallic* arsenic is *not* poisonous." Of course, the analysis did not rule out the possibility that the bullets had been coated manually with arsenic. Hayes added that he had examined blackened wounds supposedly caused by Confederate poisoned bullets and determined that the discoloration was due to gunpowder residue on the projectiles rather than poison.[19]

Some reports of poisoned bullets were vague. J. A. Avirett Jr. told Confederate secretary of war Judah Benjamin that he was "satisfied that some of the bullets that are being fired from the other side are poisoned" and promised to send samples. Packages of poisoned bullets reportedly were found in an abandoned Union camp, and it was claimed that a "poisonous paste" had been detected on bullets used by Confederate soldiers at the Battle of Rich Mountain, Virginia. In many cases, the poor outcomes of wounded soldiers convinced surgeons that poisons must be involved. A Massachusetts soldier suffered a gunshot wound, and "immediately after the ball entered his flesh, [his body] swelled up, and the patient died." The man's surgeon considered it "a clear case of poison, contained in the ball." A Confederate soldier slightly wounded in the hand died "from the effects of the ball, which contained some poisonous matters." A Confederate officer said, "A common opinion is that the balls of the enemy were poisoned, as an unusual number of deaths have ensued from slight wounds. Some of the Surgeons, I learn, concur in this opinion."[20]

An Ohio newspaper reported that a large number of Ohio soldiers with slight wounds had died with gangrene and erysipelas (a streptococcal infection), probably caused by Confederate poisoned bullets. In reaction, another newspaper claimed that the real cause of death was "the fact that the surgeons in the army are either ignorant of their duties, or culpable of most cruel if not criminal practices," particularly the spreading of disease by use of the same sponge on numerous patients. The described practice might well spread infection, and it was an established phenomenon for people, physicians or not, to attribute the horrid nature of some gunshot wounds to the projectiles having been poisoned. An American surgeon in the War of 1812 said that there was no reason to blame poisons for the contusion, laceration, inflammation, and pus formation seen in gunshot wounds, since these effects were attributable to the bullet itself. One learned European physician was of the same opinion: "Such wounds have no need to seek for poisons from without, for they contain the principles of poisoning in themselves. The layer of tissue, ground up by the projectile, decomposes, quickly becomes putrid, and stagnates in the midst of living parts. . . . Who can contest that, in decomposing, the elements of putrefaction will not often give rise to dangerous compounds, if in some way they happen to pass into the circulation?" Another European physician attributed the belief in poisoned bullets to "the local inflammation and gangrene, induced by the improper applications used in dressing gunshot wounds."[21]

There is no convincing proof that poisoned projectiles of any sort were used in the Civil War, and reasonable explanations existed for patients who did poorly after receiving apparently minor gunshot wounds. Allegations that one side or the other used poison on projectiles got a good deal of attention, in large part because such acts were considered morally reprehensible. If the use of poisons by the North was proved, said a Confederate officer, "there will be such a wail of horror and cry for vengeance on the part of the South as will make the yankees tremble for ages to come for such savage atrocities. The cry will be, no quarter to the demons, and poison should meet poison. We should not cease until we crush every reptile invader beneath the sod." A story in a Northern newspaper about the alleged Confederate use of arsenic bullets was titled "The Southern Barbarians."[22]

The general opposition to poison as a weapon of war did not stop one citizen from sending his ideas to the US secretary of war. In September 1861, Frederick C. Buckelew, a seventy-five-year-old physician from New Brunswick, New Jersey, put forward "several plans by which the enemy may be damaged, while they will be unable to retaliate by the same means." One idea, unaccompanied by details, was that "large numbers of men may be temporarily blinded so as to be helpless." Buckelew claimed, "The plan is quite feasible if carefully carried out." His last sentence was terse: "Would it be too cruel to make all lead, used in battle, fatally poisonous?" No response from the Ordnance Department was recorded.[23]

Even in the absence of ethical concerns, poisoned bullets may have presented practical problems. The amount of poison that could be transmitted by a bullet was small and might take some time to kill a wounded soldier or to make him less able to fight or recover, so the tactical value of a poisoned bullet was limited. Soldiers used their teeth to tear open paper cartridges while loading their muskets, so they might ingest poison that was on the bullet or that had migrated to the paper. Poisoned bullets could be fired with no special equipment or training, so captured poisoned ammunition might be used by the enemy. Much would also have gone to waste. Estimates put the number of musket rounds expended to produce one casualty at about two hundred, and a poisoned bullet would have had to actually strike a soldier, rather than just land close by, to cause harm. Poisons, if used, may have increased the death rate from wounds, but the overall efficiency of poisoned bullets would still have been quite low, and applying poison to millions of rounds would have been expensive and probably dangerous. Thus military officials had ample reason to disregard Buckelew's proposal, and it is doubtful that they approved the use of poisoned bullets during the war.[24]

11

VULGAR POISONS IN HONOURABLE WARFARE

> Whether the proposers of such asphyxiating projectiles have considered the metaphysical distinction between different modes of compassing death, or whether it has weighed at all with those whose office it is to decide as to their adoption, we have no means of knowing. According to the received form of retribution, however, in all such cases, the chemist who first suggested the use of such poisons to manufacturers of ammunition, is destined to perish by his own new weapon of destruction. —James F. W. Johnston, 1855

THE AMERICAN CIVIL WAR HAS been called the first modern war, in part because of the military technologies that were first employed during the conflict. Historian Robert V. Bruce, however, pointed out that many innovations commonly associated with the war had actually been developed or introduced many years earlier. He attributed the relative lack of true wartime breakthroughs to a widespread assumption that the war would not last long and thus did not justify investment in research and development by the governments or by private industry. Union ordnance officers were consumed with supplying troops with proven weapons, and their Confederate counterparts, who shared the same concerns, also had to worry about the South's limited industrial capacity and constant shortages of raw materials. Thus the governments—on their own or in collaboration with the scientific community—did relatively little to find new applications of science to the battlefield. To be sure, formulations of Greek fire were tested and used by Federal forces, but the impetus was largely that of aggressively self-promoting inventors rather than ordnance personnel searching for more effective weapons. The origin of Confederate general Beauregard's initiative to develop unconventional incendiary weapons is unclear, since it began well before Greek fire shells were thrown into Charleston; he may have been reacting to the earlier and sporadic use of liquid fire by Union forces. In any event, the various formulations of Greek fire, said Bruce, "seem to have been concocted through trial and error by unschooled tinkerers." The other chemical weapons tested or readied for use during the war—chloroform, a stink shell, and a fume-producing countermining cartridge—could hardly be called exemplars of innovation or technological advances.[1]

Indeed, "tinkerers" seems an apt description of the civilian proponents of chemical weapons described in the preceding chapters; most of these advocates were, in fact, unschooled as far as weapons expertise was concerned. The information sources for this book consisted largely of citizens' correspondence to government officials or to periodicals, with only an occasional idea submitted by individuals in the armed forces. The military men known to have had ideas for chemical weapons, all of whom happened to be Confederates, included Joseph Jones for phosphorus and hydrogen cyanide, Beverly Kennon for incendiary shells and grenades, Gabriel Rains for incendiary devices, a Captain Holden for a stink shell, and unnamed persons for the countermining cartridge and chloroform. If Union military personnel also suggested chemical weapons, they were no more successful than their Confederate military counterparts in having their ideas accepted and implemented.

Physicians were unusually common among individuals advocating, researching, or patenting chemical weapons. John Cheves, who tested and advised General Beauregard about chemical weapons, was a civilian physician, and Joseph Jones, who advocated phosphorus and hydrogen cyanide, had been a civilian physician before being appointed a surgeon in the Confederate army. Among the thirty-one civilian proponents of chemical weapons whose occupation could be determined, ten—or eleven if pepper advocate D. A. Pease had been a medical man, which was likely—had a medical degree or practiced medicine.

Economist B. Zorina Khan studied a random sample of persons who had filed patents between 1855 and 1870 and found that 5.2 percent of those with a patent for a weapon (including firearms, cannon, ordnance, and explosives) had a medical occupation in 1860. In comparing that 5.2 percent with the more than 30 percent of physicians among the civilian advocates of chemical weapons, it should be noted that the latter, for the most part, did not seek legal protection for their ideas by patenting them, but rather offered them freely. Moreover, most of the chemical weapons proposals could not rightfully be called inventions, since they were usually meager in detail about how the apparatus for delivering the poison should be constructed. The proportion of physicians in both of these samples was much larger than in the general population. The 1860 census of the United States showed that among the seven million white males at least twenty years of age—the presumed demographic category of most proponents or patentees of weapons—only about fifty-six thousand (0.8 percent) were physicians.[2]

Among advocates of chemical weapons, why were physicians overrepresented, compared with both the general population and with inventors of nonchemical weapons? One possible explanation is that most of the chemicals suggested as weapons had medicinal uses, so physicians would have been more familiar than laypeople with the agents' toxic potential and thus more likely to propose their use. One might expect, however, that physicians should have been more concerned with preserving than disrupting health. This paradox can be partially addressed by examining medical education and practice as they existed in the Civil War era.

There was little regulation of medical practice at the time, so practically anyone could claim to be a physician, medical diploma or not. Graduation from a medical school generally required an apprenticeship, attendance at two usually identical terms of lectures that lasted several months each, and completion of a thesis; admission to a medical school often required no more than the ability to pay the necessary fees. Thus becoming a physician did not require nearly the sacrifice in time, money, and effort that it does today. Many persons who obtained a medical degree or practiced medicine in the mid-1800s did not devote their lives to that calling but had other or simultaneous occupations and may not have had ethical reservations about suggesting ways to harm enemy soldiers. Paul Steiner, in a study of physicians who became Civil War generals, identified patriotism and a weak commitment to medicine as contributors to physicians' decisions to serve the military in a nonmedical role; the same factors may have applied to physicians as proponents of weapons. In some instances, physicians may have thought that their proposed weapons would make wars more humane. For example, medical graduate and chlorine advocate John Doughty, who did not practice medicine, held this view.[3]

Among the nonphysician proponents of chemical weapons, a few had occupations—chemist, druggist, teacher—that might have provided them with more than common knowledge of poisons. Many proponents of chemical weapons were prominent enough in their communities to appear in the following decades in local published histories. Some had patents for inventions unrelated to weapons or to the military. Only two of the known advocates of chemical weapons were women. Among the proponents whose ages could be determined, the average age when they submitted their suggestions was forty-five, with a range of twenty-two to eighty.

The motives behind the proposals were usually unstated. Most proponents advocated their ideas as making warfare more efficient and safer for friendly troops. They may have been responding to published calls for inventions, such as this one in *Scientific American*: "A new and more formidable battle weapon than any now known is greatly wanted. All patriotic inventors have here an opportunity of doing their country good service." Indeed, patriotism was sometimes evident in suggestions submitted to that publication and to government officials. Some proponents of chemical weapons expressed indignation or outright hostility toward the enemy or its civilian or military leaders. A few expected payment for adoption of their proposals, even those that were not patented, or threatened to offer them to other governments. Some were self-effacing and apologetic for claiming the time of harried officials, whereas others were assertive and name-dropped or enlisted the assistance of persons whom they considered influential. A few wished to be on hand for testing of their proposals or even to direct their use in combat.[4]

Other than the unconventional incendiaries, which may have been inspired by historical accounts of Greek fire, most of the proposed chemical agents were familiar in everyday life. People knew from personal experience, for example, that cayenne pepper and snuff could be irritating, and many had read that chloroform could cause unconsciousness, that chlorine was dangerous to breathe, and that acids could produce frightful burns. The fact that some substances, such as cayenne pepper and sulfur, had been used as weapons by various civilizations may have been known to some well-informed persons but was certainly not needed to verify that the agents could produce unpleasant or dangerous effects. Thus citizens who suggested these familiar substances did not necessarily realize that they were resurrecting old ideas. That many proponents had the same idea—whether it was packaging poisons in artillery shells or spraying them with a fire engine—suggests a common and rather basic level of sophistication about weapons and warfare. A relatively high degree of knowledge was displayed in Joseph Jones's phosphorus and hydrogen cyanide proposals and in John Doughty's chlorine proposal. Alkarsin and the cacodyl derivatives, which were probably unfamiliar to persons with an average education, were suggested by a few well-read individuals, but it took specialized knowledge like Jones's to realize that the chemicals were too dangerous to consider.

Most of the proposed means of deploying the suggested poisons reflected the sensible notion that the agents should be released at a safe distance from friendly troops. The proponents, however, generally seemed to believe that merely suggesting a poison was enough to make a workable weapon possible and that ordnance experts would find ways to weaponize the proposed chemicals. It would probably not have been a simple matter to produce artillery shells to deliver the poisonous payloads or to develop firing patterns that would produce effective concentrations of the chemicals. As was demonstrated by the liquid-fire shells fired at Charleston, it could not be assumed that a projectile would arrive at its target intact and explode when it should. Accuracy would have been a major concern if kites or balloons—manned or unmanned—had been used. Pouring chloroform or forcing hydrogen cyanide gas into an ironclad vessel made sense because the poisons would be confined to a closed space and pose little immediate danger to friendly troops, but delivering noxious substances by fire or garden engines would expose the device's operators to short-range enemy fire and other friendly troops to errant sprays of the liquids. The technical challenges alone would have been enough to persuade ordnance officials to lay the well-meant proposals aside.

Despite the almost universal impracticability of the proposed weapons, some could be said to have been ahead of their time. John Doughty's chlorine shell would have been unworkable because of limitations in Civil War technology—for example, the difficulty of producing large amounts of liquid chlorine and the excessive pressure it would exert within artillery shells—yet his general concept was realized in World War I projectiles filled with liquid poisons. Joseph Jones's cyanide shell closely resembled future binary weapons developed for the delivery of nerve agents, and his concept for a portable hydrogen cyanide generator has been duplicated almost exactly by terrorists (and before that by orchardists for combating insects). The pumps and shells intended to deliver the Civil War's Greek fire had their counterparts in modern flamethrowers and napalm-containing bombs. In some cases, proponents' ideas appeared later as devices—pepper spray and "pepper balls," for example—intended for nonlethal use at close ranges against adversaries other than enemy combatants. While it would be too generous to label many of the Civil War's chemical weapons advocates as true innovators, advances in technology and the emergence of new tactical applications allowed some of their visions to be realized. Because most of the ideas discussed here were not used or publicized, they cannot be said to have inspired future weapons developers. Rather, the Civil War ideas that reappeared in later years were resurrected independently.[5]

Even if some of the ideas had seemed workable and tactically advantageous, military officials might have had ethical concerns about their use. American lawyer, jurist, and diplomat Henry Wheaton, who summarized in 1866 the usages of war, concluded that weapons were not objectionable merely because of their destructiveness; he also considered incendiary projectiles like hot shot allowable. Greek fire, though, seemed different, at least to some. A Copperhead New York newspaper asserted, in reference to Greek fire, that "unnatural weapons" were uncivilized, and this view was shared early in the Civil War by General George McClellan and apparently by British officials when considering incendiary compounds during the Crimean War. In 1861, however, Henry Halleck, who the next year became commanding general of the Union army, stated that military inventions were justifiable and supported his view with a quotation from an 1838 address by former US attorney general Benjamin F. Butler: "Every great discovery in the art of war, has a life-saving and peace-promoting influence. . . . By perfecting ourselves in military science—paradoxical as it may seem—we are therefore assisting in the diffusion of peace."[6]

Thus, for some, the novelty or destructive capacity of chemical weapons was not necessarily the primary ethical issue; it was also problematic that poisoned weapons caused death or additional suffering in soldiers who were already disabled. This viewpoint assumed that poisoned weapons consisted of poison-treated projectiles and blades that could wound on their own; it seemed not to apply to most of the Civil War's proposed chemical weapons, which would incapacitate or kill by being inhaled even if its victims were unharmed by the means used to deliver the poison. Chemical weapons might be covered by the common opinion that "instruments of wholesale slaughter which cannot be foreseen or avoided by flight, are against the customs of most kinds of warfare." Once a chemical weapon was successfully employed, however, future uses might be foreseen, and they might be no less avoidable than, say, barrages of conventional artillery, so in this regard, the distinction between chemical and conventional weapons was not clear.[7] Wheaton tried to provide guidance about what weapons were allowable in war:

Perhaps the only test, in cases of open contests between acknowledged combatants, is, that the material shall not owe its efficacy, or the fear it may inspire, to a distinct quality of producing pain, or of causing or increasing the chances of death to individuals, or spreading death or disability, if this quality is something else than the application of direct force, and of a kind that cannot be met with countervailing force, or remedied by the usual medical and surgical applications for forcible injuries, or averted by retreat or surrender.[8]

It may have been simplest for military officials to accept the pat but prevalent sentiment that poisons in warfare were "prohibited by the law of nature" and thus avoid troubling comparisons with the destructive and misery-producing conventional munitions they were supplying to their troops. Military men who saw war as a chivalrous affair may have agreed with the British commentator James Hain Friswell, who said, "Degrade the soldier to the mere chemical sneak, the poisoner in uniform, the town-burner, and the death-fumigator, and '*glorious* war' will soon be over." Scottish chemist James F. W. Johnston called chemical weapons "vulgar poisons in honourable warfare."[9]

In any event, poisons—depending on one's definition of that term—in warfare were formally prohibited in April 1863 by General Order No. 100 of the US Army's Adjutant General's Office, prepared by lawyer and ethicist Francis Lieber and approved by President Lincoln: "The use of poison in any manner, be it to poison wells, or food, or arms, is wholly excluded from modern warfare. He that uses it puts himself out of the pale of the law and usages of war." (The bombardment of Charleston with Greek fire began four months later, in August 1863, so either that substance was not considered a poison or the act was in violation of the prohibition.) Paradoxically, the same document, which became known as the Lieber Code, made a point that would have found agreement among the proponents of chemical weapons: "The more vigorously wars are pursued, the better it is for humanity. Sharp wars are brief."

The US government's general indifference toward the chemical weapons proposed during the Civil War may have stemmed in part from the assumption that they were not practicable and thus not worth worrying about. Later in the nineteenth century, the blossoming of the chemical industry and marked advances in the technology of artillery made large and long-range chemical shells much more imaginable. Thus chemical warfare became a topic of international discussion at the First Hague Peace Conference in 1899, during which countries were asked to "agree to abstain from the use of all projectiles, the sole object of which is the diffusion of asphyxiating or deleterious gases." Although no such weapon had been used in war, most participating nations agreed to the provision, but the United States did not.[10] The American delegation was instructed by Secretary of State John Hay—who, as President Lincoln's secretary thirty-seven years earlier, had ridiculed John Brigham's proposal for a shell containing cayenne pepper— not to support measures limiting the use of destructive agents:

> It is doubtful if wars are to be diminished by rendering them less de-
> structive, for it is the plain lesson of history that the periods of peace
> have been longer protracted as the cost and destructiveness of war have
> increased. The expediency of restraining the inventive genius of our
> people in the direction of devising means of defense is by no means
> clear, and considering the temptations to which men and nations may be
> exposed in a time of conflict, it is doubtful if an international agreement
> to this end would prove effective.[11]

Thus Hay not only took note of the American inventiveness he had previously derided but also reiterated the "sharp wars" sentiment of Lieber and acknowledged, as did some of the Civil War's advocates of chemical weapons, that circumstances might force the use of unusually destructive weapons.

In voting against the resolution, US delegate Alfred Thayer Mahan, a former naval officer and a renowned naval strategist and historian, noted that nobody knew whether gas shells would create decisive results or excessive injury or be more or less merciful than existing weapons. Mahan, who had served in the US Navy during the Civil War, added "that it was illogical, and not demonstrably humane, to be tender about asphyxiating men with gas, when all were prepared to admit that it was allowable to blow the bottom out of an ironclad at midnight, throwing four or five hundred men into the sea, to be choked by water, with scarcely the remotest chance of escape." This argument sounded much like those voiced before and during the Civil War in opposition to views that chemical weapons were inhumane. It is notable that although most participant nations were willing to ban chemical shells—they were not, after all, sacrificing armaments currently in production or development—they were not agreeable to prohibiting improvements that had reached the stage of apparent usefulness, such as more powerful explosives or upgraded field guns and rifles.[12]

The Second Hague Conference, held in 1907, contained an article, to which the United States agreed, stating that "in addition to prohibitions provided by special conventions, it is especially forbidden to employ poison or poisoned weapons." Since a prohibition of chemical shells already existed (although not agreed to by the US delegation), the United States viewed the additional prohibition as applying to the poisoning of water supplies and not to chemical weapons as they came to be used in World War I; British officials concluded that the article did not prohibit certain nonlethal chemicals. Such reasoning or rationalization about what exactly constituted a poison may have been in play during the Civil War and removed ethical barriers to the use of Greek fire by the Union and to the preparation or testing of chloroform and other agents by the Confederates.[13]

Of course, the civilians who suggested chemical weapons during the Civil War thought them acceptable, but some nevertheless indicated that ethical implications had occurred to them. John Condon thought using strychnine or arsenic was "a horrid remedy," wanted to reserve the poison until the enemy had opened fire, and advised that the letter describing his idea be burned. Nathaniel Harris, in proposing snuff-filled bladders, asserted that "any mode of Warfare is honorable in putting down open rebellion." William Beals thought that rockets with poisonous spears were allowable against an enemy already using (unnamed) dishonorable means of warfare. John Doughty thought chlorine shells would reduce the "sanguinary character of the battlefield" and make warfare "more decisive," a sentiment consistent with the "sharp wars" view of the Lieber Code. Compared with chemical weapons meant to be lethal, those intended to temporarily incapacitate the enemy were less ethically troubling. John Cheves, for example, expressed no reservations about working on phosphorous shells as "stifling" weapons but objected to using lethal hydrogen cyanide against ironclad vessels when a nonlethal agent would be just as effective in making their crews incapable of performing their duties.[14]

When ideas for chemical weapons appeared in periodicals, they were justified, if at all, by citing the desperate situation or the dishonorable acts that the enemy had committed. The use of poisoned bullets was considered particularly despicable, and claims by both sides that the enemy was guilty of the act provoked much agitation and name-calling as well as vigorous denials by the accused. On the other hand, writers of newspaper articles seemed amused by the idea that cayenne pepper could be effective in warfare, possibly because the compound seemed so harmless.

It is impossible to say how chemical weapons could have swayed the outcome of battles or campaigns because the battlefield effectiveness of unmade weapons cannot be judged. Had the proposed chemical agents worked as intended, they at least would have caused casualties, and physicians would have been hard-pressed to provide the victims with much relief. Even today, with the exception of cyanide poisoning, for which an antidote kit exists, treatment for exposure to the agents suggested during the war would consist primarily of supportive care. Primitive gas masks had been developed for mining and industrial purposes, and if made available in large numbers, they may have provided soldiers with some protection.

The use of chemical weapons would likely have spurred retaliation. The eighteenth-century Swiss diplomat Emmerich de Vattel had warned, "If you poison your weapons, the enemy will follow your example; and thus, without gaining any advantage on your side for the decision of the contest [because the enemy was already disabled without the application of poison], you have only added to the cruelty and calamities of war." Indeed, General Beauregard stated that he would use phosphorous shells against Union positions "chiefly in the event an attempt shall be made to bombard this city [Charleston] especially with incendiary shells."[15]

Nor can it be determined how the world powers would have reacted to either the Union or Confederacy employing chemical weapons. The London press largely deplored the bombardment of Charleston with Greek fire, but Confederate retaliation with phosphorous shells would have made it difficult to label one side or the other as ethically culpable. There was, in fact, a call in Great Britain for British military officials to quit disregarding Greek fire as a weapon of war, as had been done repeatedly, and to start research into incendiary compounds before the Americans, a potential enemy, achieved a substantial technological advantage from the practical experience gained in the Civil War.[16]

Might the more widespread use of chemical weapons, such as they were, during the Civil War have hastened the use of chemical agents in subsequent conflicts? Probably not, because the crude methods suggested during the Civil War likely would have produced militarily disappointing results not worthy of replication. It took a degree of maturation of the chemical industry and ordnance technology to allow chemical warfare as it occurred in World War I; even in 1899, when nations convened at the First Hague Conference, the real effects of chemical shells were difficult to imagine. In the unlikely scenario of gas shells proving to be at least feasible during the Civil War, nations in addition to the United States may have been unwilling to prohibit them, just as they balked at banning improvements in explosives, artillery, and firearms in 1899. In the even more unlikely case of the Civil War proving chemical weapons to be horrific agents of destruction, steps to prohibit them might have been taken earlier than 1899. The chemical-shell prohibition of the First Hague Conference did not stop signatories Germany, France, and Great Britain from employing such weapons in World War I, however, and the subsequent prohibition of chemical weapons by the 1925 Geneva Protocol did not prevent the use of such weapons by signatory Italy in the Italo-Ethiopian War (1935–36) or signatory Japan in the Second Sino-Japanese War.[17]

How, then, do the Civil War's real and proposed chemical agents fit in the timeline of weaponry and warfare? Chemical weapons had been used for many centuries, so there was nothing groundbreaking about their being suggested during the Civil War. Historical accounts of Greek fire were common, and two weapons prepared for use—countermining cartridges and a stink shell—were likely based on textbook knowledge widely available to ordnance and artillery officers. Proposals for other agents most likely arose without reference to similar weapons in history.

The only World War I chemical weapons that could have been inspired by Civil War events were the incendiaries. However, weapons developers of World War I would not have been encouraged by the sorry performance of the Civil War's Greek fire; they formulated improved incendiary compounds by using newer chemical knowledge and processes. Phosphorus was investigated during the Civil War as an incendiary agent, but documentation of its actual use on the battlefield is lacking, so the World War I use of phosphorus—primarily for producing smoke screens—cannot be said to have been inspired by the Civil War experience. The Civil War's innovative ideas, such as the chlorine shell, mixing chemicals to produce hydrogen cyanide, and the cloud of acid gas, were not publicized and could not have spawned later weapons. Thus the Civil War's concepts for chemical agents did not materially improve on the past and contributed little if anything to the future of weapons development.

The ideas for chemical weapons during the Civil War can nonetheless be appreciated for what they illustrate about the era and its people. It was a time when invention was encouraged, and citizens felt free to suggest to the government ways to bring the great crisis to a speedier end. Newspapers and magazines described experiments and improvements in armaments, and interest in chemical weapons was great enough to elicit commentary and even, in the case of Greek fire, to inspire political cartoons and poetry. Considering specific proposals allows us to study the individuals behind these ideas; learn about their scientific knowledge, ethical concerns, and views of the war; and determine whether any common factors help explain their advocacy of chemical weapons. Although no such markers stand out—except perhaps for the study or practice of medicine—the proponents emerge as real people, ranging from learned and cogent to clearly unbalanced but on the whole seemingly ordinary.

Examining the proposals themselves in detail lets us speculate about their origins and judge their feasibility. Many of the ideas, though impracticable, were not as outlandish as they might seem at first glance—most, at least, reflected common knowledge of the times. The response, or lack of it, by government officials to the proposals shows that their priorities lay elsewhere—an understandable position given their onerous assignment of arming the troops and the apparent impracticality of the submitted ideas.

Studying chemical warfare as an aspect of Civil War history provides a window through which to examine some of the thoughts, values, knowledge, and technology of the time and assists in understanding the era in historical context. It was probably for the best that the ideas for chemical weapons proposed during the war went no further than they did. Resurrected now, they have much to teach us.

GLOSSARY

NOTES

BIBLIOGRAPHY

INDEX

GLOSSARY

alkarsin. A reddish-brown arsenic-containing liquid with an extremely repulsive odor and flammable fumes. Also called *Cadet's fuming liquid*. See also *cacodyl*.

antimony. A chemical element, forms of which could be added to incendiary mixtures to produce more heat or facilitate ignition.

arseniuretted hydrogen. See *arsine*.

arsine. A highly toxic gaseous arsenic compound. Also called *arseniuretted hydrogen*.

asphaltum. A dry, black, flammable substance occurring in petroleum wells.

benzene. The modern name for *benzole*.

benzine. See *benzole*.

benzole. A colorless, flammable liquid obtained, during the Civil War era, from coal tar. It was sometimes used as an inhalable anesthetic during the Civil War era. Also called *benzene* (its modern name) or *benzine*.

binary weapon. A device in which two relatively safe substances are packaged separately in the same weapon, such as a bomb or artillery projectile, and combine to form a more dangerous product after the weapon is deployed.

bisulphide of carbon. See *carbon disulfide*.

bitumen. A flammable substance occurring in petroleum wells. It may be liquid (*naphtha*) or solid (*asphaltum*).

cacodyl. A constituent of *alkarsin*. Cacodyl vapors burst into flames when exposed to air and release arsenic fumes. Also called *kakodyl* (meaning "bad smell").

Cadet's fuming liquid. See *alkarsin*.

camphene. A colorless, flammable liquid obtained from the resin of certain trees. It was commonly used as a lamp fuel. Also called *oil of turpentine* or simply *turpentine*.

caoutchouc. See *India rubber*.

carbon disulfide. A volatile liquid solvent in which *phosphorus* can be dissolved (see *volatility*). If this mixture is exposed to air, the carbon disulfide evaporates quickly and the phosphorus bursts into flames. Also called *bisulphide of carbon*.

carcass. An incendiary artillery shell containing *portfire*.

cayenne pepper. The fruits of *Capsicum annuum* and related species, commonly called chili or red peppers. The fruits were usually dried and ground before use. Exposure to ground or burning cayenne pepper is extremely irritating to the eyes, nose, and throat.

cevadilla. See *veratria*.

chlorate of potash. See *potassium chlorate.*

chlorine. A chemical element that is poisonous at high concentrations. At room temperature, it exists as a gas. Liquefying chlorine requires a low temperature, high pressure, or both. At room temperature, the vapor above liquid chlorine exerts a high pressure, which necessitates a strong container for storage of the liquid. Chlorine gas is heavier than air but dissipates quickly when released into the atmosphere at room temperature.

chloroform. A liquid commonly used as an anesthetic during the Civil War era. The anesthetic effects are cause by inhaling fumes that are given off by the highly volatile liquid (see *volatility*).

coal oil. A flammable substance obtained from certain types of shale.

coal tar. A thick, viscous, dark brown or black flammable fluid obtained from coal. Distillation of coal tar yields coal-tar naphtha, a colorless flammable fluid whose major constituent is *benzene.*

combustible sugar. A *resin*-like substance obtained by treating sugar with sulfuric and nitric acid. The product is extremely flammable and explosive, and its fire is almost inextinguishable.

flowers of sulfur. A purified form of *sulfur.*

garden engine. A portable device used for watering gardens. It often resembled a wheelbarrow and included a water reservoir and hand-operated pump.

Greek fire. A catchall term for liquid or solid incendiary substances that can burn in or under water and are difficult to extinguish.

gutta-percha. A rigid latex, often used as a sealant or insulator, formed from the sap of certain Asian trees. See also *India rubber.*

hydrochloric acid. A caustic liquid with industrial and medicinal uses. Also called *muriatic acid.*

hydrocyanic acid. See *hydrogen cyanide.*

hydrogen chloride. A toxic, colorless gas that forms *hydrochloric acid* when dissolved in water. Hydrogen chloride can be formed by mixing common salt or hydrochloric acid with *sulfuric acid.*

hydrogen cyanide. A deadly poison that is a highly volatile liquid below its boiling point of 78 degrees Fahrenheit (see *volatility*). The vapor is lighter than air and dissipates quickly when released. Hydrogen cyanide can be formed by mixing *potassium cyanide* or *sodium cyanide*, which are both poisonous, with *sulfuric acid* or *hydrochloric acid.* Also called *hydrocyanic acid* or *prussic acid.*

hydrogen sulfide. A colorless, poisonous gas with the characteristic odor of rotten eggs.

India rubber. An elastic latex, with uses similar to those of *gutta-percha*, formed from the sap of certain Asian trees. Also called *caoutchouc.*

kakodyl. See *cacodyl.*

muriatic acid. See *hydrochloric acid.*

naphtha. A flammable liquid collected from petroleum wells.

niter. Potassium nitrate, one of the three constituents (with charcoal and sulfur) of black powder. Also called *saltpeter*.

oil of turpentine. See *camphene*.

oil of vitriol. See *sulfuric acid*.

phosphorus. A highly reactive element that can ignite spontaneously in air. It could be dissolved in *carbon disulfide* or submerged in water and packaged in incendiary weapons. Phosphorus was a component in incendiary and smoke-producing munitions in World War I and later conflicts.

pitch. A solid, black, flammable substance obtained from the burning of certain varieties of pine trees.

portfire. A flammable, slow-burning substance made of *niter, sulfur*, and mealed powder (a form of gunpowder), sometimes containing *antimony* or steel filings. The composition was packed into small paper cases, pieces of which could be placed into incendiary shells called *carcasses*.

potassium chlorate. A solid substance used in matches and explosives. Also called *chlorate of potash*.

potassium cyanide. See *hydrogen cyanide*.

prussic acid. See *hydrogen cyanide*.

resin. A solid, brittle, flammable substance obtained from certain varieties of trees.

rosin. A *resin* yielded in the processing of *turpentine*.

sabadilla. See *veratria*.

saltpeter. See *niter*.

sodium cyanide. See *hydrogen cyanide*.

sublimed sulfur. A purified form of *sulfur*.

sulfur. A chemical element that, when burned, produces noxious fumes, including *sulfur dioxide*. Sulfur was a key component of black powder. A purified form of sulfur was called *sublimed sulfur* or *flowers of sulfur*.

sulfur dioxide. A poisonous gas resulting from the burning of *sulfur*.

sulfuric acid. A caustic liquid with industrial and medical uses. Also called *oil of vitriol* or *vitriolic acid*.

turpentine. See *camphene*.

veratria. A medicinally used powder derived from the seeds (*sabadilla* or *cevadilla*) of *Veratrum sabadilla* (a species also known as *Schoenocaulon officinale*) and related Latin American plants. If inhaled, veratria causes violent sneezing.

vitriolic acid. See *sulfuric acid*.

volatility. The tendency of a substance to vaporize. A volatile solid or liquid readily gives off vapor.

NOTES

1. IMPROVEMENTS IN WARLIKE INSTRUMENTALITIES

1. Live Yankee to unknown, August 24, 1861, class misc., letter 213, Correspondence Relating to Inventions (hereafter cited as CRI); Bruce, *Lincoln and the Tools of War.*

2. "National Encouragement to the Novelties of Inventors," *Philadelphia Inquirer*, July 17, 1861, 4; "Impertinence of the Ordnance Department"; James W. Ripley to Simon Cameron, June 11, 1861, *War of the Rebellion*, ser. 3, vol. 1, 264–65; Bruce, *Lincoln and the Tools of War*; Testimony of Maj. T. J. Rodman, February 6, 1864, S. Comm. Rep. No. 38-121, at 107–8 (1865).

3. Vandiver, *Ploughshares into Swords*; Brian to Pemberton, November 28, 1862, file for Brian, Confederate Papers Relating to Citizens or Business Firms, roll 150 (hereafter cited as Confederate Papers).

4. Rhodes, "Report of the Commissioner of Patents."

5. Samuel Small to Abraham Lincoln, [1861], Abraham Lincoln Papers, accessed February 6, 2014, http://memory.loc.gov/ammen/alhtml/alhome.html (hereafter cited as ALP).

6. Musick, "War in an Age of Wonders."

7. Bruce, *Lincoln and the Tools of War*, 59.

2. GREEK FIRE, AMERICAN STYLE

1. "Application of Uriah Brown for Patronage to His Invention of a Composition for the Destruction of Vessels, Similar to the 'Greek Fire,'" February 18, 1828, *American State Papers: Naval Affairs* 3:141–42; "On the Expediency of Testing Uriah Brown's System of Coast and Harbor Defence by Fire Ships," May, 10, 1828, ibid. 3:201–4; "On the Expediency of Authorizing Experiments, to Test the Efficacy of Uriah Brown's System of Defence for Bay and Harbors, by Means of Impregnable and Irresistible Fire Ships," March 24, 1836, ibid. 4:876–79. There was also interest in Greek fire in the British Isles, where in 1812, an Irishman named Maguire demonstrated his formula for British military officials. *War* (New York), December 5, 1812, 2.

2. Report of the Secretary of the Navy, S. Exec. Doc. No. 30-1, at 953, 1306–10 (1847); "Greek Fire," *Evening Post* (New York), October 19, 1847, 2.

3. *H.R. Journal*, 30th Cong., 1st sess., 272–73 (1848); H.R. Rep. No. 30-294 (1848); Hodges to Lincoln, April 17, 1863, ALP.

4. *H.R. Journal*, 24th Cong., 1st sess., 99 (1835); William J. Kellogg, "A New Destroyer," *Rockford (IL) Republican*, August 1, 1855, 1; *H.R. Journal*, 34th Cong., 3rd sess., 121 (1856); *H.R. Journal*, 35th Cong., 1st sess., 732 (1857); Short to E. M. Stanton, March 2, 1862, class 8, letter 176, CRI.

5. Cutbush, "Remarks"; Richardson, "Greek Fire"; "Greek-Fire," *Chambers's Journal*; "Greek Fire or Pyrophori"; Boynton, "Greek Fire, and Other Inflammables"; Needham, *Science and Civilisation in China*, 5:73–94. For a modern summary of ancient incendiary weapons, see Mayor, *Greek Fire*, 207–50.

6. "Greek Fire—Shell and Shot"; Gibbon, *Artillerist's Manual*, 322–30; Roberts, *Hand-Book of Artillery*, 100–124; Bragg et al., *Never for Want of Powder*, 128–30; "Greek-Fire," *Chambers's Journal*.

7. Richardson, "Greek Fire"; Odling, *Manual of Chemistry*, 275–80; Reid, *Memoirs and Correspondence*, 159; Subcommittee on Military Smokes and Obscurants, *Toxicity*; *Abridgments*, 229; "New War Projectile," *Times* (London), July 31, 1855, 12; "Captain Disney's War Projectile," *Times* (London), August 9, 1855, 12; Norton, *List of Captain Norton's Projectiles*, 6. Snuff as a chemical weapon is described in chapter 6.

8. *Abridgments*, 228.

9. Benjamin W. Richardson, "Captain Disney's Projectile," *Times* (London), August 2, 1855, 10; "Has Russia Obtained a New Projectile of War?" *Newfoundlander* (St. John's), April 20, 1854, 2; "Destructive Fire Shells"; "War Projectiles."

10. Huff to Thomas A. Scott, October 29, 1861, with endorsement by McClellan, October 31, 1861, *War of the Rebellion*, ser. 3, vol. 1, 606.

11. Live Yankee to unknown, August 24, 1861, class misc., letter 213, CRI; Hunt, *Ure's Dictionary*, 816; Spear to Simon Cameron, December 3, 1861, class misc., letter 251, CRI; Glezen to Edwin M. Stanton, April 30, 1862, class misc., letter 299, CRI; Ramsbrok, "Dr. Glezen."

12. McIntyre to General Dyer, December 30, 1864, classes 4 & 5, letter 884, CRI; Lewis to Simon Cameron, December 18, 1861, class misc., letter 258, CRI; "Scientific News"; Crary to E. M. Stanton, September 3, 1863, class misc., letter 413, CRI; Davis, *History of Clarion County*, 117; Edward Harrison, Improved Inflammable Composition for Filling Projectiles, US Patent 41,577, February 9, 1864; Mills L. Callender, Improved Material for Filling Shells, US Patent 43,667, August 2, 1864; H. W. Libby, Improved Incendiary Compound, US Patent 48,187, June 13, 1865; William Wheeler Hubbell, Improvement in Incendiary Shells, US Patent 50,711, October 31, 1865. The handwriting in Lewis's letter to Secretary Cameron matches that in known correspondence of the conchologist. Lewis to Annie Law, September 28, 1868, James Lewis Letters.

13. "Boston Light House"; Hamilton, "Report on Greenough's Patent Lamp"; Benjamin F. Greenough, Lamp, US Patent 2,039, April 10, 1841; B. F. Greenough, Mode of Using Volatile Oils for Purposes of Illumination, US Patent 3,339, November 15, 1843; Woodcroft, *Chronological Index*, 84; "New Weapon of Warfare"; "Destructive Fire Shells"; Badger to Wise, April 27, 1862, *Official Records of the Union*

and Confederate Navies, ser. 1, vol. 7, 285–86. Wise was appointed acting chief of the navy's Bureau of Ordnance in 1863 and chief in 1864.

14. "Destroying Angels, Greenough's Liquid Fire," *Aegis and Transcript* (Worcester, MA), January 4, 1862, 1; R. H. Wyman to Gideon Welles, January 3, 1862, *Official Records of the Union and Confederate Navies*, ser. 1, vol. 5, 15; "Commodore Tatnall Shelled," *New York Daily Reformer* (Watertown), January 4, 1862, 3; Badger to Wise, April 27, 1862, *Official Records of the Union and Confederate Navies*, ser. 1, vol. 7, 285–86; Wise to Badger, April 30, 1862, ibid., 293–94; "Greek Fire—Incendiary Shells."

15. "Mrs. Greenough Dead," *New York Times*, January 12, 1909; Obituary for Mrs. Elizabeth P. Greenough, *Standard* (Chicago), January 23, 1909, 4.

16. 1860 US Census, Erie County, NY, population schedule, Buffalo, third ward, 464 (112 penned), dwelling 891, family 941, Levi Short; Levi Short, Apparatus for Manufacture of Illuminating-Gas, US Patent 28,720, June 12, 1860; Short to Stanton, March 2, 1862, class 8, letter 176, CRI; "The Greek Fire Bomb Shell," *Evening Star* (Washington, DC), January 22, 1862, 2; "The Greek Fire Bombshell," ibid., January 24, 1862, 3; Levi Short and Lyman B. Smith, "Greek Fire Bomb Shells Correction," ibid., January 25, 1862, 3. The machinations by which Short and his competitors got their inventions tried and purchased are described masterfully in Bruce, *Lincoln and the Tools of War.*

17. Short to Stanton, March 2, 1862, class 8, letter 176, CRI; William D. Whipple for J. E. Wool, General Orders no. 23, Department of Virginia, March 19, 1862, *War of the Rebellion*, ser. 1, vol. 51, 555.

18. Short to Stanton, March 2, 1862, class 8, letter 176, CRI. Despite Short's imaginative spelling, the only word that may need clarification is *orriflammy*, a reference to the battle standard of the king of France during the Middle Ages, known as the oriflamme.

19. "Greek Fire," *Philadelphia Inquirer*, January 1, 1864, 4; Levi Short, Improved Composition for Filling Shells, US Patent 38,424, May 6, 1863; "Progress of the Siege Operations," *New York Times*, October 7, 1863.

20. "Greek Fire," *Evening Star* (Washington, DC), March 14, 1862, 2; "From Fortress Monroe," *Daily Evening Traveller* (Boston), March 27, 1862, 1; "From Below," *Daily Constitutionalist* (Augusta, GA), May 1, 1862, 3.

21. Advertisement for Nixon's Cremorne Gardens, *Frank Leslie's Illustrated Newspaper*, August 2, 1862, 7.

22. "The Incendiary Shell," *Milwaukee Sentinel*, April 15, 1863, 2; "Sailing of One of the New Monitors," *Boston Evening Transcript*, February 11, 1863, 2; Short to Porter (with enclosures), October 26, 1863, *Official Records of the Union and Confederate Navies*, ser. 1, vol. 25, 517–18.

23. Eleventh Maine, *Story of One Regiment*, 143–46; Gillmore, *Engineer and Artillery Operations*, 81, 114–16, 147; Stryker, "Swamp Angel"; "The Bombardment," *Charleston Daily Courier*, August 24, 1863, 1; "Charleston Again Shelled," *Charleston*

Mercury, August 25, 1863; "The Bombardment," *Charleston Daily Courier*, August 25, 1863, 1. Gillmore referred to incendiary shells prepared at the West Point Foundry without identifying them further, but evidence points to their containing Berney's incendiary fluid. O. S. Halsted Jr. to J. G. Foster, January 15, 1865, *War of the Rebellion*, ser. 1, vol. 47, pt. 2, 58; J. W. Ripley to R. P. Parrott, June 3, 1863, H.R. Exec. Doc. No. 40–99, at 353 (1868).

24. Stryker, "Swamp Angel"; Gillmore, *Engineer and Artillery Operations*, 81, 115–16, 147; Eleventh Maine, *Story of One Regiment*, 145; "The Bombardment," *Charleston Daily Courier*, August 24, 1863, 1; "Charleston Again Shelled," *Charleston Mercury*, August 25, 1863; "The Greek Fire," *Patriot Union* (Harrisburg, PA), 1; Boynton, "Greek Fire, and Other Inflammables"; "The Bombardment," *Charleston Daily Courier*, August 25, 1863, 1.

25. Gillmore, *Engineer and Artillery Operations*, 114–16.

26. Short to E. M. Stanton, October 13, 1863, class 8, letter 250, CRI; "Death of the Inventor of Greek Fire," *Daily National Republican* (Washington, DC), November 27, 1863, 2.

27. "Devil versus Lincoln," *Charleston Daily Courier*, July 27, 1864, 2.

28. Halsted to Lincoln, April 25, 1863, ALP; Alfred Berney, Improved Liquid-Fire Shell or Projectile, US Patent 36,934, November 11, 1862; Bureau of Ordnance, Navy Department, Memorandum in Relation to Birney's Inflammable Fluid, February 20, 1863, ALP. Berney's name was often misspelled as Birney.

29. Wise to O.C. Badger, April 30, 1862, *Official Records of the Union and Confederate Navies*, ser. 1, vol. 7, 293–94; S. Nicholson to William Smith, May 1, 1862, ibid., 299; S. Nicholson to John A. Dahlgren, February 20, 1863, ALP; William F. Barry to S. Williams, May 5, 1862, *War of the Rebellion*, ser. 1, vol. 11, pt. 1, 338–49; Bureau of Ordnance, Navy Department, Memorandum in Relation to Birney's Inflammable Fluid, February 20, 1863, ALP.

30. Benét to J. W. Ripley, April 10, 1863, ALP. Captain Benét was the grandfather of the author bearing the same name.

31. Halsted to Lincoln, April 25, 1863, ALP.

32. "Why the Shelling of Charleston Was Discontinued" and "The Greek Fire Shells," *Daily Evening Traveller* (Boston), September 16, 1863, 2; Alfred Berney, Improved Liquid-Fire Shell or Projectile, US Patent 36,934, November 11, 1862; Halsted to J. G. Foster, January 5, 1865, *War of the Rebellion*, ser. 1, vol., 47, pt. 2, 58; Benét to J. W. Ripley, April 10, 1863, ALP.

33. Advertisement for Alfred Berney & Co., *Philadelphia Inquirer*, May 23, 1864, 7; Mohr, *Timber Pines*, 67–72; "Some of the Benefits of War," *North American and United States Gazette* (Philadelphia), October 24, 1864, 2; *Annual Report of the American Institute*, 273–75.

34. Abbot, *Siege Artillery*, 97–98; H. H. Pierce to H. L. Abbot, November 19, 1864, *War of the Rebellion*, ser. 1, vol. 42, pt. 3, 664–65; "The Army of the James," *New York Daily Tribune*, December 1, 1864, 1; Lyman, *Meade's Headquarters*, 282–84.

35. Fleming to Abraham Lincoln, February 8, 1864, ALP; advertisement for "Gen. Fleming's wonderfully destructive shell," *Daily National Intelligencer* (Washington, DC), March 12, 1862, 3.

36. Fleming to Abraham Lincoln, February 8, 1864, ALP.

37. Abbot, *Siege Artillery*, 97–99.

3. THE TORCH FOR THE TORCH

1. Gillmore to Beauregard, August 21, 1863, *War of the Rebellion*, ser. 1, vol. 28, pt. 2, 57; Beauregard to Gillmore, August 22, 1863, ibid., 58–59.

2. Gillmore to Beauregard, August 22, 1863, ibid., 59–60; "The Duty of the Hour," *Charleston Daily Courier*, July 10, 1863, 1; Barnes and Barnes, *American Civil War through British Eyes*, 98–99.

3. "Particulars of the Bombardment of the City," *Daily Evening Traveller* (Boston), August 31, 1863, 2; C. C. Fulton, "Siege of Charleston," *New York Daily Reformer*, August 27, 1863, 3; R. S. Ripley to unknown, April 16, 1861, *War of the Rebellion*, ser. 1, vol. 1, 39–43; "Greek Fire," *Boston Evening Transcript*, August 29, 1863, 1; "Greek Fire—What It Is—Its History," *Nashville Daily Union*, September 11, 1863, 3.

4. Oscar G. Sawyer, "Mr. Oscar G. Sawyer's Dispatches," *New York Herald*, January 19, 1864, 3.

5. "Prenticeania," *Evening Star* (Washington, DC), September 10, 1863, 4.

6. "Halleck Improved," *Nashville Daily Union*, September 6, 1863, 2. The poem was a parody of Fitz-Greene Halleck's "Marco Bozzaris."

7. "Greek Fire Thrown into Charleston," *New York Daily News*, August 28, 1863, 4.

8. "Latest Intelligence: America," *Times* (London), September 9, 1863, 6; "The Civil War in America," *Illustrated Times* (London), September 12, 1863, 2.

9. "The Spirit of the Siege," *Charleston Daily Courier*, June 29, 1864, 1.

10. "An Eye for an Eye," *Richmond Whig*, December 4, 1863, 2.

11. "Greek Fire," *New York Daily Tribune*, October 8 1863, 4; "John Bull's Horror of Greek Fire," *New York Ledger*, December 19, 1863, 4; "Greek-Fire," *Chambers's Journal*; "The Southern Confederacy," *Times* (London), January 23, 1864, 25.

12. Friswell, *About in the World*, 199; "A Plan to Raise the Blockade," *Macon (GA) Telegraph*, July 4, 1861; "Southern Greek Fire," *New Age* (Philadelphia), November 5, 1863, 2; "Liquid Fire," *Charleston Mercury*, March 22, 1862, 2. Travis was called both "Captain" and "Colonel." He reportedly claimed that he had been a Confederate ordnance officer, but no confirmatory service record has been found. "Sporting Sundries," *Daily Illinois State Register* (Springfield), February 25, 1883, 1; Ben C. Truman, "Some Glances Backward," *New York Times*, October 17, 1886; Anderson to Gist, November 27, 1860, file for Hester Anderson, Confederate Papers, roll 17.

13. Investigation of Navy Department, September 19 and 26, 1862, *Official Records of the Union and Confederate Navies*, ser. 2, vol. 1, 521, 558–59; voucher, December 5, 1861, file for Quinby & Robinson, Confederate Papers, roll 831.

14. Special Orders no. 54, paragraph 2, March 2, 1863, Special Orders and Circulars, Department of South Carolina, Georgia, and Florida, Military Commands, War Department Collection of Confederate Records (RG 109), vol. 40, ch. 2; Cheves to Beauregard, February 10, 1864, *War of the Rebellion*, ser. 1, vol. 35, pt. 1, 595–97; O'Neall, *Biographical Sketches*, 133–39; "Captains Langdon Cheves, Charles T. Haskell, Jr., and William T. Haskell," *Charleston Mercury*, July 23, 1863, 2; "Balloons for the South," *Charleston Daily Courier*, July 8, 1862, 4; Ward, *List of Cadets*, 19; "Medical College of the State of South-Carolina," *Charleston Courier*, March 15, 1838, 2; Leo. D. Walker for R. S. Ripley, Special Orders no. 355, May 8, 1862, *War of the Rebellion*, ser. 1, vol. 14, 496–97; Cheves to Rachel Susan Cheves, June 7, 1862, Rachel Susan (Bee) Cheves Papers; Cheves to Beauregard, December 9, 1862, *War of the Rebellion*, ser. 1, vol. 14, 705–7; Thomas Jordan to Cheves, December 18, 1862, ibid., 723–24.

15. Cheves to Beauregard, February 10, 1864, *War of the Rebellion*, ser. 1, vol. 35, pt. 1, 595–97; Norton, "Liquid Fire and Spherical Shells"; Jones to Beauregard, March 30, 1863, Compiled Service Records of Confederate General and Staff Officers, and Nonregimental Enlisted Men (hereafter cited as Compiled Service Records); Breeden, *Joseph Jones*.

16. Jones to Beauregard, March 30, 1863, Compiled Service Records.

17. Cheves to Thomas Jordan, April 2, 1863, file for Cheves, Confederate Papers, roll 161; Charles C. Jones Jr. to George A. Mercer, September 5, 1863, *War of the Rebellion*, ser. 1, vol. 28, pt. 2, 340–42.

18. Cheves to Thomas Jordan, April 2, 1863, file for Cheves, Confederate Papers, roll 161; Cheves to Jordan (with endorsements), September 12, 1863, *War of the Rebellion*, ser. 1, vol. 28, pt. 2, 357–58; Riethmiller, "Charles H. Winston"; Hasegawa, "'Absurd Prejudice'"; I. M. St. John to James A. Seddon, *War of the Rebellion*, ser. 4, vol. 3, 695–702; Beauregard to Gorgas, October 25, 1863, file for Cheves, Confederate Papers, roll 161.

19. Cheves to Thomas Jordan, October 1, 1863, *War of the Rebellion*, ser. 1, vol. 28, pt. 2, 386; Cheves to Jordan, April 2, 1863, file for Cheves, Confederate Papers, roll 161; Cheves to Beauregard, February 10, 1864, *War of the Rebellion*, ser. 1, vol. 35, pt. 1, 595–97; Beauregard to Cheves, February 24, 1864, ibid., 641; Jordan to J. F. Gilmer, January 8, 1864, ibid., 513; Cheves to Jordan, November 1, 1863, file for Cheves, Confederate Papers, roll 161.

20. Beauregard to Cheves, February 24, 1864, *War of the Rebellion*, ser. 1, vol. 35, pt. 1, 641; Lawton to A. S. Pendleton, ibid., vol. 11, pt. 2, 594–96; John R. Cheves to Langon Cheves, July 2, 1862, Rachel Susan (Bee) Cheves Papers; "Captains Langdon Cheves, Charles T. Haskell, Jr., and William T. Haskell," *Charleston Mercury*, July 23, 1863, 2.

21. "Siege Matters," *Charleston Mercury*, October 13, 1863, 2; Beauregard to Joseph R. Anderson, November 12, 1863, *War of the Rebellion*, ser. 1, vol. 28, pt. 2, 501.

22. E. G. Parrott to S. F. DuPont, March 5, 1863, *Official Records of the Union and Confederate Navies*, ser. 1, vol. 13, 592–93; "Wounds and Complications: Firearms

and Their Projectiles," *Medical and Surgical History*, pt. 3, vol. 2., 695–701; Gibbon, *Artillerist's Manual*, 336–37, 466; "Gen. Beauregard's Greek Fire," November 5, 1863, *Daily National Intelligencer* (Washington, DC), 2; "Destruction of Georgetown, S.C.," *New York Daily Tribune*, December 25, 1863, 1; Crowley, "Confederate Torpedo Service."

23. William Rodgers Taylor, William Reynolds, and A. S. Mackenzie to S. F. DuPont, June 30, 1863, *Official Records of the Union and Confederate Navies*, ser. 1, vol. 14, 278–79; "The Rebels Purpose to Burn Philadelphia and New York with Greek Fire," *Daily National Republican* (Washington, DC), October 6, 1863, 2.

24. Rains and Michie, *Confederate Torpedoes*, 21–22, 66–68, 77–78. An even earlier concept for a binary weapon, employing phosphorus and potassium chlorate, has been attributed to chemist Frederick Accum for use in the early 1800s by the British against French naval vessels. Browne, "Early References."

25. Thomas Jordan to R. S. Ripley, January 15, 1863, *War of the Rebellion*, ser. 1, vol. 14, 749–50; Mallory to William A. Webb, February 19, 1863, *Official Records of the Union and Confederate Navies*, ser. 1, vol. 13, 820–21.

26. Sengstack to Gorgas (with endorsements), November 2, 1863, Sengstack to unknown, July 23, 1863, and receipt, November 5, 1863, all in file for C. P. Seugstack [*sic*], Compiled Service Records of Confederate Soldiers Who Served in Organizations from the State of Virginia (hereafter cited as Compiled Service Records Virginia); Special Orders no. 36, para. 2, February 13, 1862, Adjutant and Inspector General's Office; Special Orders no. 103, para. 12, May 5, 1862, Adjutant and Inspector General's Office; Special Orders no. 262, para. 29, November 4, 1863.

27. File 6975, November 21, 1863, Union Provost Marshal's File of Papers Relating to Individual Citizens; News item, *Alexandria (VA) Gazette*, November 23, 1863, 2; voucher, January 4, 1864, file for C. P. Seugstack [*sic*], Compiled Service Records Virginia.

28. "The Plot," *New York Times*, November 27, 1864; Walling, *Recollections*, 93; Seddon to McCulloh, January 19, 1865, *War of the Rebellion*, ser. 4, vol. 3, 37–38; Oldham to Davis, February 11, 1865, ibid., 1078–79; "Washington Notes," *New York Times*, August 6, 1872, 4; Thomas, "Professor McCulloh"; *Resolutions*, 120; vouchers, file for Richard S. McCulloh, Confederate Papers, roll 623; McCulloh to Davis (with endorsements), July 29, 1864, file for Richard S. McCulloch [*sic*], Confederate Papers, roll 623; Singer, *Confederate Dirty War*, 98–117.

29. Auld, *Gas and Flame*, 185–201; "German Account of the Flame Throwers"; Rottman, *Vietnam Riverine Craft*, 12, 47; Department of the Army, *Chemical Weapons and Munitions*, 2-3-2-4; Report of the Secretary of the Navy, S. Exec. Doc. No. 30-1 at 1306–10 (1847); Department of the Army, *Military Explosives*, 2-1-2-23.

30. "Fenian Fire"; "A Greek Fire Manufactory Discovered in Dublin," *New York Times*, December 13, 1866; Fries and West, *Chemical Warfare*, 311–12, 336, 393.

4. NO LIVING BEING WILL ESCAPE

1. Jones to Beauregard, March 30, 1863, Compiled Service Records.

2. Cheves to Thomas Jordan, April 2, 1863, file for Cheves, Confederate Papers, roll 161.

3. "A Novel Method of Taking Pickens," *Daily Dispatch* (Richmond), June 4, 1861, 1.

4. Baskin et al., "Cyanide Poisoning," 372–73; Curry, *Volunteers' Camp and Field Book*, 42; Breeden, *Joseph Jones*, 115–16.

5. Jones, *Medical and Surgical Memoirs*, 296–331; Tucker, *War of Nerves*, 44–45; Moore and Gates, "Hydrogen Cyanide and Cyanogen Chloride," 7; Fries and West, *Chemical Warfare*, 365.

6. "Nevada Killer Faces Death by Lethal Gas," *Evening Repository* (Canton, OH), May 30, 1930, 12; "Colorado Will Substitute Gas for Death Knot," *San Diego Union*, October 22, 1933, 7; "Moroccan Authorities"; "Special Report"; "How Tokyo Barely Escaped Even Deadlier Subway Attack," *New York Times*, May 18, 1995.

7. Tucker, *War of Nerves*, 160–61, 178–80, 224–26, 246–47; Browne, "Early References"; Haber, *Poisonous Cloud*, 62. Technical problems prevented production of the Bigeye bomb, whereas production of the M687 shell began in late 1987. International arms-reduction agreements led to destruction of the weapons' munitions bodies (completed in 1999) and their precursor chemicals (completed in 2006). U.S. Army Chemical Materials Activity, Treaty Milestones.

8. Haber, *Poisonous Cloud*, 41–42, 62–63; Fries and West, *Chemical Warfare*, 21–27; Lefebure, *Riddle of the Rhine*, 22; Moore and Gates, "Hydrogen Cyanide and Cyanogen Chloride," 8; War Department, *Handbook on Japanese Military Forces*, 214; "Chemical Warfare," 15.

9. Tucker, *War of Nerves*, 225–26.

10. Young, *Generation of Hydrocyanic Acid Gas*.

11. Bache, *System of Chemistry*, 235; Mitchell, *Elements of Chemical Philosophy*, 256; Christison, *Treatise on Poisons*, 598; Jones, *Medical and Surgical Memoirs*, 296–97.

12. Faraday, "On Fumigation"; Bentley and Redwood, *Dr. Pereira's*, 218.

13. Jones to Beauregard, March 30, 1863; Morgan, *Organic Compounds*, 1–19; Roscoe, "Robert Wilhelm Bunsen"; Johnston, *Chemistry of Common Life*, 294–96.

14. "Captain Warner's Invention."

15. Reid, *Memoirs and Correspondence*, 159–160.

16. "Naval and Military Intelligence," *Times* (London), September 18, 1854, 10; Johnston, *Chemistry of Common Life*, 294; Miles, "Chemical Warfare in the Civil War."

17. "Asphyxiating Explosions," *Daily Dispatch* (Richmond), May 14, 1861, 2; "Asphyxiating Shells against Iron-Clads," *Daily Chronicle & Sentinel* (Augusta, GA), March 25, 1863, 2; Boynton, "Greek Fire, and Other Inflammables"; Nutt, *Newburgh*, 191–92.

18. Jones to Beauregard, March 30, 1863.

19. "Resources of Modern Warfare," 694.

20. Haber, *Poisonous Cloud*, 26; Lefebure, *Riddle of the Rhine*, 31.

21. "Washington Notes," *New York Times*, August 6, 1872, 4; Bunsen, "Researches on the Cacodyl Series," 297.

22. "A Novel Method of Taking Pickens," *Daily Dispatch* (Richmond), June 4, 1861, 1; Centers for Disease Control and Prevention, "Facts about Arsine"; Condon to Pickens, January 11, 1861, Papers of David Flavel Jamison.

23. Haber, *Poisonous Cloud*, 62, 114–16, 211; Fries and West, *Chemical Warfare*, 22–27, 180–89; Gates et al., "Arsenicals," 98–99.

5. PORTENDING THE GREEN CLOUD

1. Doughty to Lincoln, April 5, 1862, special file 26-B (TR-3), Special Files, 1790–1946, entry 286, Records of the Adjutant General's Office (RG 94); Doughty to Lincoln (with endorsement), May 1, 1862, class 8, letter 191, CRI; Doughty to Ripley, July 11, 1862, classes 4 & 5, letter 636, CRI; Doughty to Ripley, August 1864, classes 4 & 5, letter 859, CRI.

2. Doughty to Lincoln, April 5, 1862; Coxe, "Reminiscences of the Effects of Chlorine."

3. Doughty to Lincoln, April 5, 1862; Doughty to Ripley, July 11, 1862; Doughty to Ripley, August 1864, CRI; Tutton, "Properties of Liquid Chlorine." Where Doughty got his information about "chemical shell & stink-pots" is unknown; the terms do not describe anything known to have been used in the Civil War.

4. Nutt, *Newburgh*, 112–13; Medical Department of the University of the State of New-York, *Annual Catalogue*, 7; John W. Doughty and B. F. Olmstead, Improvement in Boiler Feeders, US Patent 62,258, February 19, 1867; *Proceedings of the American Association for the Advancement of Science*, 81.

5. Haber, *Poisonous Cloud*, 22–42; "What Gas Means: A Visit to a French Hospital," *Times* (London), May 7, 1915, 25.

6. Haber, *Poisonous Cloud*, 22–40, 151–52; Ornstein, "Liquid Chlorine"; Newman, *Metallic Structure*, 23–25; Gibbon, *Artillerist's Manual*, 153.

7. Haber, *Poisonous Cloud*, 64, 93; Fries and West, *Chemical Warfare*, 16, 395; Tutton, "Properties of Liquid Chlorine"; Fries, "Gas in Attack"; Prentiss, *Chemicals in War*, 75.

8. Doughty to Ripley, August 1864. In his calculations, Doughty rounded upward by assuming that each of the one hundred shells would cover a square of 100 feet per side (10,000 square feet, or 0.23 acre) rather than a circle with a 100-foot diameter (7,854 square feet, or 0.18 acre). He also misstated the dimensions of the line of fortifications; it would have been 100 rather than 200 feet wide. The calculations assumed no overlap of shell bursts.

9. Ibid.; Haber, *Poisonous Cloud*, 43–44, 64, Prentiss, *Chemicals in War*, 35, 76. The chlorine concentration currently indicated by the National Institute

for Occupational Safety and Health as being "immediately dangerous to life or health" is 10 parts per million (ppm) (29 mg/m³). Centers for Disease Control and Prevention, "Immediately Dangerous to Life or Health Concentrations (IDLH): Chlorine."

10. Doughty to Ripley, August 1864; Haber, *Poisonous Cloud*, 64, 193–94; Fries, "Gas in Attack."

11. Doughty to Lincoln, April 5, 1862.

12. Ibid.; Prentiss, *Chemicals in War*, 496; Haber, *Poisonous Cloud*, 64; Gibbon, *Artillerist's Manual*, 250.

13. Doughty to Lincoln, April 5, 1862.

14. Wakabayashi, "Documents on Japanese Poison Gas"; Jones et al., "Chlorine Gas"; *Bulk Storage of Liquid Chlorine*, 4; Loveday Morris, "U.S. Looks into Syrian Claims of Gas Attack," *Washington Post*, April 14, 2014, A8.

15. Haber, *Poisonous Cloud*, 45; Nasmith, "Poison Gases in Warfare"; Wood and Bache, *Dispensatory of the United States*, 1427–28; "Improvement in Paper Manufacture"; Kahlbaum and Darbishire, *Letters of Faraday and Schoenbein*, 173–77; Stenhouse, "On the Deodorising and Disinfecting Properties"; Wilson, "Description of Dr. J. Stenhouse's Charcoal Respirator." Although Stenhouse initially claimed that his charcoal respirator was effective against chlorine, he later said in 1872 that it was not. It could be made effective, he said, by treating it with ammonia fumes. Stenhouse, "Charcoal Respirator."

16. Fries and West, *Chemical Warfare*, 116–17.

17. *Waite's Newburgh City Directory*, 194.

6. INSINUATING DUST

1. "Prof. John B. Brigham: Death of a Pioneer in Educational Matters in Syracuse," *Syracuse (NY) Weekly Express*, March 26, 1891, 7; Smith, *History of the Schools*, 54, 61, 63, 64, 70; Brigham to Hiram Putnam, June 11, 1850, Hiram Putnam Papers; Strong, *Early Landmarks of Syracuse*, 271–95; Valentine, "Trial Extraordinary"; *Thirteenth Annual Report*, 35–36; Stanton et al., *History of Woman Suffrage*, 517–28; *Proceedings of the Woman's Right Convention*, 35–36, 66; Brigham to Lincoln (with endorsement), March 11, 1862, Letters Received Relating to Ordnance Inventions (entry 143), Records of the Bureau of Ordnance (RG 74).

2. Brigham to Lincoln (with endorsement), March 11, 1862.

3. Ibid.; "A Well-Seasoned Proposition," *New York Daily Tribune*, March 17, 1862, 5; "More Plans," *Plain Dealer* (Cleveland), March 19, 1862, 2.

4. "Pickens to Be Taken with Red Pepper!," *Boston Herald*, May 23, 1861, 1; Wood and Bache, *Dispensatory of the United States*, 1339–44; Harris to Simon Cameron, May 17, 1861, classes 4 & 5, letter 229, CRI; "The Very Last Military Device," *Evening Star* (Washington, DC), August 17, 1861, 2; Vincent Fountain Jr. to Lincoln, August 12, 1861, classes 4 & 5, letter 369, CRI; William Johnson to Secretary of War, September 13, 1861, classes 4 & 5, letter 410, CRI; J. T. Vanderhoof to Cameron,

September 21, 1861, classes 4 & 5, letter 397, CRI; H. C. Comegys to Cameron, October 28, 1861, classes 4 & 5, letter 434, CRI; D. A. Pease to Cameron, November 29, 1861, class misc., letter 249, CRI; "Notes and Queries," May 24, 1862.

5. Fountain to Lincoln, August 12, 1861, classes 4 & 5, letter 369, CRI; Harris to Simon Cameron, May 17, 1861, classes 4 & 5, letter 229, CRI.

6. Pease to Cameron, November 29, 1861, class misc., letter 249, CRI; Pease and Pease, *Genealogical and Historical Record*, 230–31.

7. G. W. Foster [on behalf of Orman Coe] to Alexander W. Randall, August 23, 1864, ALP.

8. Birbeck to Edwin M. Stanton, August 19, 1862, class misc., letter 337, CRI; Comegys to Cameron, October 28, 1861, classes 4 & 5, letter 434, CRI; *Portrait and Biographical Record*, 407–8; "Hammond General Hospital"; Vanderhoof to Cameron, September 21, 1861, classes 4 & 5, letter 397, CRI; *Trow's New York City Directory*, 872; Fountain to Lincoln, August 12, 1861, classes 4 & 5, letter 369, CRI; Isaac Clough and Vincent Fountain Jr., Automaton-Dancer, US Patent 43759, August 9, 1864; Vincent Fountain Jr., Improved Potato Masher, US Patent 60355, December 11, 1866; Babcock to Secretary of War, January 5, 1863, classes 4 & 5, letter 710, CRI; *History of Fond du Lac County*, 939–40; Johnson to Secretary of War, September 13, 1861, classes 4 & 5, letter 410, CRI.

9. De, *Capsicum*, 5; Andrews, *Peppers*, 85; Needham, *Science and Civilization in China*, vol. 5, pt. 7, 268; "A Sneezing Court," *Rock River Democrat* (Rockford, IL), May 2, 1854, 1; "A Novel Finale," *Cleveland Daily Plain Dealer*, May 2, 1857, 2; news item, *Daily Evening Traveller* (Boston), October 22, 1863, 1; "An Ugly Trick," 136; Birbeck to Edwin M. Stanton, August 19, 1862, class misc., letter 337.

10. Wood and Bache, *Dispensatory of the United States*, 179–82, 716–20, 755–60; Dunglison, *New Remedies*, 680; Gordon & Bro., *Prices Current*, 14.

11. D. A. Pease to Cameron, November 29, 1861, class misc., letter 249, CRI; William Johnson to Secretary of War, September 13, 1861, classes 4 & 5, letter 410, CRI; Adelia Babcock to Secretary of War, January 5, 1863, classes 4 & 5, letter 710, CRI; G. W. Foster to Alexander W. Randall, August 23, 1864, ALP; Vincent Fountain Jr. to Lincoln, August 12, 1861, classes 4 & 5, letter 369; W. C. Kellogg to H. B. Stanton, February 23, 1863, classes 4 & 5, letter 726, CRI.

12. Maisch, "Report on the Drug Market"; "Wanted," *Hillsborough (NC) Recorder*, November 5, 1862, 4; "Wilmington Auction Sales," *Daily Chronicle & Sentinel* (Augusta, GA), June 11, 1863. In November 1862, the price of a federal greenback dollar was $2 in Confederate notes, and in May 1863, the price was $3.25. Lancaster & Co., Table of Prices in Confederate Currency of Gold and Greenbacks, February 19, 1866, Burton Norvell Harrison Family Papers, accessed December 25, 2013, http://prod.myloc.gov/Exhibitions/civil-war-in-america/december-1862-october-1863/ExhibitObjects/Inflation-in-the-Confederacy.aspx.

13. PepperBall FAQs, accessed December 25, 2013, http://pepperballproducts.com/PepperBall_FAQ_s.html.

14. Advertisement for Sayle's Garden Engine, *New England Farmer, and Horticultural Register*, May 31, 1843, 383; advertisement for Garden Engine, *Newark (NJ) Daily Advertiser*, March 15, 1853, 3; Henderson, *Gardening for Pleasure*, 375; Lyman, *Meade's Headquarters*, 282–84.

15. Wood and Bache, *Dispensatory of the United States*, 1113, 1294; Salem et al., "Inhalation Toxicology," 502–5; Reilly et al., "Quantitative Analysis."

16. *Treatise of Walter de Milemete*, xxxiv–xxxv, 154–55; Loades, "*History Channel*,"; Cochrane, *Autobiography of a Seaman*, 201; Page, *Letters of a War Correspondent*, 164–65; "General Butler an Inventor"; Reeves, "Military Use of Kites."

17. "Bombardment by Electro-Magnetism," *Boston Courier*, March 1, 1849, 4; "Aerial Warfare," *Daily Evening Transcript* (Boston), July 18, 1849, 1; Charles Perley, Improvement in Discharging Explosive Shells from Balloons, US Patent 37,771, February 24, 1863; Mikesh, *Japan's World War II Balloon Bomb Attacks*.

18. Wise, *Lifeline of the Confederacy*, 245.

19. "Going to Nassau," *Daily Dispatch* (Richmond), January 25, 1864, 1.

20. Taylor, *Running the Blockade*, 80.

21. "Antiquity of Military Asphyxiation"; Report of the Board of Ordnance and Fortification, H.R. Exec. Doc. No. 52-12 at 2 (1892); "Military Use of Sabadilla"; Haber, *Poisonous Cloud*, 51; "India Deploys World's Hottest Chilli to Fight Terrorism," *Guardian* (London), March 23, 2010, accessed December 21, 2013, http://www.theguardian.com/world/2010/mar/23/india-chilli-jolokia-terrorism.

22. Fries, "Gas in Attack."

23. Pease to Simon Cameron, November 29, 1861, class misc., letter 249, CRI; Harris to Cameron, May 17, 1861, classes 4 & 5, letter 229, CRI.

7. PROSTRATED BY INHALING IT

1. Foute, "Echoes from Hampton Roads."

2. Ibid.; "Local Intelligence," *Philadelphia Inquirer*, May 20, 1862, 8; Byers, "Statement Relating to the 'Merrimac,' etc."; Parker, *Recollections of a Naval Officer*, 273; Bennett, *Monitor and the Navy*, 136–37.

3. Thompson and Wainwright, *Confidential Correspondence*, 263–65. The Goldsborough correspondence appears to have drawn the attention of US chemical weapons personnel in 1937. "Early Projected Gas Attack."

4. Wood and Bache, *Dispensatory of the United States*, 884–94; Chapman, *Chloroform and Other Anaesthetics*, 20–22; Bollet, *Civil War Medicine*, 76–81; "Ether vs. Chloroform," *Evening Bulletin* (San Francisco), September 26, 1859, 4; advertisement for P. H. Derby, Dentist, *Springfield (MA) Republican*, February 2, 1861, 3; "Scientific Robbery," *North American and United States Gazette* (Philadelphia), April 8, 1851, 2; "Garroted by Means of Chloroform," *Cleveland Daily Plain Dealer*, November 3, 1857, 2; Warren, *Effects of Chloroform*, 35–36.

5. Bennett to Stanton, August 6, 1862, classes 4 & 5, letter 656, CRI; F. A. Stanton to E. M. Stanton, January 28, 1864, class 8, letter 279, CRI.

6. Coulter to Stanton (with endorsements), July 11, 1862, and Watson to Coulter, July 24, 1864, class misc., letter 322, CRI; "Notes and Queries," May 24, 1862; "Notes and Queries," June 15, 1861.

7. Freedley, *Leading Pursuits and Leading Men*, 172, 176; Robert B. Potts and Frederick K. Klett, Improved Apparatus for the Manufacture of Superphosphate of Lime, US Patent 45631, December 27, 1864; advertisement for Rhodes' Super-Phosphate, *Charleston Mercury*, March 14, 1862, 4; Jones, *First Report*, 57–91; "Terrible Tornado!," *Philadelphia Inquirer*, July 27, 1860, 1.

8. *Report of the Philadelphia College of Pharmacy*, 16; Potts, *Historical Collections*, 499; *University of Pennsylvania: Biographical Catalogue*, 149; England, *First Century of the Philadelphia College of Pharmacy*, 56, 107.

9. Potts & Klett's Chemical Works to Simon Cameron, November 22, 1861, classes 4 & 5, letter 452, CRI; Potts & Klett's to Edwin M. Stanton, June 10, 1862, classes 4 & 5, letter 624, CRI. The letters were signed "Pott's & Klett" in handwriting that matches a known sample of Potts's signature. Potts, *Historical Collections*, 499.

10. Baskerville, "Chemistry of Anesthetics"; Gregory, "Notes on the Purification and Properties of Chloroform"; Rabald, *Corrosion Guide*, 179.

11. "Notes and Queries," June 15, 1861.

12. Sansom, *Chloroform*, 25.

13. "Chloroform amongst Thieves"; Snow, "Further Remarks on the Employment of Chloroform by Thieves"; Sansom, *Chloroform*, 28; Amoore and Hautala, "Odor as an Aid to Chemical Safety." The belief that chloroform acts instantaneously and is thus useful in crime persists today. Payne, "Criminal Use of Chloroform."

14. Centers for Disease Control and Prevention, "Immediately Dangerous to Life or Health Concentrations (IDLH): Chloroform"; Featherstone, "Chloroform"; Haber, *Poisonous Cloud*, 41–44. Concentrations given by Haber in milligrams per cubic meter were converted to parts per million.

15. Haydon, "Proposed Gas Shell"; *Caoutchouc and Gutta Percha*, 177; "Shand and Mason's Steam Fire Engine"; United States Vulcanized Gutta Percha Belting and Packing Co., *Gutta Percha*, 27. The citation here of Haydon's article, which contains an account of Lott's proposal, is the only instance in this book in which the primary source for a proposal submitted as a letter to a government official is not cited; Lott's letter could not be located in archival repositories.

16. Potts & Klett's Chemical Works to Simon Cameron, November 22, 1861; Squibb, "Report on the Drug Market."

17. "Running the Blockade—Sale of the Goods," *Daily Richmond Examiner*, March 13, 1862, 3; "Auction Prices in Charleston of Foreign Importations," *Daily Chronicle & Sentinel* (Augusta, GA), May 3, 1863, 3; "Blockade Sale," *Charleston Mercury*, June 20, 1863, 1; "Wilmington Auction Sales," *Daily Chronicle & Sentinel* (Augusta, GA), June 11, 1863, 3; Ashhurst & Co. to William H. Prioleau, July 8, 1862, Letters, Telegrams, Orders, and Circulars Received at Savannah and Macon, 1862–65, Medical Department, War Department Collection of Confederate Records

(RG 109), vol. 566, ch. 6; Riethmiller, "Charles H. Winston"; Hasegawa, "'Absurd Prejudice'"; Hasegawa and Hambrecht, "Confederate Medical Laboratories." In March 1862, the price of a federal greenback dollar was $1.15 in Confederate notes; in May 1863, the price was $3.25; and in June 1863, the price was $4.00. Lancaster & Co., Table of Prices in Confederate Currency of Gold and Greenbacks, February 19, 1866, Burton Norvell Harrison Family Papers, accessed December 25, 2013, http://prod.myloc.gov/Exhibitions/civil-war-in-america/december-1862-october-1863/ExhibitObjects/Inflation-in-the-Confederacy.aspx.

8. DESTROYING FLUIDS

1. *History of Cincinnati and Hamilton County*, 1009; Coffin, *Reminiscences*, ii–iii, 147; Siebert, *Underground Railroad*, 64; "Cincinnati Anti-Slavery Convention," *Anti-slavery Bugle* (Salem, OH), April 5, 1851, 115; "Anti-Slavery Convention in Cincinnati," April 12, 1854, *Boston Herald*, 2; Goss, *Cincinnati*, 193–94; Message of the President of the United States, S. Exec. Doc. No. 38-1 (1864). One of Levi Coffin's efforts to assist a runaway slave was dramatized in Harriet Beecher Stowe's *Uncle Tom's Cabin*.

2. Harwood to Stanton, November 13, 1862, classes 4 & 5, letter 695, CRI.

3. Meader to Chief of Ordnance, September 6, 1862, classes 4 & 5, letter 681, CRI.

4. 1860 US Census, Philadelphia County, PA, population schedule, First Division, Fourteenth Ward, 230 (230 penned), dwelling 1465, family 1631, Meader family; "Catalogue of the Class of the Philadelphia College of Pharmacy."

5. Sutherland, *Indianapolis Directory*, 133; Fahnestock to Chief of Ordnance, August 15, 1861, classes 4 & 5, letter 372, CRI.

6. "First Artificial Leg on Display at Dyke Museum, Other Exhibits," *Wellsville (NY) Daily Reporter*, May 27, 1975, 5; Tuttle, *Descendants of William and Elizabeth Tuttle*, 268–69; David B. Marks, Artificial Leg, US Patent 10611, March 7, 1854; Marks, *Treatise on Artificial Limbs*, 11; *Encyclopedia of Connecticut Biography*, 12; Eisenstadt, *Encyclopedia of New York State*, 1703; Smythe to Lincoln, August 20, 1861, classes 4 & 5, letter 380, CRI.

7. 1860 US Census, Bracken County, KY, population schedule, District no. 1, 179 (35 penned), dwelling 238, family 238, John Dobyns; Dobyns to Cameron, August 17, 1861, class misc., letter 218, CRI.

8. *Obituary Record of Graduates of Yale University*, 490; Chapman, *Sketches of the Alumni of Dartmouth College*, 239; Forrest Shepherd, White Paint, US Patent 284, March 18, 1835; Forrest Shepherd, Improved White Water-Color Paint, US Patent 285, July 17, 1837; Forrest Shepherd, Tree-Protector, US Patent 44,667, October 11, 1864.

9. Shepherd to Lincoln, June 22, 1864, special file 26-A (TR-2), entry 286, Special Files, 1790–1946, Records of the Adjutant General's Office (RG 94). The first public mention of Shepherd's idea may have been in a short newspaper article, "Urged Use of Gas at Petersburg," *Saturday Star* (Washington, DC), November 19, 1933, A-13.

10. Wood and Bache, *Dispensatory of the United States*, 39.

11. Cheves to Thomas Jordan, September 12, 1863, *War of the Rebellion*, ser. 1, vol. 28, pt. 2, 357–58; Freedley, *Philadelphia and Its Manufactures*, 109–10; James Guthrie, Letter from the Secretary of the Treasury, H.R. Exec. Doc. No. 33-74, at 22–23, 187–91 (1854); *Industry of Nations*, 332–39.

12. "A Flare Up—Throwing Vitriol," *Newport (RI) Mercury*, April 6, 1850, 3; "A Fiendish Outrage," *Evening Bulletin* (San Francisco), August 19, 1856, 2; "An Actor Throws Vitriol in His Wife's Face," *Daily Ohio Statesman* (Columbus), June 27, 1860, 2; "A Fiendish Act—A Pound of Vitriol Thrown in a Man's Face!," *Rockford (IL) Republican*, November 8, 1860, 1; "Shocking Charge If True," *Daily Picayune* (New Orleans), April 8, 1853, 4; "Examination of Margaret Desmond for an Assault with Nitric Acid," *Evening Bulletin* (San Francisco), February 27, 1857, 3; "Desperation of a Jealous Girl," *American Traveller* (Boston), September 26, 1863, 4.

13. Taylor, *Medical Jurisprudence*, 419.

14. Cooper, *Wounds and Injuries of the Eye*, 265.

15. Smythe to Lincoln, August 20, 1861; Harwood to Stanton, November 13, 1862, CRI; Dobyns to Cameron, August 17, 1861; Meader to Chief of Ordnance, September 6, 1862.

16. Gardner, *Medical Chemistry*, 197; Fahnestock to Chief of Ordnance, August 15, 1861; Shepherd to Lincoln, June 22, 1864.

17. Richardson, "Greek Fire"; Meader to Chief of Ordnance, September 6, 1862; Dobyns to Cameron, August 17, 1861.

18. Fahnestock to Chief of Ordnance, August 15, 1861.

19. Auld, *Gas and Flame*, 125.

20. Bullock and Crenshaw, *Catalogue*, 3; Freedley, *Philadelphia and Its Manufactures*, 206–11; Accounts, Account Books, Depot of the Macon Office, 1862–65, Medical Department, War Department Collection of Confederate Records (RG 109), vol. 623, ch. 6. The cost of sulfuric acid to the purveyor contrasts with the $7.50 per pound cited by John Cheves. Cheves to Jordan, September 12, 1863, *War of the Rebellion*, ser. 1, vol. 28, pt. 2, 357–58.

21. Tracy Wilkinson, "Iraq Frees 1,135 Kuwaiti Captives; 3,865 Still Held," *Los Angeles Times*, March 22, 1991; Steven R. Hurst and Lauren Frayer, "4 Blasts in Baghdad Kill at Least 183," *Washington Post*, April 19, 2007; "Tanzania Says 15 Are Linked to Acid Attacks," *New York Times*, September 17, 2013.

22. Kalantry and Kestenbaum, "Combating Acid Violence"; "Homemade Chemical Bomb Events and Resulting Injuries"; "Homemade Chemical Bomb Incidents."

9. FIRE AND BRIMSTONE

1. Burton, *Siege of Charleston*, 16–23; "The Tortugas Garrisoned, War Preparations at Charleston, A Night Attack on Fort Sumter, Col. Hayne Still in Washington," *Evening Post* (New York), January 31, 1861; "Letter from Charleston," *Daily National Intelligencer* (Washington, DC), February 4, 1861, 3.

2. "Our Charleston Correspondent," *New York Times*, January 30, 1861.

3. Burton, *Siege of Charleston*, 23, G. T. Beauregard to Samuel Cooper, April 27, 1861, *War of the Rebellion*, ser. 1, vol. 2, ch. 1, 30–35.

4. Mayor, *Greek Fire*, 210–11; James, "Stratagems."

5. Stephenson, *Admiral's Secret Weapon*; Douglas and Ramsay, *Panmure Papers*, 340–42.

6. "How to Destroy Bark-Lice," *California Farmer and Journal of Useful Sciences* (San Francisco), March 21, 1862, 186; "Items," *Boston Recorder*, June 16, 1865, 95; "Kill the Worms," *Evening Post* (New York), June 18, 1858, 2; Miner, *Miner's Domestic Poultry Book*, 177; "Gophers," *Southern Cultivator* (Augusta, GA), March 1859, 94.

7. Riell to Secretary of War, April 25, 1862, class 4&5, letter 576, CRI; Peter and George Lorillard, "Notice," *New York Speculator*, November 5, 1822, 4; Henry Riell and Caleb Williams, "A Card to the Messrs. Lorillards," *Dutchess Observer* (Poughkeepsie, NY), March 12, 1823, 1; Barrett, *Old Merchants of New York City*, 331. Riell's name was often misspelled as Reill.

8. Riell to Secretary of War, April 25, 1862.

9. Fahnestock to Chief of Ordnance, August 15, 1861, class 4&5, letter 372, CRI; Live Yankee to unknown, August 24, 1861, letter 213, class misc., CRI; Read to Secretary of War, March 14, 1863, class 4&5, letter 733, CRI; H. A. Allen, "Do You Know," *Oregon Guardsman* (Salem), October 15, 1929; "Urged Use of Gas at Petersburg," *Sunday Star* (Washington, DC), November 19, 1933.

10. Blackford, *War Years with Jeb Stuart*, 262–63.

11. Needham and Yates, *Science and Civilisation in China*, vol. 5, pt. 6, 464–65; Needham, *Science and Civilisation in China*, vol. 4, pt. 2, 137–38; Lindberg, "Use of Riot Control Agents"; Papacino d'Antoni, *Treatise on Gun-Powder*, 326.

12. Duane, *Military Dictionary*, 322; Cutbush, *System of Pyrotechny*, 506–7.

13. Oliphant, *China*, 180; Simienowicz, *Great Art of Artillery*, 296–97; [Knowlton and Kinsley], *Military Pyrotechny*, 34–35; Brewster, *Edinburgh Encyclopaedia*, 276–77; Cutbush, *System of Pyrotechny*, 506–7.

14. Simienowicz, *Great Art of Artillery*, 296; Johnston, *Chemistry of Common Life*, 294.

15. "The Defenses of Richmond," *World* (New York), May 17, 1864, 6.

16. "A Singular Defense," *Alexandria (VA) Gazette*, May 18, 1864; "Rebel Asphixiated Balls"; Pendleton to Baldwin (with endorsements), June 10, 1864, *War of the Rebellion*, ser. 1, vol. 36, pt. 3, 888–89; Broun, *Dr. William LeRoy Broun*, 1–2.

17. Johnston, *Chemistry of Common Life*, 283–84; "Asphyxiating Shells against Iron-Clads," *Daily Chronicle & Sentinel* (Augusta, GA), March 25, 1863, 2; Short to E. M. Stanton, October 13, 1863, class 8, letter 250, CRI.

18. Fries and West, *Chemical Warfare*, 416; Aaron Zitner, "Best Defense May Be a Good, Offensive Stench," *Los Angeles Times*, November 10, 2002, http://articles.latimes.com/print/2002/nov/10/nation/na-odors10; David Hambling, "US Weapons Research Is Raising a Stink," *Guardian* (London), July 9, 2008, http://

www.theguardian.com/science/2008/jul/10/weaponstechnology.research; David Hambling, "US Military Malodorant Missiles Kick Up a Stink," *New Scientist*, June 4, 2012, http://www.newscientist.com/article/mg21428676.800-us-military-malodorant-missiles-kick-up-a-stink.html; Wyre Davies, "New Israeli Weapon Kicks Up Stink," *BBC News*, October 8, 2008, http://news.bbc.co.uk/2/hi/middle_east/7646894.stm.

10. SHARP HORRORS OF SUNDRY WEAPONS

1. Wells, *History of Newbury, Vermont*, 483; Jordan, *Century and a Half*, 23.

2. Burbank to Cameron, October 24, 1861, class 4&5, letter 429, CRI.

3. Beard, "Examination Questions"; Paris, *Life of Sir Humphry Davy*, 67–69; Christison, *Treatise on Poisons*, 622–24; Taylor, *Medical Jurisprudence*, 841–42; Traill, *Outlines*, 140–41, "Death from Carburetted Hydrogen," *Massachusetts Spy* (Worcester), February 18, 1852, 2; Fries and West, *Chemical Warfare*, 190–91.

4. McGillivray to the President, November 20, 1864, class 8, letter 293, CRI.

5. Hamilton to Stanton, June 18, 1864, class 8, letter 284, CRI.

6. 1860 US Census, Macoupin County, IL, population schedule, Town 11, Range 9, 171, dwelling 1248, family 1196, William B. Stultz; entry for W. B. Stutts, *Illinois State Business Directory*, 370.

7. Walker to L. P. Walker, June 4, 1861, Letters Received by the Confederate Secretary of War, microfilm M437, roll 3, letter 1455, War Department Collection of Confederate Records (RG 109); file for Isham Walker, Compiled Service Records of Confederate Soldiers Who Served in Organizations from the State of Mississippi; *H.R. Journal*, 33rd Cong., 2nd sess., 146 (1854); "Steiner's Balloon Outdone," *Daily Illinois State Register* (Springfield), August 10, 1858, 2; *Journal of the Congress of the Confederate States of America, 1861–1865*, vol. 5, S. Doc. No. 58-234, at 350 (1905); "A Flying Machine," *Daily Graphic* (New York), September 6, 1873.

8. Walker to L. P. Walker, June 4, 1861.

9. Wise, *System of Aeronautics*, 257–59; Beaumont, "Balloon Reconnaissances"; Glassford, "Balloon in the Civil War"; John Randolph Bryan, "Balloon Used for Scout Duty," *Times Dispatch* (Richmond), September 24, 1905, C2; Gallagher, *Fighting for the Confederacy*, 115–17; Scott, *Instructions to the American Delegates*, 30–31.

10. "Poison Tree of Java"; "Upas-Tree of Fact and Fiction"; Burnett, *Outlines of Botany*, 551–55.

11. "Recent Deaths: Colonel William Beals," *Boston Evening Transcript*, May 17, 1902, 17; Advertisement for Beals's 4th of July Fire Works, *Springfield (MA) Daily Republican*, June 24, 1853, 3. Starting some years before the Civil War, Beals attached the title colonel to his name, but he is not known to have served in the military.

12. *Third Exhibition*, 25–26; "Fire-Ship," *Portland (ME) Advertiser*, July 26, 1842, 1; "An Infernal Machine," *Daily Evening Transcript* (Boston), June 15, 1842, 2; *Fifth Exhibition*, 186.

13. Beals to unknown, August 1861, class 4&5, letter 463, CRI.

14. Ibid.

15. Mayor, *Greek Fire*, 63–97; "Indian Arrow," *Wooster (OH) Republican*, July 23, 1863, 1; news item, *Newport (RI) Mercury*, November 29, 1856, 2; "Poisoned Arrows," *New York Ledger*, November 13, 1858, 2; Wood and Bache, *Dispensatory of the United States*, 57–61, 397–99, 785–87.

16. "Poisoned Cannon Balls," *Daily Dispatch* (Richmond), April 22, 1862, 2; "Manufacturing Poisoned Bullets," *Age* (Philadelphia), August 22, 1863, 2; "Poisoned Yankee Ball," *Memphis Daily Appeal*, June 10, 1864, 1; Elijah D. Williams, Improvement in Elongated Bullets, US Patent 37,145, December 9, 1862; Kern, "Bullets Used in the Civil War"; Hayden, "Explosive or Poisoned Musket or Rifle Balls."

17. "Poisoned Bullets," *Lowell (MA) Daily Citizen & News*, September 16, 1862, 2; Reuben and Ira W. Shaler, Improvement in Compound Bullets for Small-Arms, US Patent 36,197, August 12, 1862; "Poisoned Bullets a Humbug," *Lowell (MA) Daily Citizen & News*, September 18, 1862, 2; Kern, "Bullets Used in the Civil War"; Hayden, "Explosive or Poisoned Musket or Rifle Balls."

18. "Manufacturing Poisoned Bullets," *Age* (Philadelphia), August 22, 1863, 2; "Items," *Fremont (OH) Journal*, May 22, 1863, 2; Taylor, *Medical Jurisprudence*, 122–26, 140–41; Treves, "Wounded in the Transvaal War"; Whitelock, *Memorials of the English Affairs*, 349–50.

19. "The Southern Barbarians," *Boston Evening Transcript*, September 18, 1861, 2; "Poisonous Missiles," *Colorado Republican and Rocky Mountain Herald* (Denver), June 19, 1862, 2; Abel, "Some of the Applications."

20. Avirett to Benjamin, October 1, 1861, *War of the Rebellion*, ser. 1, vol. 1, pt. 2, 329; "Further from Corinth," *Daily Dispatch* (Richmond), April 16, 1862, 3; "Miscellaneous War News," *Springfield (MA) Republican*, August 10, 1861, 8; "The Southern Barbarians," *Boston Evening Transcript*, September 18, 1861, 2; "Fatal Affair," *Daily Dispatch* (Richmond), November 10, 1863, 1; "Poisoned Balls," *Western Democrat* (Charlotte), July 29, 1862, 3.

21. "A Brave Regiment," *Crisis* (Columbus, OH), December 23, 1863, 381; Trowbridge, "Gunshot Wounds"; Longmore, *Gunshot Injuries*, 89–92.

22. "Poisoned Balls," *Western Democrat* (Charlotte), July 29, 1862; "The Southern Barbarians," *Boston Evening Transcript*, September 18, 1861, 2.

23. Buckelew to Simon Cameron, September 24, 1861, class 8, letter 164, CRI.

24. Broun, "Richmond Arsenal"; Griffith, *Battle Tactics*, 84–85.

11. VULGAR POISONS IN HONOURABLE WARFARE

1. Bruce, *Launching of Modern American Science*, 306–12.

2. Khan, "Impact of War"; Kennedy, *Population of the United States*, 592–93, 670–71, 676–77.

3. Bollet, *Civil War Medicine*, 57–61; Steiner, *Physician-Generals*, 147–64.

4. "Improvements for the Times"; Schmidt, "'Multiplicity of Ingenious Articles.'"

5. According to Haber (*Poisonous Cloud*, 15), the first successful use of poison gas in World War I "had no precursors" and differed from most other weapons, which could be "traced over decades if not centuries."

6. Wheaton, *Elements of International Law*, 428n; "Greek Fire Thrown into Charleston," *New York Daily News*, August 28, 1863, 4; G. Huff to Thomas A. Scott, October 29, 1861, with endorsement by McClellan, October 31, 1861, *War of the Rebellion*, ser. 3, vol. 1, 606; Richardson, "Greek Fire"; Halleck, *International Law*, 398–99; Butler, *Military Profession*, 25. The former attorney general was not the same Benjamin F. Butler who was a politician and Union general.

7. Halleck, *International Law*, 399; Woolsey, *Introduction to the Study of International Law*, 294–96.

8. Wheaton, *Elements of International Law*, 428n.

9. Vattel, *Law of Nations*, 361; Friswell, *About in the World*, 199–209, Johnston, *Chemistry of Common Life*, 296–97.

10. Prentiss, *Chemicals in War*, 685–86.

11. Scott, *Instructions to the American Delegates*, 6–9.

12. Ibid., 35–38; Prentiss, *Chemicals in War*, 686.

13. Prentiss, *Chemicals in War*, 687; Haber, *Poisonous Cloud*, 19–21.

14. Condon to Francis Pickens, January 11, 1861, Papers of David Flavel Jamison; Harris to Simon Cameron, May 17, 1861, class 4&5, letter 229, CRI; Beals to unknown, August 1861, class 4&5, letter 463, CRI; Doughty to Abraham Lincoln, April 5, 1862, special file 26-B (TR-3), Special Files, 1790–1946 (entry 286), Records of the Adjutant General's Office (RG 94); Cheves to Thomas Jordan, April 2, 1863, Confederate Papers, roll 161.

15. Vattel, *Law of Nations*, 361; Beauregard to Josiah Gorgas, October 25, 1863, file for John Cheves, Confederate Papers, roll 161.

16. "Greek Fire—Alarm in England," *Portrait Monthly of the New York Illustrated News*, January 1864, 111.

17. Haber, *Poisonous Cloud*, 308; Wakabayashi, "Documents on Japanese Poison Gas."

.

BIBLIOGRAPHY

ARCHIVES

Cheves, Rachel Susan (Bee), Papers, David M. Rubenstein Rare Book and Manuscript Library, Duke University, Durham, NC.

Compiled Service Records of Confederate General and Staff Officers, and Nonregimental Enlisted Men. Microfilm M331, roll 144, RG 109. National Archives and Records Administration, Washington, DC.

Compiled Service Records of Confederate Soldiers Who Served in Organizations from the State of Mississippi. Microfilm M269, roll 181, RG 109. National Archives and Records Administration, Washington, DC.

Compiled Service Records of Confederate Soldiers Who Served in Organizations from the State of Virginia. Microfilm M324, roll 360, RG 109. National Archives and Records Administration, Washington, DC.

Confederate Papers Relating to Citizens or Business Firms. Microfilm M346, RG 109. National Archives and Records Administration, Washington, DC.

Correspondence Relating to Inventions (entry 994), RG 156. National Archives and Records Administration, Washington, DC.

Harrison, Burton Norvell, Family Papers. Library of Congress, Washington, DC.

Jamison, David Flavel, Papers, 1810–64. Leyburn Library, Washington and Lee University, Lexington, VA.

Lewis, James, Letters. Department of Special Collections, Stanford University Libraries, Stanford, CA.

Lincoln, Abraham, Papers. Manuscript Division, Library of Congress, Washington, DC.

Putnam, Hiram, Papers. Mortimer Rare Book Room, Neilson Library, Smith College, Northampton, MA.

Records of the Adjutant General's Office (RG 94). National Archives and Records Administration, Washington, DC.

Records of the Bureau of Ordnance (RG 74). National Archives and Records Administration, Washington, DC.

Records of the Office of the Chief of Ordnance (RG 156). National Archives and Records Administration, Washington, DC.

Union Provost Marshal's File of Papers Relating to Individual Citizens. Microfilm M345, roll 241, RG 109. National Archives and Records Administration, Washington, DC.

War Department Collection of Confederate Records (RG 109). National Archives and Records Administration, Washington, DC.

NEWSPAPERS

Aegis and Transcript (Worcester, MA)
Age (Philadelphia)
Alexandria (VA) Gazette
American Traveller (Boston)
Anti-slavery Bugle (Salem, OH)
Boston Courier
Boston Evening Transcript
Boston Herald
Boston Recorder
California Farmer and Journal of Useful Sciences (San Francisco)
Charleston Courier
Charleston Daily Courier
Charleston Mercury
Cleveland Daily Plain Dealer
Colorado Republican and Rocky Mountain Herald (Denver)
Crisis (Columbus, OH)
Daily Chronicle & Sentinel (Augusta, GA)
Daily Constitutionalist (Augusta, GA)
Daily Dispatch (Richmond)
Daily Evening Transcript (Boston)
Daily Evening Traveller (Boston)
Daily Graphic (New York)
Daily Illinois State Register (Springfield)
Daily National Intelligencer (Washington, DC)
Daily National Republican (Washington, DC)
Daily Ohio Statesman (Columbus)
Daily Picayune (New Orleans)
Daily Richmond Examiner
Daily Richmond Inquirer
Duchess Observer (Poughkeepsie, NY)
Evening Bulletin (San Francisco)
Evening Post (New York)
Evening Repository (Canton, OH)
Evening Star (Washington, DC)
Frank Leslie's Illustrated Newspaper
Fremont (OH) Journal
Guardian (London)
Hillsborough (NC) Recorder

Illustrated Times (London)
Los Angeles Times
Lowell (MA) Daily Citizen & News
Macon (GA) Telegraph
Massachusetts Spy (Worcester)
Memphis Daily Appeal
Milwaukee Sentinel
Nashville Daily Union
New Age (Philadelphia)
Newark (NJ) Daily Advertiser
New England Farmer, and Horticultural Register (Boston)
Newfoundlander (St. John's)
Newport (RI) Mercury
New York Daily News
New York Daily Reformer (Watertown)
New York Daily Tribune
New York Herald
New York Ledger
New York Speculator
New York Times
North American and United States Gazette (Philadelphia)
Oregon Guardsman (Salem)
Patriot Union (Harrisburg, PA)
Philadelphia Inquirer
Plain Dealer (Cleveland)
Portland (ME) Advertiser
Portrait Monthly of the New York Illustrated News
Richmond Whig
Rockford (IL) Republican
Rock River Democrat (Rockford, IL)
San Diego Union
Saturday Star (Washington, DC)
Southern Cultivator (Augusta, GA)
Springfield (MA) Daily Republican
Springfield (MA) Republican
Standard (Chicago)
Star (Washington, DC)
Sunday Star (Washington, DC)
Syracuse (NY) Weekly Express
Times (London)
Times Dispatch (Richmond)
War (New York)

Washington Post
Wellsville (NY) Daily Reporter
Western Democrat (Charlotte)
Wooster (OH) Republican
World (New York)

OTHER PRINTED AND ONLINE MATERIAL

Abbot, Henry L. *Siege Artillery in the Campaigns against Richmond*. Washington, DC: Government Printing Office, 1867.

Abel, F. A. "On Some of the Applications of Chemistry to Military Purposes." In *Notices of the Proceedings at the Meetings of the Members of the Royal Institution of Great Britain*, 2:283–88. London: William Clowes and Sons, 1858.

Abridgments of the Specifications Relating to Fire-Arms and Other Weapons, Ammunitions, and Accoutrements. London: George E. Eyre and William Spottiswoode, 1859.

Adjutant General's Office. General Order No. 100: Instructions for the Government of Armies of the United States, in the Field. New York: D. Van Nostrand, 1863.

American State Papers, 1789–1838. 38 vols. Washington, DC: Library of Congress. Accessed May 24, 2013. http://memory.loc.gov/ammem/amlaw/lwsplink.html #anchor6.

Amoore, John E., and Earl Hautala. "Odor as an Aid to Chemical Safety: Odor Thresholds Compared with Threshold Limit Values and Volatilities for 214 Industrial Chemicals in Air and Water Dilution." *Journal of Applied Toxicology* 3 (December 1983): 272–90.

Andrews, Jean. *Peppers: The Domesticated Capsicums*. New ed. Austin: University of Texas Press, 1995.

Annual Report of the American Institute, of the City of New York, for the Years 1864, '65. Albany, NY: G. Wendell, 1865.

"Antiquity of Military Asphyxiation." *Army and Navy Register* 57 (May 29, 1915): 683.

Auld, S. J. M. *Gas and Flame in Modern Warfare*. New York: George H. Doran, 1918.

Bache, Franklin. *A System of Chemistry for the Use of Students of Medicine*. Philadelphia: William Fry, 1819.

Barnes, James, and Patience Barnes. *The American Civil War through British Eyes*. Vol. 3, February 1863–December 1865. Kent, OH: Kent State University Press, 2005.

Barrett, Walter. *The Old Merchants of New York City*. 3rd ser. New York: Carleton, 1865.

Baskerville, Charles. "The Chemistry of Anesthetics." *Science*, n.s., 34 (August 11, 1911): 161–76.

Baskin, Steven I., James B. Kelly, Beverly I. Maliner, Gary A. Rockwood, and Czaba K. Zoltani. "Cyanide Poisoning" In *Medical Aspects of Chemical Warfare*, edited by Shirley D. Tuorinsky, 371–410. Washington, DC: Borden Institute, 2008.

Beard, J. T., ed. "Examination Questions for Mine Managers, Mine Foremen, Fire Bosses, etc." *Mines and Minerals* 20 (September 1899): 85.

Beaumont, F. "On Balloon Reconnaissances." In *Papers on Subjects Connected with the Duties of the Corps of Royal Engineers*, n.s., 12:94–103. Woolwich, England: W. P. Jackson, 1863.

Bennett, Frank M. *The Monitor and the Navy under Steam*. Boston: Houghton, Mifflin, 1900.

Bentley, Robert, and Theophilus Redwood, eds. *Dr. Pereira's Elements of Materia Medica and Therapeutics*. London: Longmans, Green, 1872.

Benton, J. G. *Course of Instruction in Ordnance and Gunnery; Compiled for the Use of the Cadets of the United States Military Academy*. 2nd ed. New York: Van Nostrand: 1862.

Blackford, W. W. *War Years with Jeb Stuart*. Baton Rouge: Louisiana State University Press, 1993.

Bollet, Alfred Jay. *Civil War Medicine: Challenges and Triumphs*. Tucson, AZ: Galen, 2002.

"Boston Light House." *Army and Navy Chronicle* 9 (October 3, 1839): 222.

Boynton, Edward C. "Greek Fire, and Other Inflammables." *United States Service Magazine* 1 (January 1864): 50–55.

Bragg, C. L., Charles D. Ross, Gordon A. Blaker, Stephanie A. T. Jacobe, and Theodore P. Savas. *Never for Want of Powder: The Confederate Powder Works in Augusta, Georgia*. Columbia: University of South Carolina Press, 2007.

Breeden, James O. *Joseph Jones, M.D.: Scientist of the Old South*. Lexington: University Press of Kentucky, 1975.

Brewster, David. *The Edinburgh Encyclopaedia*. Vol. 17. Edinburgh: William Blackwood, 1830.

Broun, Thomas L., comp. *Dr. William LeRoy Broun*. New York: Neale, 1912.

Broun, W. Le Roy. "The Richmond Arsenal." *New Eclectic Magazine* 4 (April 1869): 455–58.

Browne, C. A. "Early References Pertaining to Chemical Warfare." *Journal of Industrial and Engineering Chemistry* 14 (July 1, 1922): 646.

Bruce, Robert V. *The Launching of Modern American Science, 1846–1876*. New York: Alfred A. Knopf, 1987.

———. *Lincoln and the Tools of War*. Indianapolis: Bobbs-Merrill, 1956.

Bulk Storage of Liquid Chlorine. Pamphlet 5. 7th ed. Arlington, VA: Chlorine Institute, 2005.

Bullock and Crenshaw. *Catalogue of Drugs, Pharmaceutical Preparations, Utensil, Apparatus, Surgical Instruments, etc.* Philadelphia: Bullock and Crenshaw, 1857.

Bunsen, Rud. "Researches on the Cacodyl Series." In *Scientific Memoirs*, edited by Richard Taylor, 3:281–318. London: Richard and John E. Taylor, 1843.

Burnett, Gilbert T. *Outlines of Botany*. Vol. 2. London: John Churchill, 1835.

Burton, E. Milby. *The Siege of Charleston*. Columbia: University of South Carolina Press, 1970.

Butler, Benjamin F. *The Military Profession in the United States, and the Means of Promoting Its Usefulness and Honour.* New York: Samuel Colman, 1839.

Byers, James. "Statement Relating to the 'Merrimac,' etc." In *A Brief Sketch of the First Monitor and Its Inventor,* by Ebenezer P. Dorr, 50–52. Buffalo: Matthews and Warren, 1874.

Caoutchouc and Gutta Percha. London: Society for Promoting Christian Knowledge, 1852.

"Captain Warner's Invention." *Mechanics' Magazine, Museum, Register, Journal, and Gazette* 41 (August 10, 1844): 88–91.

"Catalogue of the Class of the Philadelphia College of Pharmacy." *American Journal of Pharmacy* 23 (January 1860): 95–96.

Centers for Disease Control and Prevention. "Facts about Arsine." Accessed November 29, 2013. http://emergency.cdc.gov/agent/arsine/facts.asp.

———. "Immediately Dangerous to Life or Health Concentrations (IDLH): Chlorine." Accessed December 18, 2013. http://www.cdc.gov/niosh/idlh/7782505 .html.

———. "Immediately Dangerous to Life or Health Concentrations (IDLH): Chloroform." Accessed December 27, 2013. http://www.cdc.gov/niosh/idlh/67663.html.

Chapman, George T. *Sketches of the Alumni of Dartmouth College.* Cambridge, MA: Riverside, 1867.

Chapman, John. *Chloroform and Other Anaesthetics: Their History, and Use during Childbirth.* London: Williams and Norgate, 1859.

"Chemical Warfare." *Tactical and Technical Trends,* no. 14 (December 17, 1942): 12–16.

"Chloroform amongst Thieves." *Lancet* 2 (October 28, 1865): 490–91.

Christison, Robert. *A Treatise on Poisons.* Philadelphia: Ed. Barrington and Geo. D. Haswell, 1845.

Cochrane, Thomas. *The Autobiography of a Seaman.* London: Richard Bentley, 1861.

Coffin, Levi. *Reminiscences of Levi Coffin, the Reputed President of the Underground Railroad.* 2nd ed. Cincinnati: Robert Clark, 1880.

Cooper, William White. *On Wounds and Injuries of the Eye.* London: John Churchill, 1859.

Coxe, John Redman. "Reminiscences of the Effects of Chlorine, Largely Inhaled, with the Favourable Result of Copious Bleeding," *Medical Examiner and Record of Medical Science,* n.s., 60 (April 1848): 211–22.

Crowley, R. O. "The Confederate Torpedo Service." *Century Magazine* (June 1898): 290–300.

Curry, John P. *Volunteers' Camp and Field Book.* New York: D. Appleton, 1862.

Cutbush, James. "Remarks Concerning the Composition and Properties of the Greek Fire." *American Journal of Science, and Arts* 6 (1823): 302–15.

———. *A System of Pyrotechny.* Philadelphia: Clara F. Cutbush, 1825.

Davis, A. J., ed. *History of Clarion County, Pennsylvania.* Syracuse: D. Mason, 1887.

De, Amit Krishna. *Capsicum: The Genus* Capsicum. New York: Taylor and Francis, 2003.

Department of the Army. *Chemical Weapons and Munitions.* Technical Manual TM 43-0001-26-2. Washington, DC: Government Printing Office, 1982.

———. *Military Explosives.* Technical Manual TM 9-1300-214. Washington, DC: Government Printing Office, 1984.

"Destructive Fire Shells." *Scientific American,* n.s., 6 (January 11, 1862): 25.

Douglas, George, and George Dalhousie Ramsay, eds. *The Panmure Papers.* Vol. 1. London: Hodder and Stoughton, 1908.

Duane, William. *A Military Dictionary.* Philadelphia: William Duane, 1810.

Dunglison, Robley. *New Remedies: With Formulae for Their Preparation and Administration.* 7th ed. Philadelphia: Blanchard and Lea, 1856.

"Early Projected Gas Attack." *Chemical Warfare Bulletin* 23 (July 1937): 119–20.

Eisenstadt, Peter, ed. *The Encyclopedia of New York State.* Syracuse, NY: Syracuse University Press, 2005.

Eleventh Maine Regimental Association. *The Story of One Regiment.* Astor Place, NY: J. J. Little, 1896.

Encyclopedia of Connecticut Biography. Vol. 10. New York: American Historical Society, n.d.

England, Joseph W., ed. *The First Century of the Philadelphia College of Pharmacy, 1821–1921.* Philadelphia: Philadelphia College of Pharmacy and Science, 1922.

Faraday, M. "On Fumigation." *Quarterly Journal of Science, Literature, and the Arts* 18 (1825): 92–95.

Featherstone, H. W. "Chloroform." *Anesthesiology* 8 (July 1947): 362–71.

"The Fenian Fire." *London Lancet* (March 1867): 196–97.

The Fifth Exhibition of the Massachusetts Charitable Mechanic Association, at Faneuil and Quincy Halls, in the City of Boston, September 1847. Boston: Dutton and Wentworth, 1848.

Flagg, Edmund. *Venice: The City of the Sea.* Vol 2. New York: Charles Scribner, 1853.

Foute, R. C. "Echoes from Hampton Roads." *Southern Historical Society Papers* 19 (January 1891): 246–48.

Freedley, Edwin T. *Leading Pursuits and Leading Men: A Treatise on the Principal Trades and Manufactures of the United States.* Philadelphia: Edward Young, 1856.

———. *Philadelphia and Its Manufactures: A Hand-Book Exhibiting the Development, Variety, and Statistics of the Manufacturing Industry of Philadelphia in 1857.* Philadelphia: Edward Young, 1860.

Fries, Amos A. "Gas in Attack." Pts. 1 and 2. *National Service with the International Military Digest* 5 (June 1919): 327–36; (July 1919): 7–12.

Fries, Amos A., and Clarence J. West. *Chemical Warfare.* New York: McGraw-Hill, 1921.

Friswell, James Hain. *About in the World.* London: Sampson Low, Son, and Marston, 1864.

Gallagher, Gary W., ed. *Fighting for the Confederacy: The Personal Recollections of General Edward Porter Alexander*. Chapel Hill: University of North Carolina Press, 1989.

Gardner, D. P. *Medical Chemistry for the Use of Students and the Profession*. Philadelphia: Lea and Blanchard, 1848.

Gates, Marshall, Jonathan W. Williams, and John A. Zapp. "Arsenicals." In *Chemical Warfare Agents, and Related Chemical Problems*, parts 1–2: *Summary Technical Report of Division 9, NDRC*, National Defense Research Committee, 1:83–114. Washington, DC: Government Printing Office, 1946.

"General Butler an Inventor." *Scientific American*, n.s., 11 (August 6, 1864): 82.

"A German Account of the Flame Throwers." In *The New York Times Current History: The European War*, 16:397. New York: New York Times, 1918.

Gibbon, John. *The Artillerist's Manual, Compiled from Various Sources, and Adapted to the Service of the United States*. 2nd ed. New York: D. Van Nostrand, 1863.

Gillmore, Q. A. *Engineer and Artillery Operations against the Defences of Charleston Harbor in 1863*. New York: D. Van Nostrand, 1865.

Glassford, W. A. "The Balloon in the Civil War." *Journal of the Military Service Institution of the United States* 18 (March 1896): 255–66.

Gordon, W. J. M., & Bro. *Prices Current to Physicians*. Cincinnati: W. J. M. Gordon, 1864.

Goss, Charles Frederic. *Cincinnati: The Queen City*. Chicago: S. J. Clarke, 1912.

"Greek-Fire." *Chambers's Journal of Popular Literature Science and Arts*, n.s., 40 (October 24, 1863): 260–61.

"Greek Fire—Incendiary Shells." *Scientific American*, n.s., 9 (September 19, 1863): 81.

"Greek Fire or Pyrophori." *Scientific American*, n.s., 9 (December 19, 1863): 391.

"Greek Fire—Shell and Shot." *Scientific American*, n.s., 9 (October 24, 1863): 265.

Gregory, William. "Notes on the Purification and Properties of Chloroform." *Monthly Journal of Medical Science* 10 (May 1850): 414–22.

Griffith, Paddy. *Battle Tactics of the Civil War*. New Haven, CT: Yale University Press, 1989.

Haber, L. F. *The Poisonous Cloud: Chemical Warfare in the First World War*. Oxford: Oxford University Press, 1986.

Halleck, H. W. *International Law; or, Rules Regulating the Intercourse of States in Peace and War*. New York: D. Van Nostrand, 1861.

Hamilton, William. "Report on Greenough's Patent Lamp and Chemical Oil." *Journal of the Franklin Institute*, 3rd ser., 1 (1842): 50–53.

"Hammond General Hospital." *Medical and Surgical Reporter*, n.s., 9 (November 29 and December 6, 1862): 244.

Hasegawa, Guy R. "'Absurd Prejudice': A. Snowden Piggot and the Confederate Medical Laboratory at Lincolnton." *North Carolina Historical Review* 81 (July 2004): 313–34.

———. "Proposals for Chemical Weapons during the American Civil War." *Military Medicine* 173 (May 2008): 499–506.

Hasegawa, Guy R., and F. Terry Hambrecht. "The Confederate Medical Laboratories." *Southern Medical Journal* 96 (December 2003): 1221–30.

Hayden, Horace Edward. "Explosive or Poisoned Musket or Rifle Balls." *Southern Historical Society Papers* 7 (January 1880): 18–28.

Haydon, F. Stansbury. "A Proposed Gas Shell, 1862." *Chemical Warfare Bulletin* 24 (July 1938): 115–19.

Henderson, Peter. *Gardening for Pleasure*. New York: Orange Judd, 1891.

History of Cincinnati and Hamilton County, Ohio: Their Past and Present. Cincinnati: S. B. Nelson, 1894.

The History of Fond du Lac County, Wisconsin. Chicago: Western Historical, 1880.

"Homemade Chemical Bomb Events and Resulting Injuries: Selected States, January 1996–March 2003." *Morbidity and Mortality Weekly Reports* 52 (July 18, 2003): 662–64.

"Homemade Chemical Bomb Incidents: 15 States, 2003–2011." *Morbidity and Mortality Weekly Reports* 62 (June 21, 2013): 498–500.

"How Many Have Heard of This?" *Chemical Warfare* 10 (November 15, 1924): 11–12.

Hunt, Robert, ed. *Ure's Dictionary of Arts, Manufactures, and Mines*. Vol. 1. London: Longman, Green, Longman, and Roberts, 1860.

Illinois State Business Directory, 1860. Chicago: J. C. W. Bailey, 1860.

"Impertinence of the Ordnance Department toward Inventors." *Scientific American*, n.s., 9 (September 19, 1863): 178.

"An Improvement in Paper Manufacture." *Scientific American*, n.s., 2 (April 14, 1860): 246.

"Improvements for the Times—Suggestions to Inventors." *Scientific American*, n.s., 4 (May 4, 1861): 277.

The Industry of Nations, as Exemplified in the Great Exhibition of 1851: The Materials of Industry. London: Society for Promoting Christina Knowledge, 1852.

James, Simon. "Stratagems, Combat, and 'Chemical Warfare' in the Siege Mines of Dura-Europos." *American Journal of Archaeology* 115 (January 2011): 69–101.

Johnston, James F. W. *The Chemistry of Common Life*. Vol. 2. Edinburgh: William Blackwood and Sons, 1855.

Jones, Joseph. *First Report to the Cotton Planters' Convention of Georgia, on the Agricultural Resources of Georgia*. Augusta, GA: Chronicle and Sentinel, 1860.

———. *Medical and Surgical Memoirs*. Vol. 1. New Orleans: Clark and Hofeline, 1876.

Jones, Robert, Brandon Wills, and Christopher Kang. "Chlorine Gas: An Evolving Hazardous Material Threat and Unconventional Weapon." *Western Journal of Emergency Medicine* 11 (May 2010): 151–56.

Jordan, John W. *A Century and a Half of Pittsburg and Her People*. Vol. 3. [New York]: Lewis, 1908.

Kahlbaum, Georg W. A., and Francis V. Darbishire, eds. *The Letters of Faraday and Schoenbein, 1836–1862*. London: Williams and Norgate, 1899.

Kalantry, Sital, and Jocelyn Getgen Kastenbaum. "Combating Acid Violence in Bangladesh, India, and Cambodia." Avon Global Center for Women and Justice and Dorothea S. Clarke Program in Feminist Jurisprudence, paper 1. Accessed January 15, 2014. http://scholarship.law.cornell.edu/avon_clarke/1.

Kennedy, Joseph C. G., comp. *Population of the United States in 1860; Compiled from the Original Returns of the Eighth Census, under the Direction of the Secretary of the Interior.* Washington, DC: Government Printing Office, 1864.

Kern, Albert. "Bullets Used in the Civil War." *Confederate Veteran* 24 (July 1916): 310–11.

Khan, B. Zorina. "The Impact of War on Resource Allocation: 'Creative Destruction' and the American Civil War." NBER Working Paper 20944, National Bureau of Economic Research, Cambridge, MA, 2015. http://www.nber.org/papers/w20944.

[Knowlton, Miner, and James Duncan Zebina Kinsley]. *Military Pyrotechny for the Use of the Cadets of the U.S. Military Academy.* N.p.: George Aspinwall, 1835.

Lefebure, Victor. *The Riddle of the Rhine: Chemical Strategy in Peace and War.* London: W. Collins Sons, 1921.

Lindberg, Kip. "The Use of Riot Control Agents during the Vietnam War." *Army Chemical Review* (January–June 2007): 51–55.

Loades, Mike. "*History Channel* & the Experiments with Walter de Milemete's Kite Bomb." *Christ Church Library Newsletter* 5 ([January–March] 2009): 1–4.

Longmore, T. *Gunshot Injuries: Their History, Characteristic Features, Complications, and General Treatment.* London: Longmans, Green, 1877.

Lyman, Theodore. *Meade's Headquarters, 1863–1865.* Boston: Massachusetts Historical Society, 1922.

Maisch, John M. "Report on the Drug Market." In *Proceedings of the American Pharmaceutical Association at Its Twelfth Annual Meeting, Held in Cincinnati, O., September, 1864.* Philadelphia: Merrihew and Son, 1864.

Marks, George Edwin. *A Treatise on Artificial Limbs with Rubber Hands and Feet.* New York: A. A. Marks, 1896.

Mayor, Adrienne. *Greek Fire, Poison Arrows, and Scorpion Bombs: Biological & Chemical Warfare in the Ancient World.* New York: Overlook Duckworth, 2009.

Medical Department of the University of the State of New-York. *Annual Catalogue.* New York: Adee and Estabrook, 1844.

Medical and Surgical History of the War of the Rebellion. Washington, DC: Government Printing Office, 1875–85.

Mikesh, Robert C. *Japan's World War II Balloon Bomb Attacks on North America.* Washington, DC: Smithsonian Institution Press, 1973.

Miles, Wyndham D. "Chemical Warfare in the Civil War." *Armed Forces Chemical Journal* 12 (March–April 1958): 26, 27, 33.

———. "The Civil War: A Discourse on How the Conflict Was Influenced by Chemistry and Chemists." *Chemical and Engineering News* 39 (April 3, 1961): 108–15; (April 10, 1961): 116–23.

———. "Suffocating Smoke at Petersburg." *Armed Forces Chemical Journal* 13 (July–August 1959): 34–35.

"Military Use of Sabadilla in the Manufacture of Tear-Producing Gases." *Scientific American* 115 (July 15, 1916): 56.

Miner, T. B. *Miner's Domestic Poultry Book*. Rochester, NY: Geo. W. Fisher, 1853.

Mitchell, Thomas D. *Elements of Chemical Philosophy*. Cincinnati: Corey and Fairbank, 1832.

Mohr, Charles. *The Timber Pines of the Southern United States*. Washington, DC: Government Printing Office, 1896.

Moore, Stanford, and Marshall Gates. "Hydrogen Cyanide and Cyanogen Chloride." In *Chemical Warfare Agents, and Related Chemical Problems*, parts 1–2: *Summary Technical Report of Division 9, NDRC*, National Defense Research Committee, 1:7–16. Washington, DC: Government Printing Office, 1946.

Morgan, Gilbert T. *Organic Compounds of Arsenic & Antimony*. London: Longmans, Green, 1918.

"Moroccan Authorities Foil Terrorist Cell Pursuing Chemical Weapons." *WMD Insights*, February 2006. Accessed November 23, 2013. http://cns.miis.edu/wmd_insights/WMDInsights_2006_02.pdf.

Musick, Michael P. "War in an Age of Wonders." *Prologue* 27 (Winter 1995): 348–67.

Nasmith, George G. "Poison Gases in Warfare." *Medical Record* 96 (July 26, 1919): 146–57.

Needham, Joseph. *Science and Civilisation in China*. Vol. 4, *Physics and Physical Technology*. Part 2, *Mechanical Engineering*. Cambridge: Cambridge University Press, 1965.

———. *Science and Civilisation in China*. Vol. 5, *Chemistry and Chemical Technology*. Part 7, *The Gunpowder Epic*. Oxford: Cambridge University Press, 1986.

Needham, Joseph, and Robin D. S. Yates. *Science and Civilisation in China*. Vol. 5, *Chemistry and Chemical Technology*. Part 6, *Military Technology: Missiles and Sieges*. Cambridge: Cambridge University Press, 1994.

Newman, John. *Metallic Structures: Corrosion and Fouling, and Their Prevention*. London: E. and F. N. Spon, 1896.

"A New Weapon of Warfare." *Medical and Surgical Reporter*, n.s., 7 (December 21, 28, 1861): 310.

Norton, J. "Liquid Fire and Spherical Shells." *Mechanics' Magazine* 64 (January 12, 1856): 39.

Norton, John. *A List of Captain Norton's Projectiles, and His Other Naval and Military Inventions; with Original Correspondence*. Gravesend, England: Caddel and Son, 1860.

"Notes and Queries." *Scientific American*, n.s., 4 (June 15, 1861): 382; 6 (May 24, 1862): 334.

Nutt, John J. *Newburgh: Her Institutions, Industries, and Leading Citizens*. Newburgh, NY: Ritchie and Hull, 1891.

Obituary Record of Graduates of Yale University Deceased from June, 1880, to June, 1890. New Haven, CT: Tuttle, Morehouse and Taylor, 1890.

Odling, William. *A Manual of Chemistry, Descriptive and Theoretical.* London: Longman, Green, Longman, and Roberts, 1861.

Official Records of the Union and Confederate Navies in the War of the Rebellion. Washington, DC: Government Printing Office, 1894–1922.

Oliphant, Oscar. *China: A Popular History.* London: J. F. Hope, 1857.

O'Neall, John Belton. *Biographical Sketches of the Bench and Bar of South Carolina.* Vol. 1. Charleston, SC: S. G. Courtenay, 1859.

Ornstein, G. "Liquid Chlorine." *Metallurgical and Chemical Engineering* 14 (February 15, 1916): 215–19.

Pabst, G., ed. *Köhler's Medizinal-Pflanzen in naturgetreuen Abbildungen mit kurz erläuterndem Texte* [Köhler's medicinal plants]. Vol. 2. Gera-Untermhaus, Germany: Fr. Eugen Köhler, 1887.

Page, Charles A. *Letters of a War Correspondent.* Boston: L. C. Page, 1899.

Papacino d'Antoni, Alessandro Vittorio. *A Treatise on Gun-Powder; a Treatise on Fire-Arms; and a Treatise on the Service of Artillery in Time of War.* Translated by [J.?] Thomson. London: T. and J. Egerton, 1789.

Paris, John Ayrton. *The Life of Sir Humphry Davy.* London: Henry Colburn and Richard Bentley, 1831.

Parker, William Harwar. *Recollections of a Naval Officer, 1841–1865.* New York: Charles Scribner's Sons, 1883.

Payne, J. P. "The Criminal Use of Chloroform." *Anaesthesia* 53 (July 1998): 685–90.

Pease, David, and Austin S. Pease. *A Genealogical and Historical Record of the Descendants of John Pease, Sen., Last of Enfield, Conn.* Springfield, MA: Samuel Bowles, 1869.

"Poison Tree of Java." *North American Review and Miscellaneous Journal* 6 (January 1818): 276–77.

Portrait and Biographical Record of Lackawanna County, Pennsylvania. New York: Chapman, 1897.

Potts, Thomas Maxwell, comp. *Historical Collections Relating to the Potts Family.* Canonsburg, PA: Thomas Maxwell Potts, 1901.

Prentiss, Augustin M. *Chemicals in War: A Treatise on Chemical Warfare.* New York: McGraw-Hill, 1937.

Proceedings of the American Association for the Advancement of Science, Fifty-Fifth Meeting Held at New Orleans, LA., December, 1905–January, 1906. Washington, DC: Gibson Bros., 1906.

The Proceedings of the Woman's Rights Convention, Held at Syracuse, September 8th, 9th & 10th, 1852. Syracuse: J. E. Masters, 1852.

Rabald, Erich. *Corrosion Guide.* 2nd ed. Amsterdam: Elsevier Science, 1968.

Rains, Gabriel J., and Peter S. Michie. *Confederate Torpedoes.* Edited by Herbert M. Schiller. Jefferson, NC: McFarland, 2011.

Ramsbrok, C. R. "Dr. Glezen, of Huntingburg." *Indiana Medical Journal* 19 (March 1901): 356.

"Rebel Asphixiated Balls." *Scientific American*, n.s., 10 (June 11, 1864): 376.

Reeves, Dache McClain. "Military Use of Kites." *Air Service Journal* 1 (October 25, 1917): 501–2.

Reid, Wemyss. *Memoirs and Correspondence of Lyon Playfair*. New York: Harper and Brothers, 1899.

Reilly, Christopher A., Dennis J. Crouch, and Gerald S. Yost. "Quantitative Analysis of Capsaicinoids in Fresh Peppers, Oleoresin Capsicum and Pepper Spray Products." *Journal of Forensic Sciences* 46 (May 2001): 502–9.

Report of the Philadelphia College of Pharmacy, with a Catalogue of Its Members and Graduates. Philadelphia: Merrihew and Thompson, 1846.

Resolutions Passed by the Trustees of Columbia College. New York: D. Van Nostrand, 1868.

"Resources of Modern Warfare: Shells, Fuses, and Enfield Cartridges." *Dublin University Magazine* 53 (June 1859): 686–95.

Rhodes, Rufus R. "Report of the Commissioner of Patents." Richmond, 1862

Richardson, B. W. "Greek Fire: Its Ancient and Modern History." *Popular Science Review* 3 (1864): 164–77.

Riethmiller, Steven. "Charles H. Winston and Confederate Sulfuric Acid." *Journal of Chemical Education* 72 (July 1995): 575–77.

Roberts, Joseph. *The Hand-Book of Artillery, for the Service of the United States (Army and Militia)*. 5th ed. New York: D. Van Nostrand, 1863.

Roscoe, H. E. "Robert Wilhelm Bunsen." *Nature* 23 (April 28, 1881): 597–600.

Rottman, Gordon L. *Vietnam Riverine Craft, 1962–75*. Oxford: Osprey, 2006.

Salem, Harry, Bryan Ballantyne, and Sidney A. Katz. "Inhalation Toxicology of Riot Control Agents." In *Inhalation Toxicology*, 2nd ed., edited by Harry Salem and Sidney A. Katz, 485–520. Boca Raton, FL: CRC Press, 2006.

Sansom, Arthur Ernest. *Chloroform: Its Action and Administration*. London: John Churchill and Sons, 1865.

Schmidt, James M. "'A Multiplicity of Ingenious Articles': Civil War Medicine and *Scientific American* Magazine." In *Years of Change and Suffering: Modern Perspectives on Civil War Medicine*, edited by James M. Schmidt and Guy R. Hasegawa, 37–55. Roseville, MN: Edinborough, 2009.

"Scientific News: Dr. James Lewis." *American Naturalist* 15 (June 1881): 506–8.

Scott, James Brown, ed. *Instructions to the American Delegates to The Hague Peace Conferences and Their Official Reports*. New York: Oxford University Press, 1916.

"Shand and Mason's Steam Fire Engine." *Practical Mechanic's Journal* 4 (August 1, 1859): 137.

Sherman, William T. *Memoirs of General William T. Sherman*. 2 vols. New York: Appleton, 1875.

Siebert, Wilbur H. *The Underground Railroad from Slavery to Freedom.* New York: Macmillan, 1899.

Simienowicz, Casimir. *The Great Art of Artillery.* Translated by George Shelvocke. London: J. Tonson, 1729.

Singer, Jane. *The Confederate Dirty War.* Jefferson, NC: McFarland, 2005.

Smart, Jeffery K. "Chemical & Biological Warfare Research & Development during the Civil War." *Chemical and Biological Defense Information Analysis Center Newsletter* 5 (Spring 2004): 3, 11–13, 15.

Smith, Edward. *A History of the Schools of Syracuse from Its Early Settlement to January 1, 1893.* Syracuse, NY: C. W. Bardeen, 1894.

Snow, John. "Further Remarks on the Employment of Chloroform by Thieves." *London Medical Gazette* 11 (November 15, 1850): 834–35.

"Special Report: Manual for Producing Chemical Weapon to Be Used in New York Subway Plot Available on al-Qaeda Websites since Late 2005." *WMD Insights,* July–August 2006. Accessed November 23, 2013. http://cns.miis.edu/wmd _insights/WMDInsights_2006_08.pdf.

Squibb, E. R. "Report on the Drug Market." In *Proceedings of the American Pharmaceutical Association at Its Eleventh Annual Meeting, Held in Baltimore, Md., September, 1863.* Philadelphia: Merrihew and Thompson, 1863.

Stanton, Elizabeth Cady, Susan B. Anthony, and Matilda Joslyn Gage, eds. *History of Woman Suffrage.* New York: Fowler and Wells, 1881.

Steiner, Paul E. *Physician-Generals in the Civil War.* Springfield, IL: Charles C. Thomas, 1966.

Stenhouse, John. "The Charcoal Respirator." *Chemical News* 25 (May 17, 1872): 239.

———. "On the Deodorising and Disinfecting Properties of Charcoal, with the Description of a Charcoal Respirator for Purifying the Air by Filtration." *Journal of the Society of Arts* 2 (February 24, 1854): 245–47.

Stephenson, Charles. *The Admiral's Secret Weapon: Lord Dundonald and the Origins of Chemical Warfare.* Woodbridge, England: Boydell Press, 2006.

Strong, Gurney S. *Early Landmarks of Syracuse.* Syracuse, NY: Times Publishing, 1894.

Stryker, William S. "The 'Swamp Angel.'" In *Battles and Leaders of the Civil War,* edited by Robert Underwood Johnson and Clarence Clough Buel, 4:72–74. New York: Century, 1888.

Subcommittee on Military Smokes and Obscurants, National Research Council. *Toxicity of Military Smokes and Obscurants.* Vol. 2. Washington, DC: National Research Council, 1999.

Sutherland, James, comp. *Indianapolis Directory, and Business Mirror, for 1861.* Indianapolis: Bowen, Stewart, 1861.

Taylor, Alfred Swaine. *Medical Jurisprudence.* London: John Churchill, 1858.

Taylor, Thomas E. *Running the Blockade.* London: John Murray, 1896.

The Third Exhibition of the Massachusetts Charitable Mechanic Association, at Quincy Hall, in the City of Boston, September 20, 1841. Boston: T. R. Marvin, 1841.

The Thirteenth Annual Report of the American & Foreign Anti-slavery Society. New York: American and Foreign Anti-slavery Society, 1853.

Thomas, Milton Halsey. "Professor McCulloh of Princeton, Columbia, and Points South." *Princeton University Library Chronicle* 9 (November 1947): 17–29.

Thompson, Robert Means, and Richard Wainwright, eds. *Confidential Correspondence of Gustavus Vasa Fox, Assistant Secretary of the Navy, 1861–1865.* Vol. 1. New York: Naval History Society, 1918.

Traill, Thomas Stewart. *Outlines of a Course of Lectures on Medical Jurisprudence.* Philadelphia: Lea and Blanchard, 1841.

The Treatise of Walter de Milemete: De Nobilitatibus, Sapientiis, et Prudentiis Regum. Oxford: Roxburghe Club, 1913.

Treves, Frederick. "On the Wounded in the Transvaal War." *Medico-Chirurgical Transactions* 83 (1900): 271–95.

Trowbridge, Amasa. "Gunshot Wounds." *American Medical Times* 2 (May 25, 1861): 334–35.

Trow's New York City Directory, for the Year Ending May 1, 1861. New York: John F. Trow, 1861.

Tucker, Jonathan B. *War of Nerves: Chemical Warfare from World War I to al-Qaeda.* New York: Pantheon, 2006.

Tuttle, George Frederick. *The Descendants of William and Elizabeth Tuttle.* Rutland, VT: Tuttle, 1883.

Tutton, A. E. "The Properties of Liquid Chlorine." *Nature* 42 (October 16, 1890): 593–95.

"An Ugly Trick." *Scientific American,* n.s., 4 (March 2, 1861): 136.

United States Vulcanized Gutta Percha Belting and Packing Co. *Gutta Percha: Its Discovery, Properties, Manufactures, &c., &c.* New York: Hosford, 1857.

University of Pennsylvania: Biographical Catalogue of the Matriculates of the College. Philadelphia: Society of the Alumni, 1894.

"The Upas-Tree of Fact and Fiction." *National Magazine* 10 (June 1857): 495–98.

U.S. Army Chemical Materials Activity. Treaty Milestones. Accessed August 16, 2014. http://www.cma.army.mil/completedmissions.aspx.

Valentine, T. W. "Trial Extraordinary." *New York Teacher* 1 (March 1853): 188–89.

Vandiver, Frank E. *Ploughshares into Swords: Josiah Gorgas and Confederate Ordnance.* College Station: Texas A&M University Press, 1994.

Vattel, Emmerich de. *The Law of Nations; or, Principles of the Law of Nature, Applied to the Conduct and Affairs of Nations and Sovereigns.* Edited by Joseph Chitty. Philadelphia: T. and J. W. Johnson, 1861.

Waite's Newburgh City Directory for 1906. Newburgh, NY: L. P. Waite, 1906.

Wakabayashi, Bob Tadashi. "Documents on Japanese Poison Gas Warfare in China." *Sino-Japanese Studies* 7 (October 1994): 3–33.

Walling, George W. *Recollections of a New York City Chief of Police.* New York: Caxton, 1887.

Ward, William. *List of Cadets Admitted into the United States Military Academy, West Point, N.Y., from Its Origin till September 1, 1886.* Washington, DC: Government Printing Office, 1887.

War Department. *Handbook on Japanese Military Forces.* Technical Manual TM-E30-480. Washington, DC: Government Printing Office, 1944.

War of the Rebellion: A Compilation of the Official Records of the Union and Confederate Armies. Washington, DC: Government Printing Office, 1880–1901.

"War Projectiles." *Scientific American* 11 (September 29, 1855): 21.

Warren, John C. *Effects of Chloroform and of Strong Chloric Ether, as Narcotic Agents.* Boston: William D. Ticknor, 1849.

Wells, Frederic P. *History of Newbury, Vermont.* St. Johnsbury, VT: Caledonian, 1902.

Wheaton, Henry. *Elements of International Law.* Edited by Richard Henry Dana. London: Sampson, Maw, Son, 1866.

Whitelock, Bulstrode. *Memorials of the English Affairs.* Vol. 2. Oxford: Oxford University Press, 1853.

"Why the Shelling of Charleston Was Discontinued." *Scientific American,* n.s., 9 (September 19, 1863), 180–81.

Wilson, George. "A Description of Dr. J. Stenhouse's Charcoal Respirator for Breathing without Danger Infectious Atmospheres." *Transactions of the Royal Scottish Society of Arts* 4 (1856): appendix O, 198–200.

Wise, John. *A System of Aeronautics, Comprehending Its Earliest Investigations, and Modern Practice and Art.* Philadelphia: Joseph A. Speel, 1850.

Wise, Stephen R. *Lifeline of the Confederacy: Blockade Running during the Civil War.* Columbia: University of South Carolina Press, 1988.

Wood, George B., and Franklin Bache. *The Dispensatory of the United States of America.* 11th ed. Philadelphia: J. B. Lippincott, 1858.

Woodcroft, Bennet. *Chronological Index of Patents Applied for and Patents Granted.* London: George Edward Eyre and William Spottiswoode, 1860.

Woolsey, Theodore D. *Introduction to the Study of International Law, Designed as an Aid in Teaching, and in Historical Studies.* Boston: James Munroe, 1860.

Youmans, Edward L. *A Class-Book of Chemistry.* New York: Appleton, 1867.

Young, H. D. *The Generation of Hydrocyanic Acid Gas in Fumigation by Portable Machines.* Circular No. 139, Agricultural Experiment Station. Berkeley: University of California College of Agriculture, 1915.

INDEX

Italicized page numbers indicate figures.

acids: in arts and industry, 95; in civilian attacks, 95–96, 99; cost, *76*, 98; in homemade bombs, 99; production, *77*, 98; as proposed Civil War weapons, 91–99; risks to munitions workers, 98. *See also individual acids*
aconite, 116
alcohol, 10, 11, 39, 59, 61
alkarsin, 39, 40, 41, 42, 107, 124
al-Qaeda, 36
Anderson, Homer, 7, 23
Antiaris toxicaria, 113
antimony, 8, 13, 28
Arago, 17
arsenic: in artillery shells, 42, 128; in bullets, 116, 117, 119; as stabilizer for hydrogen cyanide, 37; in toxic compounds, 37, 39–42, 43
arseniuretted hydrogen, 37, 42, 43
arsine, 37, 42, 43
arson, 29, 30, 32
artemisia, 104
artillery projectiles, 8, 25, *66*, *67*, *68*, *69*, *71*, *73*; firing pattern and rate, 48–50, 51, 88, 97, 124, 147n8; poisoned, 116; suitability for chemical weapons, 48, 50–51, 59, 87, 88, 97, 98, 107–8, 110, 124. *See also* binary weapons; bladders as projectiles; glass; Greek fire; mortars
asafetida, 104
Aum Shinrikyo, 36
Austria, 62
Avirett, J. A., Jr., 118

Babcock, Adelia, 58
Badger, O. C., 11
Baldwin, Briscoe G., 106
balloons: for delivering bombs, 28–29, 62, *80*, 112–13, 124; for delivering cayenne pepper, 57, 61; for observation, 24, 113
Battery Wagner, SC, 10, 24, 27, 28, 29
Battle of Rich Mountain, 118
Battle of the Crater, 49, *78*, 103
Beals, William, 114–16, 128, 155n11
Beauregard, Pierre Gustave Toutant (P. G. T.), *67*, 94, 110; and cacodyl derivatives, 39, 41, 43; and defense of Charleston, SC, 20–22, 27, 29; and development of incendiary weapons, 24–27, 33, 121; and hydrogen cyanide, 33–35
Beecher, Henry Ward, 91
Benét, Stephen Vincent, 17, 18, 19, 142n30
Benjamin, Judah, 118
Bennett, George, 85
benzole (also called benzene or benzine), 11, 16, 28
Berney, Alfred, 14, 15, 16–18, 19, 28, 142n23, 142n28
Bigeye bomb, 37, 146n7
binary weapons, 29, 36–37, 42, *68*, 93, 97, 103, 124, 145n24, 146n7. *See also* Bigeye bomb; M687 artillery shell
Birbeck, C. G., 57, 58
bisulphide of carbon. *See* carbon disulfide

hydrogen cyanide, 34, 38; protection against, 52, 148n15; in Second Sino-Japanese War, 52, 130; in terrorism, 52; toxicity, 45, 47, 88, 147n9; in World War I, 47, 52, *77*
chlorocyanic acid, 38
chloroform: as anesthetic, *74*, 84–85, 87–88; cost, 86, 89; criminal use, 85, 87–88, 151n13; history, 84–85; nonmedical uses, 85; physical properties, 86, 87, 88, 89; as proposed Civil War weapon, 56, 83–84, 85–90, 121, 124; toxicity, 88, 123
cloud attacks: acid, 94–95, 97–98; chlorine, 47, 52, *77*, 95, 97–98
coal oil, 10, 16, *65*
coal tar, 16, 17
Cochrane, Thomas, 61, 101, 102, 103
Coe, Orman, 57, 61
Coffin, Levi, 91, 152n1
combustible sugar, 10, 23, 103
Comegys, Henry C., 57
Condon, John, 42, 128
copper, 37, 117
copperas, 117
copper subacetate, 117
copper sulfate, 117
cotton, 2, 28, 100, 102
Coulter, Dickson B., 85–86
Coxe, John Redman, 45, 47
Crary, F. G., 10
Crimean War, 7, 8–9, 10, 40, 101, 125
CSS *Atlanta*, 28
CSS *Nashville*, 14
CSS *Virginia*, 16, 44, 55, 83–84
Curry, John P., 35
cyanide. *See* hydrogen cyanide; potassium cyanide; sodium cyanide
cyanide of potassium, 33, 34, 35, 36, 38
cyanogen chloride, 38

Dahlgren, John A., 11, 92, 93
Davis, Jefferson, 30, 94, 110, 112
Davy, Humphry, 110
Disney, Henry, 8–9, 24

Dobyns, John, 94, 96
Doughty, John W.: background, 46; and chlorine, 44–49, 50–51, 52–53, 59, 69, 123–24; ethical views, 51, 122, 128
Douglas, Stephen A., 56
Douglass, Frederick, 91
dung (in chemical weapons), 27, 105
Dura-Europos, Syria, 101, 104

edged weapons, 114–16, 125, 128
England. *See* Great Britain
erysipelas, 118
ether, 27, 85
ethics of chemical weapons, 4, 125–28, 130; and acids, 96; and arsenic, 42; and cacodyl derivatives, 40; and chlorine, 51; and chloroform, 90; and hydrogen cyanide, 34, 43; and incendiary weapons, 9, 10, 20–23, 32, 129; and physicians, 122; and poisoned projectiles, 119; and rockets, 115; and strychnine, 42

Fahnestock, Samuel, 93, 95, 97, 103
Fenians, 32
ferrous sulfate, 117
firedamp, 109–10
fire engines, *73*, 97, 123, 124; and chloroform, 88–89; and gutta-percha or India rubber, 89; and sulfuric acid, 94, 96; and turpentine, 10, 23. *See also* garden engines
First Boer War, 117
flamethrowers: ancient, 7; proposed before Civil War, 6–7; proposed during Civil War, 10, 11–12, 13, 16, 17, 18, 23, 28, 31, 65; used after Civil War, 31, 65, 124
Flammenwerfer, 31
Fleming, Robert L., 19
Fort Brady, VA, 18
Fortier, M., 9
Fort Jackson, LA, 14
Fort Pickens, FL, 35, 56, *79*, *80*, 112–13
Fort Sumter, SC, 15, 20, 21, 26, 42, 100–101
Fort Wagner, SC, 10, 24, 27, 28, 29

GUY R. HASEGAWA is an editor for the *American Journal of Health-System Pharmacy* in Bethesda, Maryland. His publications include *Years of Change and Suffering: Modern Perspectives on Civil War Medicine*, for which he was a coeditor and contributor; *Mending Broken Soldiers: The Union and Confederate Programs to Supply Artificial Limbs*; and numerous articles on Civil War medicine.